Dennis Ambrose O´Sullivan

Government in Canada. The principles and institutions of our federal and provincial constitutions

The B. N. A. act, 1867, compared with the United States Constitution, with a sketch of the constitutional history of Canada. Second Edition

Dennis Ambrose O´Sullivan

Government in Canada. The principles and institutions of our federal and provincial constitutions
The B. N. A. act, 1867, compared with the United States Constitution, with a sketch of the constitutional history of Canada. Second Edition

ISBN/EAN: 9783337207946

Printed in Europe, USA, Canada, Australia, Japan

Cover: Foto ©Suzi / pixelio.de

More available books at **www.hansebooks.com**

GOVERNMENT IN CANADA.

THE PRINCIPLES AND INSTITUTIONS
OF OUR FEDERAL AND PROVINCIAL CONSTITUTIONS.

THE B. N. A. ACT, 1867, COMPARED WITH THE UNITED
STATES CONSTITUTION,

WITH

A SKETCH OF THE CONSTITUTIONAL HISTORY OF CANADA;

BY

D. A. O'SULLIVAN, M.A., D.C.L.

Of Osgoode Hall, Barrister-at-Law.
Scholar-in-Law in University of Toronto, Hon. D. C. L. Laval.

AUTHOR OF "PRACTICAL CONVEYANCING," "HOW TO DRAW A SIMPLE WILL," "ESSAYS
ON TREATIES AFFECTING CANADA AND THE UNITED STATES," ETC.

SECOND EDITION;

ENLARGED AND IMPROVED.

TORONTO:
CARSWELL & CO., PUBLISHERS,
1887.

Entered according to Act of Parliament of Canada, in the year one thousand eight hundred and eighty-seven, by D. A. O'SULLIVAN, in the office of the Minister of Agriculture.

PRINTED BY
MOORE & CO., LAW PRINTERS,
20 ADELAIDE ST. EAST,
TORONTO.

This Work

IS,

BY KIND PERMISSION, RESPECTFULLY INSCRIBED

TO THE

HON. EDWARD BLAKE,

BY

THE AUTHOR.

THE writer took advantage of the long vacation of the present year to prepare the second edition of this work for the press. The order of the edition of 1879 has been retained but the book has been entirely re-written and enlarged to fully twice its original size. The B. N. A. Act and its amendments have been made the text of three fourths of the present volume ; no section has been omitted and in every necessary case the corresponding sections in the U. S. Constitution have been referred to. The chapters on the People and their Rights and the Courts and their Procedure will, it is trusted, be of use to the general public. The chapter on Criminal Law received many useful additions and suggestions from Mr. Irving Q. C. of the Ontario bar and the writer is glad to acknowledge this assistance from such an experienced and distinguished counsel. The history of former governments in Part II is an amplification of the introductory sketch in the former edition. It would be outside the design of the book to make this as complete as it should be. The writer may on some future occasion arrange the materials provided for this Part in a constitutional history of Canada.

During a period of twenty years the constitution of Canada has been put to many tests. It is less difficult to say now than it was ten years ago, that our federal constitution may turn out to be something different from what the framers of it intended. It cannot be at one and the same time a federation and the reproduction of a constitutional monarchy. If the provinces are not absolute within their

own legislative limits, but subject to a veto from the central
government, then there is theoretically only one Legislature
in Canada. If the central government absorbs all the
executive of the government "of and over Canada," there can
be none left for the provinces. But the writer hopes to
shew in these pages that the federation is not endangered
by a veto held over the provinces, as a similar one is held
over the Dominion, or that the executive power is not as
readily at hand for the one as the other. Over each of our
governments there is one paramount authority and the
administration that would strike at the legislative authority
of the provinces is liable to have its own rule applied to its
own legislation. The veto is an accident of the Canadian
federation as it has been of other leagues, but it no more
affects the principles of a federal union than does the absence
of sovereignty. A number of tenants may unite as well as
a number of landlords.

On the question of the executive power the reader will
notice that in the U. S. constitution it is vested in the
President. That is the executive for the *United* States.
There writs and process run in the name of The People,
and Congress enacts in that way just as we use the name
of the Queen. The individual or *separate* States have their
executive also in The People, and their process is tested in
that way, their legislation is enacted in that way, and still
there is not a word about it in the United States constitution. With us the executive power " of and over " Canada
is vested in the Queen and it is contended in these pages
that the Queen's name is as warranted in provincial matters as it is in matters in the Dominion.

On one other point the writer may be permitted to make
a remark. That is as to the reserve powers in Canadian
legislatures. It will be seen in the chapter on the distribution of legislative power (page 95) that there is no analogy

at all between our constitution and that of the American union on the delegation of powers. Two elaborate classes of subjects were prepared by the framers of our union—one to go to the central government, another to the local. It was felt that notwithstanding the particularity of these classes there might be something over and above them in both cases. What the 91st and 92nd sections then provided was that any subject not in the central class assigned to the Dominion should go to the Dominion government if it related to the peace, order and good government of all the provinces ; and that any subject not on the local list if for any matter within the provinces should go to the local government.

The reader will also see that there is no analogy between the judicial power in the United States and the judicial power in Canada, though the practical working of the two judicatures is the same so far as declaring unconstitutional laws to be void. The courts in Canada are Queen's Courts testing all Dominion and provincial legislation by the standard of an Imperial Statute—the Constitution of Canada. In the United States the judicial power is vested in the Supreme Court and that power is independent of the President and of Congress.

These are some of the points that will be found in detail in this volume. The writer studied the United States constitution with many aids, but he took the text of the Canadian constitution as his best guide. It is impossible to reconcile many of the judgments of the courts on our side of the line, the reader will not easily form an opinion from decided cases. But when the whole Act of 1867 is viewed in its history, its intentions and its language, there is no substantial desire of its promoters that may not be effected by it. It is, like every federal charter, liable to drift into pure centralism on the one hand or to exaggerated claims for State rights on the other ; over and above this it is liable to be lost in the principles of monarchy and the exercise of the veto power. Dangers such as these have been met and overcome in the American Union and they can be met and overcome in our own.

The writer hopes that this volume will be acceptable to the Canadian public as a useful book on the constitution. He does not flatter himself that the sale of the former large edition was due to anything more than the pressing necessity for some work on the subject ; but he hopes that the present edition will deserve some of the praise that its predecessor received. He is, however, willing to commit it to the public on its merits, and will be glad to learn from any one who is able or entitled to speak on the subject.

The writer is under obligations to Mr. Houston, librarian of the legislative assembly of Ontario, and to Mr. Bain, of the Toronto public library, and gladly avails himself of this opportunity to acknowledge the courtesies extended by them.

The index of this edition has been prepared by Mr. W. McBrady, B. A., student-at-law, and the proof sheets compared and corrected by him.

The Long Vacation,

TORONTO, 1887.

PREFACE TO THE FIRST EDITION.

IN the compilation of the following pages the writer has endeavoured to make a fair use of such materials as were within his reach, in order to effect the object he intended. Preceded by no writer on the subject, and desirous of rejecting such contemporary opinion as was neither judicial nor official nor otherwise authoritative, he has found the task not at all an easy one. From the number of distinguished constitutional lawyers in Canada, and especially in this province, one might have been justified in the expectation that something more permanent than a speech at the hustings or a pamphlet in some party issue would have remained as instructive reading on the subject. As to contemporary opinion, very little of it is entitled to grave consideration.

It is needless to say that the writer has carefully avoided using any public expression of opinion, no matter how authoritative it might appear, unless it bore the stamp of some authority upon it. In regard to decisions of the courts and judicial *dicta* on the subject, the former *must* of course be taken to be law; the latter carry weight proportionate to the reputation and ability of the particular judge pronouncing them. It must be admitted that a judge, in construing our Constitutional Act or any section of it or any statute in fact, familiarizes himself necessarily with the spirit of the Act; and if he goes out of his way to express an uncalled for opinion, or what may be deemed uncalled for, it is certainly because on that point he has no doubt whatever. Judges have plenty to do in deciding the disputes immediately before them ; and it is to be expected that before commenting on any foreign subject they generally will have entertained strong views on it. The writer makes no apology for regarding such *dicta* as entitled to great consideration ; and only regrets that he was unable to find more judicial utterances in the law reports than are incorporated herein.

The utterances of any of our public men, speaking in their official capacity as servants of the crown and country, are deserving of consideration next only to what must be regarded as settled law. The writer has faith in the political morality of our leading statesmen to the extent, at least, that no one of them, acting in an official or, as may be said, a judicial position—as advisers of the crown, as trustees of the constitution—would permit his judgment to be biased by a mere party spirit, or for a temporary party triumph.

If it be otherwise in Canada, then it is time we were governed without party, as that term is now understood.

Accordingly, all official papers and correspondence, both of English and Canadian ministers while in office, bearing on the subject, have been freely used.

None of the other sources need comment.

In his task the writer has consulted no one and asked no one's opinion. It is only fair to state this, as it may well happen that in a work which was the joint production of the writer and others, any excellence in it would be attributed to them and the defects to himself. Whatever there is in this book deserving either of praise or blame is attachable to the writer and to no other person.

It was originally intended to make the work complete for each province as to the executive departments and to add the courts of law thereto. This was abandoned, partly because some necessary information from professional gentlemen in the other provinces did not come to hand in time, and also because, if rumor be true, a description of the courts in Ontario as they are now constituted may not apply for any length of time.

Some other alterations were made in the plan of the work after portions of it were in type.

The indulgence of the public will have to be asked in regard to any errors in this edition. Though in contemplation for some time, it was entirely remodeled and re-written within the past two months and it was put through the press very rapidly.

The writer acknowledges with pleasure the assistance he has received, both in the preparation of the index and otherwise, from Mr. C. L. Mahoney and Mr. A. A. Archbold, students-at-law.

TORONTO, December, 1879.

LIST OF AUTHORITIES

USED IN THE IMMEDIATE PREPARATION OF THIS WORK.

BAGEHOT—The English Constitution.
BLACKSTONE's Commentaries.
BOURNE's Story of Our Colonies.
CHALMER's Opinions of Distinguished Lawyers.
CHITTY on the Prerogatives of the Crown.
CLARK's Colonial Law.
COOLEY's Constitutional Limitations.
COX's British Commonwealth.
FINLAYSON's History of the Privy Council.
HALLAM's Constitutional History of England.
HODGIN's Voters' Lists.
LATTEY's Privy Council Practice.
MACFIE's British Columbia and Vancouver's Island.
MARTIN on the Colonies.
McDONALD's British Columbia and Vancouver Island.
McGREGOR's British America.
ORDERS in Council—Imperial, Dominion and Provincial.
POMEROY's Constitutional Law.
REPORTS of English and Canadian cases in the Privy Council,
Supreme and Provincial Courts.
RULES of the Senate, Commons, and the Provincial Assemblies.
SEDGWICK's Constitutional Law.
SESSIONAL Papers—Dominion and Provincial.
STATE Papers and Opinions of Officials on Constitutional
points.
STATUTES—Imperial, Dominion and Provincial.
WATSON's Constitutional History of Canada.

CONTENTS.

PART I.

THE CONSTITUTION AS IT IS.

PART II.

FORMER GOVERNMENTS IN CANADA AND IN THE PROVINCES.

PLAN OF THE WORK.

GOVERNMENT IN CANADA.

PART I.

THE CONSTITUTION AS IT IS.

CHAPTER I.

THE MONARCHIC FEDERATION.

The intention of the provinces in forming a union—The preamble of the B. N. A. Act—General view of the Act—The executive—Sovereignty—What is a federal union—The division of powers in it—What is the British constitution—The unity of the powers in it—Opinion of Mr. Blake—Mr. Dicey and others.

THE present constitution of Canada was framed with a view of protecting the diversified interests of the several provinces composing it and of securing efficiency, harmony and permanency, in the working of a union of these provinces. With that view representatives of those colonies which originally formed the union, agreed to a general government charged with matters of common interest to the whole country, and local governments charged with the control of local matters within their respective sections, for each of the provinces. It was desired as far as the circumstances would permit, to follow the British constitution as a model ; and the executive authority or government was agreed to be vested in the Sovereign of Great Britain and Ireland and to be administered according to the principles of the British constitution. There was to be a general legislature or parliament for the federated provinces, empowered to make laws for the peace, welfare and good government of the federation—so far as a colony could go —but to have no legislative control over a class of specified subjects. This excepted class of subjects was reserved to the legislatures of the provinces, and these legislatures were to have exclusive control over them. The local governments and legislatures were created at the same time and were to have the power of constructing their own constitutions as they thought best ; the local legislatures were to have the power of amending them from time to time. Where concurrent jurisdiction obtained over any one subject, the laws of the general parliament were to prevail over those of the local legislature (a).

These wishes of the representatives of the provinces were drafted into an Imperial statute called " The British North America Act, 1867, " and came into force on the 1st of July of that year. The preamble of the Act states that,

" Whereas the provinces of Canada, Nova Scotia and New Brunswick have expressed their desire to be federally united into one Dominion, under the crown of the United Kingdom of Great Britain and Ireland, with a constitution similar in principle to that of the United Kingdom, and

" Whereas such a union would conduce to the welfare of the provinces and promote the interests of the British Empire,

(a) See Quebec Resolutions, 1 to 7.

"And Whereas on the establishment of the union by authority of parliament it is expedient not only that the constitution of the legislative authority in the Dominion be provided for, but also that the nature of the executive government therein be declared,

"And Whereas it is expedient that provision be made for the eventual admission into the union of other parts of British North America,

"Be it therefore enacted, etc."

Then follow the terms of the union—the executive government and authority of and over Canada, the privy council, the Governor-General, the legislative powers of the parliament of Canada—occupying some fifty-seven sections of the Act; then the executive and legislative powers of the provinces, and the last third of the Act to matters of common interest, to the judicature, assets, etc., of the Dominion and the provinces.

The preamble of the Act has been given in its exact words, because there are two ideas in it that must be kept constantly in view in any discussion upon it (b).

(a) The provinces desire to be federally united; with (b) A constitution similar in principle to that of the United Kingdom of Great Britain and Ireland.

(b) Mr. Dicey in his "Law of the Constitution" says: The preamble to the British North America Act, 1867, asserts with official mendacity that the provinces of the present Dominion have expressed their desire to unite into one Dominion, with a constitution similar in principle to that of the United Kingdom. If preambles were intended to express the truth, for the word "Kingdom," ought to have been substituted "States." Mr. H. Jenkins, C. B., undertakes to answer Mr. Dicey, pointing out that "the executive is not elected by the people, nor is it independent of parliament, in the way in which the President of the United States is independent of congress, with ministers who cannot sit there. On the contrary the executive is carried on by means of ministers, responsible to parliament just as it is in England."—*Law Quarterly Review*, April, 1887.

It is not a little remarkable that the enacting part of the British North America Act should, notwithstanding the language of its preamble, contain no reference to the provinces being federally united, or to the Act itself being the consummation of a federal union.

The word union however occurs very often in the pre-amble and in the Act, and it must be taken to mean a federal union with a constitution similar to that of the United Kingdom, because the second recital of the preamble refers to " such a union," etc. The union is effected by a proclamation on a certain day ; and the Act declares that " the provinces of Canada, Nova Scotia and New Brunswick shall form and be one Dominion under the name of Canada, and on and after that day those three provinces shall form and be one Dominion accordingly." The fifth section is as follows:

Canada shall be divided into four provinces named Ontario, Quebec, Nova Scotia and New Brunswick.

Canada before the passing of the Act was itself a union of two provinces, but it did not come, as a union, into the new union : it was " deemed to be severed and shall form two separate provinces " as is the language of the sixth section,—Upper Canada constituted the province of Ontario and Lower Canada the province of Quebec. The other two provinces retained their former names and limits. The Act then proceeds in some forty subsequent sections to deal with the new Canada, giving it a constitution similar to that of Great Britain—executive, the Queen represented by a Governor-General, a privy council, and two houses of parliament.

In the twelfth section it collects together all the powers, authorities, and functions of the late Governors or Lieu-tenant-Governors of the three provinces forming the union, and vests these in the Governor-General of Canada, " as far as the same continue in existence and capable of being exercised after the union in relation to the government of Canada."

There is nothing in this one third of the British North America Act in regard to any distribution of legislative power, nor indeed anything to show that there is to be a limitation on any of the powers of the government of Canada. By the seventeenth section " there shall be one parliament for Canada consisting of the Queen, an upper house styled the senate, and the house of commons." The legislative powers of this parliament are given by the ninety-first section, and in the preceding sections the provincial constitutions are set out in detail.

The executive power in the provinces does not appear to be so clearly brought out as is the executive power over Canada. Whatever may have been in the minds of the framers of the Act this part of it is curiously worded. Even the printing is significant. The whole Act is divided in this way:

Preamble.

I. Preliminary. [*Name of the Act, application to the Queen.*]

II. Union. [*Uniting the Provinces; dividing Canada into Provinces.*]

III. Executive Power. [*Vested in the Queen; Privy Council; Governor.*]

IV. Legislative Power. [*Parliament at Ottawa; Queen, Senate, and Commons.*]

V. Provincial Constitutions. *Executive Power.*

VI.   Distribution of the Legislative Power.   *Powers of the Parliament; exclusive powers of the Provincial Legislatures.*

VII.   Judicature.

VIII.   Revenue; Debts; Assets; Taxation.

IX.   Miscellaneous Provisions.

X.   Intercolonial Railway.

XI.   Admission of other Colonies.

It is worthy of note that the first three heads seem to apply to Canada as made up of the provinces, not so evidently the Canada of one parliament.   The parliament is constituted in IV., and although the Queen is named in that head as the first element of parliament, the executive authority of and over Canada is vested in her by a preceding section.   This authority is also "continued" in the Queen, an expression that should apparently refer to something having a previous existence.   Now the Canada of the Act had no previous existence, but was created by it.   It would therefore not be a strained construction to refer the preceding section nine, to the provinces as well as to the Dominion.

The first question we have to consider is,

WHAT IS A FEDERAL UNION ?

It would appear from the preamble of the Act that the principles involved in a federation were to be of the essence of the compact, and that the principles of the British constitution were to be adjusted to that state of affairs so far as they were applicable.   This will be the more apparent when a consideration of federal principles is fully understood.   These are quite new in British institutions and we must look elsewhere for any experience in their workings.

The United States of America is offered as a convenient example of a federal union though strictly it is not a federal union. In the year 1776 the old thirteen colonies declared themselves independent sovereign states. They soon after formed a confederation but without giving it much executive power, and after an experience of ten years they found how useless it was and how necessary some adequate executive was over the whole people. In 1787 a convention met and settled the present constitution of the United States—nine states adopting it at the time and the others coming in subsequently. The States were theretofore sovereign states—they conferred certain powers on the central government and they reserved all others to themselves.

Many of the ablest men in the union were of opinion that by reason of the reserved powers and for other reasons the States remained sovereign states and could go out of the union as they pleased. It took a war to decide that this was not the case—that they were only one people (c). "We the people of the United States," are the opening words of the constitution, and these were fatal to state secession just as soon as the people of the United States vested the executive power in the President of the United States : the constitution in all its provisions looked to an indestructible union composed of indestructible states.

A federal union then means two perfectly independent co-ordinate powers in the same state. The powers of each are equally sovereign and neither are derived from the other. The state governments are not subordinate to the general government, nor the general government to the state governments. They are co-ordinate governments standing on the same level and deriving their powers from the same

(c) It is not pretended that the war of 1860-64 decided the question judicially.

sovereign authority. In their respective spheres neither yields to the other. Each is independent and complete in its own work; incomplete and dependent on the other for the complete work of government. (d).

In every federal union there are these two powers operating over the same territory and over the same people. The power of one legislature to make laws on one class of subjects for every one in its own territory, is quite consistent with the power of another legislature to make laws for the same people on all other subjects. The power of making laws is useless without an executive power to carry them out, and it follows that in every federal union there must be a division of the executive power similar to that in the legislative power. Such a division is unknown in the British constitution, where the executive power centres in the Queen. In our constitution " the executive government and authority of and over Canada is," by the Act of the Union, "declared to continue and be vested in the Queen;" but that is no more *mutatis mutandis* than the expression : "We, the people of the United States, " so far as the government of that country is concerned. The United States government and the individual state governments have each an executive, making up in the aggregate the sovereign power of the people; the central government sovereign in one set of subjects everywhere ; the state

(d) Brownson's Works, vol. 18, Politics, pp. 126, 272. Mr. Freeman gives this definition : Two requisites seem necessary to constitute a federal government in its most perfect form. On the one hand each of the members of the union must be wholly independent in these matters which concern each member only. On the other hand all must be subject to a common power in those matters which concern the whole body of members collectively. Federal government is in its essence a compromise between two opposite political systems. It is one that forms a single state in its relations to other nations, but which consists of many states with regard to its internal government.

Elsewhere Mr. Freeman describes a federation as having "a government co-ordinate with the state governments, sovereign in its own sphere, as they are sovereign in their sphere."

governments sovereign in all others within their own territorial limits.

In a colony such as the old Canada was, and the present Canada is, it makes no difference whatever, for the application of these federal principles, that we are short of the sovereign power to begin with. We are not concerned with sovereignty but only with executive power (*e*).

The imperial parliament has a portion of this sovereign power, the provinces have another portion, and the Dominion government has the remainder. From a federal point of view there are two divisions in the executive, as in the legislative branches of government. In the United States no difficulty is experienced in the executive of the nation, as contra-distinguished from the executive of the states, but with us it has been denied that the executive in the provinces is the Queen. The provinces of Ontario, Quebec, Manitoba, and British Columbia head

(*e*) Sovereignty under a federal system does not reside either in the general or in the local governments; in the United States it does not reside in fact in both of these, but is in the *Convention* which moves the constitution. All the American constitutional writers speak of a divided sovereignty, while the English writers from Austin down regard this as a contradiction in terms. Executive power may be divided, and the difficulty in Canada is in accepting any federal doctrine on a point so patent under British principles as the unity of the executive. See Chapter in the Powers of Parliament, *post.*

Mr. Jenkyns, who criticizes Mr. Dicey, brings himself however to this remarkable concession:—"A truer position would therefore seem to be to recognize that sovereignty may be divided, and that with a rigid constitution such as that of the United States each of two or more different bodies may within limits assigned to its jurisdiction be legally sovereign."

Daniel Webster says:—"The sovereignty of government is an idea belonging to the other side of the Atlantic. No such thing is known in North America. Our governments are all limited. In Europe sovereignty is of feudal origin and imports no more than the state of the sovereign. It comprises his rights, duties, exemptions, prerogatives and powers. But with us, all power is with the people. They alone are sovereign; and they erect what governments they please, and confer on them such powers as they please. None of these governments is sovereign, in the European sense of the word, all being restrained by written constitutions."

their statutes " Her Majesty, by and with the advice and consent &c., enacts as follows " : shewing that the governments in these provinces believe Her Majesty to be a part of their legislatures. On the other hand, there are many judges and statesmen who regard this as unwarranted and unauthorized; as yet no settlement of this divergence of opinion has been arrived at. The constitutions of the provincial executive authority in Nova Scotia and New Brunswick remained as before the union, while in Ontario and Quebec the new Lieutenant-Governors, though appointed by the Governor-General of Canada, have the same powers, authorities and functions as their predecessors, so far as provincial legislation goes. Besides the heading on the provincial statutes, which remains as before 1867, the grants of public lands, always made by the crown, come within the executive of the province; and this is only one of the many instances where the crown would seem to be of necessity acting immediately in the affairs reserved to the provinces (f).

It would seem then that the constitution of Canada is to be taken as on the federal basis, but that the principles of the British constitution are to be applied to the working out of government whenever and wherever such principles can be applied. It is to be a federal union " with a constitution similar in principle to that of the United Kingdom." It is difficult to conceive of forms of government more radically opposed to each other than a federal union and a constitutional monarchy. "The whole British system," says Mr. Blake, " is in contradiction to the federal system. Their system is one of legislative union; it is based upon the omnipotence of the sole and central parliament." The first thing that presents itself is, that in a federation,

---

(f) Mr. Mowat is of opinion that "it is easy to demonstrate that far more of what is prerogative falls within the acknowledged authority of the provinces than within the authority assigned to the Dominion."

there being two sets of powers in the state, there must, of necessity, be two sets of legislatures, and consequently be two constitutions. Are both of these constitutions to be "similar in principle to that of the United Kingdom?" Or which one of them, if not both? The central government is managed by a parliament, of which the Queen is expressly one of the component parts; but in view of the fact that the local governments have had legislatures, with officers and machinery very like a parliament, is the Queen necessarily excluded from being a part of their constitutions? But however that may be, is not this certain,—"the executive power of and over Canada is vested in the Queen;" the central government has a portion only of the legislative power, and can wield only a corresponding portion of the executive; now what power has the right to say that it is the Queen, is the executive, for the remainder? The conclusion seems to be irresistible, that for whatever purpose the executive of the legislature of a province requires the Queen, the Queen is there as amply and as necessarily as she is in the Dominion.

Whatever doubt there may be as to the executive powers, it must be conceded that all similarity between a federation and a constitutional monarchy vanishes as one comes to consider the other functions of government; it is express that the law-making function is the opposite of what obtains in England, and it is undeniable the law-interpreting function is unheard of there. The judicature in a federal constitution has very important powers and duties, and stands towards the legislatures in a way altogether unknown under the British constitution. The courts not only decide the rights of litigants before the law, but they declare whether or not any particular statute has been enacted by the legislature having the authority to pass that statute. It is their duty if an Act does not come from the proper legislature, to say that it is void, it is unconstitutional. They place an authoritative interpretation and construction upon the acts of the legislatures, judge when a given state of facts does or does not come within the purview of the law, and they decide not only as between the powers of the legislatures themselves, but also declare as between their legislation and the paramount law of the constitution whether it be compatible with the ultimate authority in the empire.

" The question never arose, " said Mr. Blake in his speech on the Supreme and Exchequer Courts Acts, " never could arise, to British statesmen or a British judge, whether an Act of the British parliament, affecting British subjects, is within the competency of that parliament or not. Such a notion is to them preposterous. It is to them incredible that such a question could be raised. "

PRINCIPLES OF THE BRITISH CONSTITUTION.

The chief features of the British constitution are very well known. Briefly, they are the unity of its executive, the omnipotence of its legislature, and the unqualified subordination of the judicature to the statute law. The Queen is the executive and the apex of constitutional power. This executive is one and indivisible, it is the head of the legislature, it is the source of the judicature. " Very few propositions in politics," says Macaulay, " can be so perfectly demonstrated as this, that parliamentary government cannot be carried on by two really equal and independent powers in one empire."

The British legislature has no division of its powers, it legislates on all classes of subjects and there is no limit to its powers. In a sense it is omnipotent—that is it can do whatever is not impossible ; it directs the executive in practice, it is practically the parliament. It rules by a committee called the privy or cabinet council, its measures must be interpreted by the judicature and carried into effect by the executive.

In Great Britain the constitution imposes no restriction on the power of government; in the United States of America, as with us, the constitution divides the powers conceded by the people to government between the general government and the particular state governments. Strictly the government is one and its powers only are divided and exercised by two sets of agents or ministries. The American system is not founded on antagonism of classes, estates or interests, and is in no sense a system of checks and balances: the British constitution trusts to that antagonism to preserve the government from pure centralism (*g*).

The judicature of England interprets the laws but does not sit in judgment on the right to make them, does not question their constitutionality in the same way as the courts do on this side of the Atlantic. A law or statute repealing the Magna Charta, or the Bill of Rights or some of the other great props of the constitution would be startling, possibly would be irregular, but it would not be unconstitutional in the sense in which we in Canada or the people of the American Union use that word. Each new session of the British legislature brings with it the power to repeal all the existing law and introduce a new order of things; and the judicature of the United Kingdom would have no alternative but to construe its meaning judicially.

From the foregoing we can appreciate how complicated and delicate are the adjustments of the machinery for government in Canada. We have a federal union with monarchic principles—one system a contradiction to another,

(*g*) Brownson's Constitution of the United States.

as Mr. Blake says; a piece of official mendacity, as Mr.
Dicey terms it. Yet Mr. Jenkyns, C.B., explains it all to
his own satisfaction by elevating the parliament of Canada
and minimizing the provincial " Councils." Mr. Freeman,
writing in 1863, thinks that a monarchic federation though
it never yet existed " is not in itself at all contradictory to
the federal ideal." Mr. Justice Story has this remark
which is at least as applicable to our country as to his own,
and which must close, for the present, any scientific exposition of the constitution : " No man who has ever studied
the subject with profound attention has risen from the
labour without an increased and almost overwhelming sense
of its intricate relations and perplexing doubts."

CHAPTER II.

THE CONSTITUTION OF CANADA.

*The constitution, the agreement of the provinces—Federal
union with monarchic principles—Executive " of and
over Canada" in the Queen—A parliament with two
houses constituted and unchangeable—A privy council
jurisdiction of parliament limited legislatively—Provincial jurisdiction defined—The executive power follows the legislative power in a federation—The provincial constitutions and their alteration—The judicature and its peculiar functions.*

The Imperial Act, known as The British North America
Act, 1867, settled and defined the present constitution of
Canada. For many years previous to that date and on
several occasions, as will be seen hereafter, the question of
uniting portions of the British possessions in America was
actively discussed. After a number of concessions from
all parties the points of agreement were laid before the
British parliament, and a written constitution drafted
thereon. The late province of Canada, comprising Upper
and Lower Canada, and the provinces of Nova Scotia and
New Brunswick were federally united into one Dominion—
Canada—under the crown of the United Kingdom of Great
Britain and Ireland, with a constitution similar in principle
to that of the United Kingdom. By it one PARLIAMENT,
consisting of the Queen, an upper house, styled the senate,
and the house of commons, was given to Canada. The
executive power of and over Canada was continued, and is

vested in the QUEEN. 'A council known as THE QUEEN'S
PRIVY COUNCIL FOR CANADA to aid and advise in the government of the country, was established, and an officer styled
the GOVERNOR-GENERAL OF CANADA, who possesses all the
powers, authorities and functions of our former governors,
so far as they can apply under the Act, represents Her
Majesty the Queen, and carries on the government in her
name and on her behalf. The SENATE was a body appointed by the first Governor-General, and intended to be
as permanent as in the nature of things it could well be.
The members of the House of COMMONS were to be elected
by the votes of the people as their representatives. These
three constituent elements of our parliament, corresponding
to the Queen, Lords and Commons in England, are to be
expected in the Canadian constitution, when it is remembered that the principle of the Dominion government
was intended to be the same as that of the United Kingdom.
Here, as in England, the executive power is declared to be
vested in the Queen, but that power is of course limited by
the two houses of parliament. The basis of the British
constitution is, that the power of making, abrogating,
changing or explaining its laws belongs to parliament
alone. Bearing in mind the power of disallowance lodged
in the Governor-General and in the Queen, and also the
fact that the parliament of Canada has power to legislate
over a limited number of subjects only, there is no doubt
but that the Canadian parliament has, under its constitution, a parallel authority. Neither in England nor here
does the legislative power reside in the crown, though the
latter possesses the whole power of carrying out the laws.
The desire of the guardians of both constitutions is said to
be to keep the exercise of the legislative and executive
powers as distinct as possible from each other. In effect,
however, they are linked together, as will be seen when the
position and the peculiar functions of the privy council

are examined. The power of the Crown being limited by its constitutional advisers, the form of government as far as it goes in that direction is a limited monarchy. The power of the Crown in England was declared in 1688 to be derived from a contract with the people. The people owe allegiance to the Crown, and the Crown grants protection in return. The Crown represents the nation—is supreme magistrate, appoints judges, distributes honors, receives and sends ambassadors, makes treaties, declares war, summons and dissolves parliament. But all acts of the Crown must be advised and transacted by ministers responsible to the people, and the King or Queen must govern according to law.

In Canada the royal authority is the same as in England—but the Queen acts here by and through a representative—a Governor-General. The contract with the people in the constitution may be traced to the cession of Canada by the Treaty of Paris in 1763, and reacknowledged in various ways since, chiefly by the Act of Confederation, which was the work of the peoples' representatives. But the functions of a Governor-General, though representing royalty, are more restricted than those appertaining to royalty itself. His duties do not involve many international offices—he has no ambassadors to send, and Canada as a colony has none to receive. There are no treaties to be made nor wars to be declared; but it is probable that all the prerogatives of royalty necessary to a colony are exerciseable by him, and attached to his person and office.

The SENATE, though corresponding largely to the House of Lords in England, yet differs in many respects from the latter body. The absence of a titled or hereditary aristocracy in Canada, to which the members of our Upper House may be supposed to belong, is one chief feature.

The duration of their patents, the limit to the term of holding office, the restriction as to their numbers, the absence of judicial functions, are a few of the points of difference between them. The chief uses of both bodies may be said to be the same—to prevent hasty legislation, and be in composition a body fearless of wrathful constituents and an equipose to preserve the balance of the constitution.

The third estate in the realm, the Commons, has fewer points of dissimilarity than either of the other two. The house of commons, under a constitutional form of government such as we possess, is the important part of parliament. The members of the privy council, if not mainly of their number, report in their house as to the manner of conducting the government. The supplies for carrying on all government originate with them. They are in fact the *people*—the supreme ruling power.

With us, as in England, the concurrence of these three elements of parliament is necessary to every measure. All must act in concert in order to produce a law. If the lords in England should refuse to act harmoniously with the commons, new peers of the realm could be created in accord with the popular wish as expressed by the action of the commons. If the commons could not agree with the lords of parliament, the former could be dissolved and new members elected by the people. But the last power would generally be found to be with the commons; who have virtually, in England at all events, the determining of the law in their own hands. In Canada it is much the same, but in case a deadlock were to occur between the senate and the commons, there could very well arise cases for which no remedy is at hand. The number of senators under our constitution cannot be increased but by a very small number, and the total number may be still too small to command a majority. If the commons and senate remained obstinately in opposition to each other the government could not go on. It would be necessary to have an Imperial Act passed to make legislation possible in any such unfortunate contingency.

In case the senate and commons agree, bills may be reserved by the Governor-General for the signification of the Queen's pleasure, or he may withhold the Queen's assent. Our position as a colony gives rise to the former case, perhaps to both cases, as the latter has no counterpart, in practice at least, in England. There, if a Bill is passed in the lords and commons, the Queen does not now refuse her assent thereto, the power of veto having fallen into disuse since the time of Queen Anne. Here, if a Governor-General refused the Queen's assent to a bill, it would be equivalent to an intimation to the ministry to resign—a hint that he refuses to take their advice. While possessing the undoubted right to refuse the Queen's assent to any bill, a Canadian Governor-General will scarcely ever refuse the Queen's assent. If he thinks the bill undesirable or objectionable he may possibly adopt the other course of reserving it for Her Majesty's pleasure.

One peculiar feature of the British constitution is its CABINET or PRIVY COUNCIL. The privy council would seem to mean the present and past advisers of the Crown. In practice, however, the past advisers, who are usually in opposition, do not tender advice till called upon in a change of ministry. The cabinet council here, as in England, means the ministry of administration for the time being— the government, in fact, of the day.

The task of government is carried on by the ministry, or government, or administration so long as they can command a majority in the two houses of parliament, and are the choice of the Crown. This is what is meant both in England and in Canada by responsible government. Parliament here has no judicial functions, nor does any of its branches form an appellate court, as in England. When a change of ministry occurs by the action of parliament, its action is administrative. The functions of Canadian parliaments otherwise are mainly legislative.

Other points of difference in the constitutions are chiefly in details, and arise from difference of position. The English constitution is for the most part unwritten. Some few of the great props, such as the Magna Charta, the Bill of Rights, the Act of Settlement, are embodied in Acts of Parliament with the other laws of the land. Under a federal constitution, the boundaries between the central and constituent powers must be committed to writing. A written constitution is essential to a federation. The Dominion has, in fact, a written and defined constitution, but it is not limited by it. It possesses powers which are neither defined nor limited, excepting by the Confederation Act and the Imperial Statute 28 and 29 Vic., ch. 63. It has general sovereignty in all matters but those from which it is expressly excluded, or in which, from the inherent condition of a dependency, it is necessarily and impliedly restricted. (*a*).

In all colonies there is a division of the sovereign power, part of it being exercised by the colonial legislature and the remainder by the imperial legislature. In Canada there is a threefold division of sovereignty—part of it imperial, part federal, and part provincial. These, although they all exist and are exercised within the same territory, are yet separate and distinct sovereignties acting separately

(*a*) Every subject proper to be legislated for in Canada falls either within the sovereignty of the provinces or of the Dominion. In two instances, that of immigration and agriculture, it may fall within both. In matters where imperial interests are in question it is likely to fall within neither.

and independently of each other within their respective spheres.

This is the basis and essence of *federal union* and by the constitution of Canada the several provinces comprising the Dominion are united together in a union of that nature· Three provinces—or we may say four provinces—that were relatively independent of each other, but all equally dependent on Great Britain, managed their own affairs up to the year 1867. By a compact ratified in that year they agreed to have one general parliament for all matters of common interest, and to retain the management of their own local and domestic concerns, virtually as they did before 1867. That is the federal union of Canada. Like the states of the American Union the provinces of the Dominion are united for some purposes, and separated for others. There is a federacy—a union for matters of general and, one might say, national interest; there is a separation for matters of local or internal interest.

In the American Union the separate states of the union surrendered to the United States government a portion of their sovereignty, and retained all the residue of it to themselves. This portion was given to the general government absolutely and irrevocably. The State governments kept the reserved powers to themselves—the central government was one of enumerated powers. Every power not expressly given to the central government was reserved to the local government. The powers of both were derived from the same source—the people—and it would require the people to act before these powers could be altered.

The action of the separate colonies of Great Britain, which now form Canada, was somewhat similar; but it is not correct to say that the principle of surrendering their legislative powers was just the reverse of what it was in the United States. The provinces, reserving for themselves the power to legislate on certain specified subjects, surrendered other specified subjects to the central government. Certain enumerated powers are allotted to each government; all powers necessary for the good government of CANADA, and not already in the Dominion list, belong to the central government : all powers of a PROVINCIAL nature and not already on the provincial list, belong to the local government. There is no reservation of provincial matters to Canada, and no reservation of Dominion affairs to the provinces. Every subject not relating to the provinces is given to the Dominion of Canada. Both powers were derived from the will of the people of Canada, acting under the British authority, and these powers cannot be altered but by that same will and authority.

The provinces being the originators and controllers of the Act of Union, assigned to themselves what they wanted—a prescribed class of subjects over which they were to have exclusive control, and they agreed that all other subjects should be dealt with by the general legislature for all the provinces. The provinces reserved to themselves the control of their own constitutions, so that they can amend them as they choose, except as regards the office of Lieutenant-Governor, who is a Dominion official. The executive power in the provinces is not said to be vested in the Lieutenant-Governor, nor is it expressly vested in the Queen. On this point there has been a great diversity of opinion. The writer can add nothing to what is said in the previous chapter on the executive power of and over Canada. The framers of the Act have left this part of it invitingly open to a difference of opinion, and various opinions have been expressed on it.

Whether or not the principles of the British constitution apply to the provinces and the provincial legislatures is another question much debated. The provinces or most of

them have gone on with the government much as before
1867—using the Queen's name as theretofore, having a
privy council, an upper house in some provinces, and a good
deal of the forms and ceremonies that appertain to parliaments and parliamentary procedure. (b).

The Lieutenant-Governor who is the head of the provincial legislature has acquiesced in all this—has indeed
been a prominent figure at all events in the forms and
ceremonies. He is a Dominion officer, appointed virtually
by the government of the Dominion. And so after an
experience of twenty years it must be concluded that if the
provincial governments ought not to be modeled on the imperial parliament, the Dominion authorities are now pre-
cluded from questioning their propriety. But there were
other grounds apart from magnifying by forms the new
Dominion; there was a new departure in the constitution
of a colony. It was to be no longer a legislative council

(b) It was much debated some years ago whether or not the provincial
legislatures were parliaments, but one circumstance will show that the
language of the Act of Union could not be otherwise than it is. A
parliament for Canada was intended; what the provinces wanted did
not appear so evident, and was not necessary to be considered as they
might not (as in Ontario) have an upper house or want one. How could
the imperial legislature recognize a parliament with only one house?
and what would be the use of decreeing them parliaments if at the next
session any one of them might declare that they required only a chairman for the purpose of their business? On the other hand it is apparent
that a parliament as nearly like the imperial one as could be under the
changed circumstances, was intended for the Dominion, not only on
account of its importance, but also that its permanence and stability
would be put beyond question. Besides it was desirable to distinguish the
legislatures in some way. Compare the permanance given in the U. S.
constitution to congress, and the senate, and the house of representatives, and sec. ii., article iv. as to the states of the union; "The United
States shall guarantee to every state in this union a republican form of
government, and shall protect each of them against invasion; and an
application of the legislature, or of the executive (when the legislature
cannot be convened), against domestic violence." Except the tenth
amendment which reserves the powers not delegated to congress, to the
states this is substantially all that is said of the states or their constitutions. The executive power is "vested in a President of the United
States of America." Yet no one will deny that the powers of the states
of the American Union are relatively of more importance towards the
United States government, than are the powers of the provinces of the
Dominion towards the parliament of Canada.

with a legislative assembly of prescribed powers, presided
over by a governor with very ample powers, but it was to
be, not only in name, but in substance a PARLIAMENT where
the power of two defined houses was to be the maximum
power of a dependency; the power of the governor a
minimum power to be the constitutional power of the
Crown in England. All this was not effected at the time
so far as the Crown is concerned, but it has been effected
since. For the first time in a British colony there was a
real parliament—one sitting in the capital of the Dominion
of Canada,—a parliament such as the fathers of confederation wanted, and without which they would not be satisfied.
They were entering on a new phase of existence; and so in
a few years later when the power of the Crown was defined.
Mr. Blake, the then Minister of Justice was able to say:
"Canada is not merely a colony or a province. She is a
Dominion composed of an aggregate of seven large provinces
federally united under one Imperial charter which expressly
recites that the constitution is to be similar to that of the
United Kingdom. Nay, more; besides the power with
which she is invested over a large part of the affairs of the
inhabitants of the several provinces, she enjoys absolute
power of legislation and administration over the people and
Territories of the North-West, out of which she has already
created one province, and is empowered to create others,
with representative institutions." (c)

The constitution while providing for these branches of
government, did not forget, that under a federal system
there ought to be some final authority to say whether or
not the different legislatures or executives have kept within
their prescribed limits.

A provincial legislature may trench on the limits of the
Dominion, and the parliament of Canada may usurp local

(c) Hon. Mr. Blake, Minister of Justice, to the Earl of Carnarvon.
sessional papers D, 1876.

rights. In either of these cases the courts must declare whether these legislative bodies have transcended their powers, and may declare acts of this nature unconstitutional and void.

The duties of the Canadian courts are relatively of more importance than those of the British courts. In England the powers of the legislature are, so far as human powers can be, omnipotent. Its acts are superior to judicial interpretation, so far as the question of their constitutionality is concerned. In Canada the courts are in a different position. Its humblest tribunal may declare an Act of Parliament unconstitutional, and may refuse to follow it. There can be no restraint put upon the due exercise of the judicial power by any authority, Dominion or Provincial ; for that would be to place these bodies above the law which created them and granted them powers which are not absolute, and which no legislation of theirs can make so. (d).

A similar judicial power exists in the United States. The supreme court is the most important judicial tribunal in the world. It is the supreme arbiter of the nation under the constitution.

Accordingly power was given to the parliament of Canada to provide for the constitution, maintenance and organization of a general court of appeal for Canada, and for the establishment of any additional courts for the better administration of the laws of Canada. This court would not of course deprive every other court of declaring in a proper case any Act to be unconstitutional, but it would afford as was hoped an ultimate court so as to bring about a uniformity of law in appeals from the various provinces. The ultimate court however, is the judicial committee of the privy council in England.

(d) Per Mr. Justice Wilson in the *Queen* v. *Taylor*, 36 U. C. R. 192.

CHAPTER III.

THE PARLIAMENT OF CANADA.—THE QUEEN.

The Queen—The first estate—The Governor-General—His Deputy—Death of Sovereign—Summons senators, speaker of senate—Calls together parliament—Other Duties — Judges — Lieutenant-Governors — Statutory Powers—Acts of 1791, 1840, 1854, 1867—Royal instructions—Mr. Blake and Earl Carnarvon—Duties of Governor—Mr. Todd's views—Duke of Newcastle's instructions.

THE first constituent element of the parliament of Canada is not only in principle, but is in reality the same as the first element of the parliament of the United Kingdom. This is the King or Queen of Great Britain and Ireland, who is the first estate in the realm.

In Canada the King or Queen is represented by a Governor-General, who is appointed by the Secretary of State for the colonies. He holds office during the pleasure of the sovereign of Great Britain ; and in the event of the sovereign's death, for six months after that date, in case no new appointment is made. An administrator or other officer may be appointed to carry on the government of Canada on behalf of and in the name of the Queen, and all the provisions of the Confederation Act, in reference to the Governor-General, apply to such administrator, or under whatever other title he may be known. The Queen may authorize the Governor-General to appoint any person or persons jointly or severally to be his deputy or deputies, within any part or parts of Canada, and the Governor-General may assign to such deputy or deputies, to exercise during his pleasure, such powers, functions and authorities of the Governor-General as the latter may deem necessary or expedient to assign to him or them, subject to any limitations or directions expressed or given by the Queen. Any such appointment, however, does not affect the powers, authorities and functions of the Governor-General himself. The death of the Governor does not dissolve the parliament. It is called to consult with the Queen, and not with him; and there might be ten governors during the reign of one Queen, with the same parliament assisting at the last as well as the first. He is not the *caput principium et finis* of the colonial constitutions. (*a*)

The Governor-General chooses and summons his privy councillors, and removes them when the government of Canada requires it.

He also summons in the Queen's name, by instrument under the Great Seal of Canada, persons of necessary qualifications for senators. At the time of the union of the provinces in 1867, Lord Monck, the first Governor-General of the Dominion of Canada, inserted the names of the senators in the Queen's proclamation of the union of the four provinces. Any additional senators are hereafter to be summoned by the Governor-General; and whenever a vacancy happens in the senate by resignation, death or otherwise, the Governor-General fills the vacancy by new appointments of qualified persons.

He also appoints a speaker in the senate, and may remove and appoint another in his place. The speaker must be a senator; and in this particular the senate, as to that officer, differs somewhat from the speaker of the House of Lords in England, who is not necessarily a peer of the

(*a*) Chalmer's opinions.

realm—or member of the house of lords. But in case he
is not a peer, he is not entitled to vote or take part in the
debates in the house.

The Governor-General summons and calls together the
house of commons in the Queen's name, and may dissolve
the same within the period of five years from its commencement. Independent of this statutory provision the
prerogative right in relation to the dissolution of general
assemblies is at least as extensive in the colonies as it ever
was in England. In respect to the English parliament
and this prerogative of the Crown, whatever the extent of
it may be, every governor by his commission is empowered
to exercise it in his particular province. (b).

He is empowered to assent in the Queen's name to bills
passed in both houses. He may also refuse the Queen's
assent to such bills, or he may reserve the bill for the signification of the Queen's pleasure. He also, when the
Queen's pleasure is signified on a reserved bill, declares by
speech or message to the houses, or by proclamation, that
it has received the assent of the Queen in council. Copies
of all bills assented to are sent to one of the secretaries of
state, and may be disallowed at any time within two years.
He must recommend to the house of commons all money
bills. He originates no measure, and by himself has no
legislative powers. He has a negative voice only in the
legislature.

The Governor-General appoints the judges for the
superior, district and county courts, except the judges of
the probate court in Nova Scotia and New Brunswick, and
may remove judges of the superior courts on address of
the senate and house of commons. He has also, until
the parliament of Canada otherwise provides, the appoint-

(b) Chalmer's opinions.

ment of such officers as may be deemed necessary and proper for the effectual execution of the Confederation Act. An appeal lies to the Governor-General in council from any act or decision of any provincial authority in reference to separate or dissentient schools in relation to education affecting the rights and privileges of any supporters of separate or dissentient schools. In case provincial law seems to the Governor-General in council requisite for this purpose, and that it is not made by the proper authorities, or in case the proper provincial authorities do not duly execute the directions of the Governor-General in council in any such appeal, the parliament of Canada may legislate thereon. (c).

The Governor-General in council appoints a Lieutenant-Governor for each province under the Great Seal of Canada, and may appoint an administrator to execute the office and functions of Lieutenant-Governor during the absence, illness or other inabilities of the latter : and the Governor-General (d) may remove a Lieutenant-Governor within five

(c) *Ex parte Renaud et al* (1 Pugsley, 273,) is a case decided in New Brunswick on a statute passed in 1871 repealing a school Act of 1858. The statute of 1858 was, or was supposed to be, one providing for denomination schools ; the Act repealing it in 1871 was upheld. In the following May the matter came up in the house of commons at Ottawa, and was referred to England 'to the crown law officers and lords of the privy council. They all declined to interfere, as the power of disallowance vested with the Governor-General absolutely and exclusively. The question came up in various ways with the same result. See Sess. papers, 1877, No. 89 ; also Sess. papers 1874, No. 25. See a similar case in Prince Edward Island Assembly Journals, 1878, page 2.

(d) In some parts of the Act of 1867 certain powers are given to the Governor-General in council, and in other parts to the Governor-General, omitting the words *in council*. This arose, it is said, from adopting the language of older Acts under which the Governor-General had unmistakeable powers apart from or independent of his council. Before the era of responsible government in Canada the Governor-General by himself had large administrative powers, and the phrase Governor-General had a different significance from what it has now. The council was then an irresponsible body ; so long as they agreed with the Royal representative they cared little for the popular element. The popular element now controls the council, and it is apprehended that any acts of a Governor-General for which an existing ministry is to be called to account by the years from his appointment, on assigning cause for such removal. In March 1878, M. Letellier was Lieutenant-Governor of Quebec and complaining that his ministers did not accept his recommendations, he dismissed them, summoned others and reported the case to the Governor-General. The dismissed premier, M. de Boucherville, sent in a counter-statement, and subsequently a petition came from certain members of the ex-ministry. The government in power at Ottawa took no action, but in the following year Sir John Macdonald, as chief minister, advised the removal of M. Letellier from office, as his usefulness was gone. (Sessional paper 1878-9). The Governor-General in council may disallow Acts of a provincial legislature within one year after their enactment in the same way as a disallowance of an Act of the parliament of Canada is signified in England, except that in the latter case two years are allowed to pass instead of one.

The power of the Governor-General in council to disallow a provincial Act is as absolute as the power of the Queen to disallow a Dominion Act, and is in each case to be the result of the exercise of a sound discretion, for which exercise of discretion the executive council for the time

people, must be done on the advice of his council, no matter whether so expressed or not. See Sir John A. Macdonald's letter to Sir Michael Hicks Beach on the Letellier question, and the Hon. Edward Blake on the Royal instructions to Lord Dufferin as to exercise of prerogative of pardon by a Governor-General. Sir John Macdonald says: "Long before confederation, the principle of what is known as 'responsible government' had been conceded to the colonies, now united in the Dominion. Whether, therefore in any case power is given to the Governor-General to act individually, or with the aid of his council, the act as one within the scope of the Canadian constitution must be on the advice of a responsible minister. The distinction drawn in the statute between the act of a Governor and an act of a Governor in council is a technical one, and arose from the fact, that in Canada for a long period before confederation, certain acts of administration were required by law to be done under the sanction of an order in council, while others did not require that formality. In both cases, however, since responsible government has been conceded, such acts have always been performed under the advice of a responsible ministry."

being is, in either case, to be responsible, as for other acts of executive administration. (e).

The twelfth section of the British North America Act relates to the general powers of the Governor-General and is as follows :

"All powers, authorities, and functions which, under any Act of the parliament of Great Britain, or of the parliament of the United Kingdom of Great Britain and Ireland, or of the legislature of Upper Canada, Lower Canada, Canada, Nova Scotia or New Brunswick, are at the Union vested in or exerciseable by the respective Governors or Lieutenant-Governors of those provinces, with the advice, or with the advice and consent, of the respective executive councils thereof, or in conjunction with those councils, or with any number of members thereof, or by those Governors or Lieutenant-Governors individually, shall, as far as the same continue in existence and capable of being exercised after the union in relation to the government of Canada, be vested in and exerciseable by the Governor-General, with the advice or with the advice and consent of or in conjunction with the Queen's privy council for Canada, or any members thereof, or by the Governor-General individually, as the case requires, subject nevertheless (except with respect to such as exist under Acts of the parliament of Great Britain or of the parliament of the United Kingdom of Great Britain and Ireland) to be abolished or altered by the parliament of Canada."

The Acts of the parliament of Great Britain which could relate to this subject are 14 Geo. III., cap. 83, and 31 Geo. III., cap. 31, both of which have already been referred to as the Quebec Act of 1774 and the constitutional Act of 1791.

(e) Per C. J. Harrison in *Leprohon* v. *Ottawa*, 40 U. C. R. And see valuable memorandum of Mr. Lash the late Deputy Minister of Justice, *post.*

There is nothing in the Quebec Act further than repealing the proclamation of October, 1763, as to the provisional government and all the powers and authorities given to the governors.

In the constitutional Act, 1791, there is for the first time a Governor or Lieutenant-Governor given to the provinces of Upper and Lower Canada, into which the former province of Quebec was divided. The powers of the Governor or Lieutenant-Governor under this Act were as follows:

(1) Bills passed by the Legislative Council and Assembly of the Provinces, were, before becoming law, to be assented to by His Majesty, or, in his name, by the Governor or Lieutenant-Governor of the provinces.

(2) It was lawful for His Majesty, by instrument under the sign manual, to authorize and direct the Governor or Lieutenant-Governor to summon the members of the legislative council—seven in Upper Canada and fifteen in Lower Canada—and also such other persons to the council as he may think fit.

(3) It was lawful for him to summon and call together the legislative assembly.

(4) It was lawful for him to divide the provinces into districts, to appoint returning officers and the time and place of holding elections.

As to assenting to bills, he declared such assent according to his discretion, but only subject to the Act. He could withhold his assent, or reserve it for His Majesty's consideration.

A feature of this Act is that the Royal instructions to three of the former Governors—Guy Carlton, Sir Frederick Haldimand and Lord Dorchester—in reference to tithes and the support of clergy were incorporated into the Act.

The Union Act 3 & 4 Victoria cap. 35 (1840), an Act of the Parliament of Great Britain and Ireland, has two sections bearing upon this subject. Sec. 40, as to the authority of the Governor is as follows :

"Nothing herein contained shall be construed to limit or restrain the exercise of Her Majesty's prerogative in authorizing, and not withstanding this Act, and any other Act or Acts passed in the parliament of *Great Britain*, or in the parliament of the United Kingdom of *Great Britain* and *Ireland*, or of the legislature of the province of *Quebec*, or of the provinces of *Upper* or *Lower Canada* respectively, it shall be lawful for Her Majesty to authorize the Lieutenant-Governor of the province of *Canada* to exercise and execute, within such parts of the said province as Her Majesty shall think fit, notwithstanding the presence of the Governor within the province, such of the powers, functions, and authority, as well judicial as other which before and at the time of the passing of this Act were and are vested in the Governor, Lieutenant-Governor or Person administering the government of the provinces of *Upper Canada* and *Lower Canada* respectively, or of either of them, and which from and after the said re-union of the said two provinces shall become vested in the Governor of the province of *Canada*; and to authorize the Governor of the province of *Canada* to assign, depute, substitute, and appoint any person or persons, jointly or severally, to be his deputy or deputies within any part or parts of the province of *Canada*, and in that capacity to exercise, perform and execute during the pleasure of the said Governor such of the powers, functions and authorities, as well judicial as other, as before and at the time of the passing of this Act were and are vested in the Governor, Lieutenant-Governor or person administering the government of the provinces of *Upper* and *Lower Canada* respectively, and which from and after the union of the said provinces shall become vested in the Governor of the province of *Canada*, as the Governor of the province of *Canada* shall deem to be necessary or expedient; provided always, that by the appointment of a deputy or deputies as aforesaid, the power and authority of the Governor of the province of *Canada* shall not be abridged, altered,

o's.g.c. 4

or in any way affected, otherwise than as Her Majesty shall think proper to direct."

Sec. 59 of the same Act reads :

" All powers and authorities expressed in this Act, to be given to the Governor of the province of Canada, shall be exercised by such Governor in conformity with and subject to such orders, instructions and directions, as Her Majesty shall from time to time see fit to make or issue."

The imperial enactment, 17 and 18 Vic., cap. 118 (1854), which altered the Union Act, has no important reference to the powers of Governor. It defines the word " Governor " as comprehending the Governor, and in his absence, the Lieutenant-Governor, or person authorized to execute the office, or the functions of the Governor of Canada.

Of the numerous references made to the Governor of the late province of Canada in the statutes from the union till confederation, no detailed statement need be made here. They refer to the necessary duties of the chief executive officer of the province, entrusted with carrying on the government under the constitution. In one place we find him made a corporation sole—empowered to issue proclamations, commissions, &c. In 1845 an Act was passed relating to commissions, in the first section of which it was enacted that on the demise of the Crown no new commissions need issue, but a proclamation continuing all public officers in their place should be sufficient. Section 2 is as follows :—" Nothing in the next preceding section shall prejudice, or in any way affect the rights or prerogative of the Crown, with respect to any office or appointment, derived or held by authority from it, nor prejudice, or affect the rights, or prerogatives thereof in any other respect whatsoever." Power is expressly reserved to Her Majesty in an Act passed in the same year to prorogue or dissolve the provincial parliament of Canada on the demise of the Crown.

The foregoing will give some idea of the statute law, on the powers of a Governor-General; and it is to this, rather than to anything else, that recourse must be had in order to discover what are his powers, authorities and functions. Such prerogative rights of the Crown in England as are called personal rights of the sovereign, are conveyed to Governors of Colonies only by express delegation. The royal commission and royal instructions generally contained the extent of these, and they are now virtually reduced to nothing.

The Governor of a British colony is in general invested with royal authority, and is the representative and deputy of the British sovereign. The sovereign alone exercises the prerogatives of the Crown, and these royal rights and powers cannot be vested in two persons at the same time. They may and are, however, delegated to colonial Governors either by the charter governments of the colony or by the royal commission and instructions, but only by express terms. The fundamental rights and principles upon which the royal authority rests, and which are necessary to maintain it, extend to the colonies. The Queen is sovereign of Great Britain and of the colonies as well. She has perpetuity, and can do no wrong constitutionally within the British Dominions. The local prerogatives in England, unless by express grant, do not extend to the colonies; but it seems on good authority that the minor prerogatives and interests of the Crown may be taken up and dealt with by the colonial legislatures. Until that happens the prerogative in England prevails. (f)

This occurred in Ontario where a Lieutenant Governor was, unless and until authorized by his legislature, held incapable of creating Queen's Counsel—the prerogative of

(f) Chitty on Prerogatives of the Crown.

fountain of honor not being within his power under the
British North America Act. (g)   This prerogative is,
however, vested in the Governor General, he being the
Queen's representative in Canada, and he is competent to
appoint Queen's Counsel.   The law on the question of prerogative is laid down in Chalmer's Opinions of Eminent
Lawyers:

"The prerogative in the colonies, unless where it is
abridged by grants, etc., made to the inhabitants, is that
power over the subjects considered either separately or
collectively, which by the common law of England abstracted from Acts of parliament, and grants of liberties,
&c., from the Crown to the subject, the King could right-
fully exercise in England."

The Common Law of England on the question of
prerogative is, therefore, the common law of the colonies
on that subject—unless where the charter or royal commission interposes to extend or restrict it—and this law is
set out in 17 Edward II., cap. 1, a statute simply declaratory
of the common law.   The Governor-General is the representative of the Queen, and the Queen is part of our
constitution.   Whatever rights are necessary or exerciseable
in a colony must vest in him as royal representative, and
it is not so obviously material that they are statutory rather
than prerogative rights.

The royal commission and royal instructions are now
reduced to the most general terms, and contain no express
delegation of any prerogative rights.   In 1875 a correspondence began between Earl Carnarvon and Mr. Blake,

(g) The judges of the supreme court appear to differ on this point with
the law officers of the Crown in England.   The latter are of opinion that
any provincial legislature might authorize by statute the Lieutenant-
Governor to make such appointments.   An arrangement seems to have
been entered into in this matter, between the federal and provincial
authorities.   See sess. papers, Canada, 1873, No. 50.   Lenoir v. Ritchie,
5 S. C. R. 575.

minister of justice, upon the commission and instructions to governors. The word colony was objected to and removed, and 'ordinances' was deemed unsuitable to a government carried on by "law." The prerogative of pardon was for a long time in dispute but finally was left as all other matters to the Governor acting on the advice of his ministers. This correspondence is very interesting and may be seen in the sessional papers of 1876, and on a return made in 1879. Not only Canada but all the British Colonies owe a debt of gratitude to the distinguished minister of justice who successfully pleaded their cause before the Colonial Secretary on this occasion. See also the correspondence on the question of disallowance of legislation, except on the advice of ministers. Sess. papers 1877, No. 89.

When the Governor-General has dismissed one set of ministers, and is about to choose another, then, and then only, does he appear to stand alone under our constitution. Even in this case, the new ministry is responsible—the Crown is never responsible. The Crown is not supposed to have ministers unless it accepts their advice. Its independent judgment seems to be called into requisition when the question is, to what party shall the reins of power be entrusted. Once having made a selection, its acts are the acts of the new ministry—it is no longer on the Governor-General's advice, but on theirs, that the country is governed. (h)

So far as legislative powers are concerned, the Governor-General possesses only a negative voice. The Queen herself

(h) Undoubtedly that theory is that the minister chosen by the King is himself responsible for every circumstance or act which led to his appointment. This principle was established in the fullest manner, in 1834, when Sir Robert Peel admitted his entire responsibility for the dismissal of Lord Melbourne, by King William IV., though it was notorious that he was in Italy at the time and had not been consulted on the matter.—*Yonge's Constitutional History*, Chap. I.

cannot be said but by fiction to possess any such powers, as the first estate in parliament would seem to imply. A measure becomes law in England, it is true, with her assent, but she would not now refuse her assent on a measure passed in both houses. The two houses of parliament could send up a bill deposing her, or altering the succession, and she would be obliged to sign it ; and if one sovereign refused his or her assent, another could be got to grant it. As a late vigorous, but rather rough and plain-spoken, writer puts it : " She must sign her own death-warrant, if the two houses unanimously send it up to her. " (i)

The Governor-General has in the reservation of bills a certain power, but beyond this and his instructions, and an undoubted right to refuse advice tendered by ministers, the principle of the British constitution leaves in him as the Queen's representative no positive legislative powers whatever.

Mr. Todd considers that a Governor must be regarded as a representative of the crown, and as the embodiment of the monarchical element in a colony. He also regards him as the source of all executive authority in a colony. But it is manifest that the Governor is not the source but the representative of executive authority in Canada. It may be otherwise in crown colonies, but certainly not in this Dominion.

The duties of a Governor may be summed up in three heads : he must always act through advisers approved of by parliament ; he must refrain from personal interference with the ministers in their direction of local affairs except to uphold the law or protect the people ; and he must consent to all acts of government except in extreme cases.

(i) Bagehot, on the English constitution.

The Duke of Newcastle as colonial secretary in 1862, wrote to the governor of Queensland in this way: " The general principle by which the governor of a colony possessing responsible government is to be guided is this : that when imperial interests are concerned he is to consider himself the guardian of these interests ; but in matters of purely local politics, except in extreme cases, to follow the advice of a ministry which appears to possess the confidence of the legislature. But extreme cases are those which cannot be reduced to any recognized principle arising in circumstances which it is impossible or unwise to anticipate, and of which the full force can, in general be estimated only by persons in immediate contact with them." (,j)

(j) See Todd, Parliamentary Government in the Colonies, pp. 432, 440.

CHAPTER IV.

THE PARLIAMENT OF CANADA—THE SENATE.

Composition of the senate—Limited to 78—The three divisions —Qualifications of a senator—How the seat becomes vacant—Title and precedence—Number in the cabinet— Speaker—Quorum—Privileges—The House of Lords— Additional senators—Rule in such a case—Reason for a second chamber—Mr. Smith's view—Mr. Todd's.

THE senate or upper house is the second element in the parliament of Canada, and was composed of 72 members when first summoned at Confederation—24 from Ontario, 24 from Quebec, and 24 from the Maritime Provinces of Nova Scotia and New Brunswick. This number from the Maritime Provinces included their share in the senate whenever Prince Edward Island should be thereafter admitted. This happened in 1873.

In relation to the senate, Canada was deemed to consist of three divisions equally represented by senators selected from these sections. It is only in Quebec that the senators represent particular localities.

Since confederation, in 1871, British Columbia has been admitted, and sends three members. Manitoba, admitted in 1870, sent two members until its population, according to a decennial census, attained 50,000 inhabitants, and it now sends three; and when the population reaches 75,000 it will be entitled to four representatives in the senate. The Territories are not yet represented. When Newfoundland is admitted it will be entitled to send four senators to the Canadian parliament. The Governor-General may recommend the appointment of three, or six senators, representing equally the three divisions of Canada, and in case the Queen thinks fit, one or two may be appointed from Ontario, Quebec, and the Maritime Provinces.

The number of senators must never exceed 78, or after the admission of Newfoundland, of 82. There should be at present 78 members in the senate, the full number, Ontario sending 24, Quebec 24, New Brunswick and Nova Scotia 10 each, Manitoba 3, British Columbia 3, and Prince Edward Island 4. (a)

The qualifications of a senator are as follows :

(1) He shall be of the full age of thirty years :

(2) He shall be either a natural born subject of the Queen, or a subject of the Queen naturalized by an Act of the parliament of Great Britain, or of the parliament of the United Kingdom of Great Britain and Ireland, or of the legislature of one of the Provinces of Upper Canada, Lower Canada, Canada, Nova Scotia, or New Brunswick, before the Union, or of the parliament of Canada after the union :

(3) He shall be legally or equitably seized as of freehold for his own use and benefit of lands or tenements held in free and common socage, or seized or possessed for his own use and benefit of lands or tenements held in franc-alleu or in roture, within the province for which he is appointed, of the value of four thousand dollars, over and above all rents, dues, debts, charges, mortgages, and incumbrances due or payable out of or charged on or affecting the same :

(4) His real and personal property shall be together worth four thousand dollars over and above his debts and liabilities :

(a) In point of fact there seem to be 22 from Ontario, the same number from Quebec, 10 each from Nova Scotia and New Brunswick, 4 from Prince Edward Island and 3 from Manitoba and British Columbia each. By the Act of 1887 the North-west Territories are entitled to two members.

(5) He shall be resident in the province for which he is appointed :

(6) In the case of Quebec he shall have his real property qualification in the electoral division for which he is appointed, or shall be resident in that division.

The first senators were summoned by the Queen by warrant under Her Majesty's sign manual, and their names were inserted in the proclamation of the union in 1867. Such persons as were called thereafter, and such persons as shall be called, to the Senate, were and shall be, by the Governor-General, in the Queen's name, by instrument under the great seal of Canada.

A senator, subject to the following provisions, holds his seat for life.

He may, by writing under his hand, resign his place in the senate.

His seat becomes vacant—

(1) If for two consecutive sessions of the parliament he fails to give his attendance in the senate :

(2) If he takes an oath or makes a declaration or acknowledgment of allegiance, obedience, or adherence to a foreign power, or does an act whereby he becomes a subject or citizen, or entitled to the rights or privileges of a subject or citizen of a foreign power :

(3) If he is adjudged bankrupt or insolvent, or applies for the benefit of any law relating to insolvent debtors, or becomes a public defaulter :

(4) If he is attainted of treason, or convicted of felony or of any infamous crime :

(5) If he ceases to be qualified in respect of property or of residence ; provided that a senator shall not be deemed

to have ceased to be qualified in respect of residence by reason only of his residing at the seat of the government of Canada while holding an office under that government requiring his presence there.

Any vacancy in the senate resulting from resignation, death, or otherwise, is filled by the Governor-General's appointment of a fit and qualified person to fill the vacancy.

Any question arising as to the qualification of a senator, or to a vacancy in the senate, shall be heard and determined by the senate.

No senator is capable of being elected, or of sitting or voting as a member of the house of commons.

No Ontario senator can be a member of the local legislature of that province.

Every senator before taking his seat in the senate must take and subscribe before the Governor-General, or some person authorized by him, a prescribed oath and declaration.

A senator is entitled to be styled honorable so long as he is a member of the senate, and no longer, and he ranks fourth in the precedence assigned to persons in Canada. (b)

A member of the senate may be a member of the ministry of administration ; and if his duties require him to live at the seat of government, it is not necessary that he should reside in his own province if appointed out of Ontario. Mr. Todd says : (c) " Following the practice previously observed from the first introduction of responsible government into the old province of Canada, it has been customary that two members of the cabinet should have seats in the

(b) See table of precedence hereafter.
(c) Parliamentary government, page 48.

upper house to take charge of public business therein, and generally to represent the administration of the legislative council or as it is now termed the senate. It is understood that less than two members would not suffice; and upon the formation of the present administration in November, 1878, the number was increased to three, the speaker of the senate being for the first time since confederation, made a cabinet minister."

The senate is summoned to Ottawa, the seat of government, at the same time as the commons is convened. The speaker of the senate is appointed by commission under the great seal by the Governor-General, and must be a senator, though the analogous course in the house of lords in England, as was observed, is not followed in this particular. There the Lord Chancellor is *ex officio* speaker in the lords, and is keeper of the Great Seal, but is not necessarily a peer of the realm.

He presides over all the deliberations of the senate except when they are in committee of the whole; he decides questions of order. He addresses the senate from the floor of the house and not from the chair, he has a vote in every case and votes before the other senators. They do not address him, though he occupies the chair in the senate, but they address the rest of the senators. Any intemperate or offensive language is dealt with by the senate, which may censure the delinquent, and may also interfere to prevent quarrels between senators. He reports the speech of the Governor-General and informs the commons of the necessity of the election of a speaker.

Fifteen members, including the speaker, form at present a quorum for the transaction of business. Questions are decided by a majority of votes; and when these are equal, the motion or bill is lost, or deemed to be in the negative.

The privileges, immunities and powers of the senate and its members are left to be defined by the parliament of Canada, but they must never exceed those held by the English house of commons and its members at the time the parliament of Canada so defines them. (*d*)

The rules of the house and the procedure will be briefly adverted to hereafter.

All bills may issue in this, or in the house of commons indifferently, (*e*) excepting money bills, which must originate in the commons. Bills of a judicial nature, such as divorce bills, etc., and bills referring to the rights and privileges of the senate, would, following the analogy of the practice in the upper house in England, have their commencement properly in the senate.

The senate does not appear to possess any other functions than those of a branch of the legislature, or law-making machinery of the state. In England the lords possess judicial functions, as well as legislative ones, and their house is the highest court for deciding cases referred to it from the English courts.

Such frequent reference has been made to the house of lords that a few words may be said here of this body, in order to contrast it with the senate of our own country.

In England the house of lords is the aristocratic element of parliament, and consists of lords temporal—that is, lay noblemen or peers—and lords spiritual—that is, archbishops and bishops. The temporal lords are called peers of the realm, and when of full age, and not imbecile, are entitled to sit in the house in virtue of their titles and ancient rights.

(*d*) See next chapter on the Commons as to the privileges of members.
(*e*) The senate alone, apparently, takes the initiative in divorce bills.

The lords are in number rather more than two-thirds of the commoners. A part of them have judicial as well as legislative functions. A special portion of them—all distinguished lawyers, or judges, form the appellate court of the house of lords. Many of them are members of the judicial committee of the privy council, which is the highest appellate court in the empire for the colonies.

There are five orders of peers—dukes, marquises, earls, viscounts and barons. This is their rank in the order of precedence, but they all sit in the house as barons, that is, as possessing a barony or landed estate. The bishops now sit in the house in virtue of their estates, and not in respect of their clerical dignities. They rank before barons and after viscounts, and are lords of parliament, though not peers of the realm. The spiritual lords number thirty— the lay lords or peers vary between four and five hundred. This number is maintained by the eldest sons of peers succeeding to their fathers' titles, and also by the crown creating peers by patent of nobility. The crown is not limited to the creation of any certain number of peers, when a collision happens between the lords and commons, but the popular element—the commons—suggests the appointment of as many as are necessary.

The house of lords in England may be said to be practically under the control of the commons. It has the power to delay bills, and power to amend them in most cases, but it has no other powers. Its political character can be changed by the creation of new peers, to make it accord with the ruling party in the commons, and so it cannot stand out against them. When the commons has made up its mind on any measure the lords are powerless to resist. As Bagehot says, their veto is:—"We reject your bill for this once, or these twice, or even these thrice, but if you keep on sending it up, at last we won't reject it."

The senate of Canada has larger powers than these. It not only can delay legislation, as it very wisely did in the Insolvency Bill of 1878, but legislation cannot be got without it. It cannot vote the supplies, but it can vote against the supplies, and put a stop to all government, as the analogous body, the legislative council, foolishly did in Quebec in 1879. Its political complexion cannot be altered by the addition of new members because the maximum number is fixed at 78 for the present provinces, and that number may now be reached. It is not controlled by the commons in a sense, but it follows the commons as the best expression of public opinion : it must be harmonized with them by administration in accordance with their views.

Any difference between the commons and senate here is not so easily adjusted, or rather will not be whenever such a contingency arises. Six members added to the senate may not be sufficient to make it accord with the majority in the commons. In 1874 six members were recommended to be appointed, but Earl Kimberley suggested that the crown should take no action until a difference had arisen, and that the creation of new members would supply a remedy in the event of an actual collision. (*f*) Our senate is in this respect differently situated from the upper house in England, and its peculiar constitution may some day give rise to a deadlock in the government.

The senate was intended to be composed of men of wealth and stake in the country who were superior to party and heedless of local or interested claims. It was thought that to be answerable to constituents was frequently to be obliged to pander to their whims—to legislate for their special interests. This, it was hoped would be obviated by

(*f*) Senate Journals, 1877, page 130.

appointments by the crown of persons whose own interests would suffer when their country's suffered ; and that the good of the country would, even for selfish motives, if for no other, be promoted by them as being largely mixed up with their own individual prosperity. A second house was needed to prevent hasty or inconsiderate legislation—a house wherein the largely increasing legislation for the provinces could be participated in and matured. It was expected to elicit the sober second thought of the people. It was felt also that some equipoise was needed to maintain the balance of the constitution.

Mr. Goldwin Smith, writing of the senate and of the patronage of the prime minister in Canada in regard to the appointments to it, has the following :

" He " the premier, " nominates for life the members of the upper house of the legislature, whereas in the United States the members of the senate are elected by the legislature of the state which they represent. The result of this theoretically conservative arrangement in Canada is practically the reverse of conservative. A nominee senate, without even a basis of landed wealth, such as is possessed by the house of lords, or any guarantee either for its reasonable agreement with public opinion or for its independence of government influence, has not, nor does it deserve to have, any sort of authority. The consequence is that, whereas in the United States power is really divided between the two houses, and the senate, with perfect freedom, controls and reverses the acts of the popular house, in Canada power centres entirely in the commons. The senate is a cipher ; it initiates nothing ; it adjourns till business comes up to it from the commons, and only shows that it is alive about once in each session by the rejection of some secondary bill. The salaries which the country pays to senators are simply wasted, and the community is led to repose in the belief that it has a conservative safeguard where it has none. It is true that the institution can scarcely be said to have had a fair trial. The patronage has been for the most part in illiberal hands, and has been systematically used for the objects of party or for narrower objects still. The framers of the constitution, the British statesmen who took part in the work at least, probably had a vision of an assembly representing the great interests and professions and eminence of all kinds, such as might have commanded the respect of the nation. They, at all events, did not mean that places in the legislature should be used as part of the bribery fund of faction and as inducements to spend money in elections. But it is more than doubtful whether, where the basis of government is popular election, real power can be conferred on any body which has not an elective title."

Mr. Todd, in his "Parliamentary Government in the Colonies," says : (g)

"A nominated upper chamber, though undoubtedly preferable in certain respects to an elected body, constitutes no efficient or effectual check to democratic ascendancy. And it is obviously not in this direction that we may expect to find the point of agreement which shall reconcile the conflicting claims of colonial legislative bodies. New South Wales, the Dominion of Canada and Queensland severally possess a nominated upper house, and yet difficulties similar to those which have so long agitated Victoria are not unknown in these colonies . . . In Canada, the senate or upper house have repeatedly exhibited an independent spirit, and the expediency of curbing their powers in respect to financial questions, has been mooted, at any rate by the party now in opposition." .

Mr. Freeman is especially favorable to a second chamber under a Federal system, because he says it is capable of representing therein the wants and wishes of the several states or provinces included in the confederation in their separate standing.

The senate is nominated in Canada because a second elective chamber would seem superfluous: because the

(g) Page 522.

o's.g.c. 5

model of the upper house in England was kept in view, and because two houses of some character were deemed necessary. An elective second house would be a second commons, and would ask and require larger powers than a nominated senate. The choice in 1867 was between a nominated senate and no senate.

CHAPTER V.

THE PARLIAMENT OF CANADA—THE COMMONS.

Former and present composition of the commons—Who may not be members—Who may and who may not vote for members—Election trials—Duration of the commons—Speaker—Quorum—Privileges of the house; of its members.

THE house of commons is the third element in the parliament of Canada, and was originally composed of 181 members, representing the four provinces as follows :

Ontario, represented by	82	members.
Quebec, "	65	"
Nova Scotia, "	19	"
New Brunswick "	15	"

Of the provinces annexed to Canada since confederation the following is the representation :

Prince Edward Island, represented by	6	members.
Manitoba, "	4	"
British Columbia, "	6	"

Provision was made at the passing of the Confederation Act for an increase of the number of members in the house, but the proportionate representation of the four provinces comprising Canada in 1867 must not be disturbed by any such increase. The parliament of Canada has power over this increased representation. It was further provided that in 1871, when a census of the people was to be taken, an adjustment of the representation of the four provinces should take place in parliament. This gave rise to a representation of 206 members, and subsequently the number was increased to 211 as follows :

Ontario	92	members.
Quebec	65	"
New Brunswick	16	"
Nova Scotia	21	"
Manitoba	5	"
Prince Edward Island	6	"
British Columbia	6	"
In all	211	"

To these must now be added as representing the North-West Territories :

Saskatchewan and Alberta, 1 each	2	members.
East and West Assiniboia, 1 each	2	"
	4	"

The different provinces are divided up into electoral districts, each of which returns a member to the commons on his having received a majority of polled votes in the riding. The writs for the election of members issue out of the office of the clerk of the crown in chancery, and are usually but not necessarily addressed to the sheriff or registrar as returning officer in the electoral district. A day for the nomination of candidates and the day and place for holding the polls are then appointed. Each candidate must deposit $200 with the returning officer to apply towards the payment of election expenses. The candidates need have no real property qualification, but must be either natural born or naturalized subjects of the Queen. No member of the senate of Canada or of the provincial legislature of Ontario is eligible to sit in the commons.

The following classes of persons are ineligible as members of the commons :

(1). No person accepting or holding any office, commission or employment, permanent or temporary, in the service of the government of Canada, or of any of its officers, at the nomination of the crown to which is attached any fee, any salary, wages, allowance, emolument or property of any kind, shall be eligible to sit or vote as a member of the commons.

(2). No sheriff, registrar of deeds, clerk of the peace or county attorney can be a member.

(3). No contractor directly or indirectly, except a contractor for a loan of money or securities to the government after public competition. But members of Her Majesty's privy council, holding offices of state in Ottawa, are not ineligible. Nor are militia officers, or men who receive their daily pay or remuneration for enrolment, or the care of arms or drill instruction.

No senator or member of the local legislature of Ontario, even before the recent legislation was eligible to sit in the commons.

Each member is allowed $10 per day in a session under thirty days—if beyond thirty days, $1,000 and not more. He is also allowed, as are the senators, ten cents a mile going and coming by the nearest mail route, for mileage.

The qualifications of voters are ranged under the following heads :

1—PERSONS ENTITLED TO VOTE.

Every person shall be entitled to be registered, in any year, upon the list of voters for the proper polling district of any electoral district or portion of an electoral district, and when so registered, to vote, if such person—

(1). Is of the full age of twenty-one years and not disqualified or prevented by dominion law from voting,

(2). Is a British subject by birth or naturalization,

(3). Is the owner of real property, actually worth—if in a city—$300 ; in a town, $200 ; elsewhere, $150,

(4). Is a tenant under a lease of $2 per month, or $6 per quarter, or $12 half-yearly, or annual rental of $20.

(5). Is a *bona fide* occupant for one year before applying to be put on the list of land valued as if he were owner. (3)

(6). Is a resident and assessed for $300 income,

(7). Is a farmer's son under certain circumstances,

(8). Is son of an owner, other than a farmer, under similar circumstances,

(9). Is a fisherman owning real property, boats, nets, fishing gear and tackle, worth at least $150,

(10). Is a life annuitant for at least $100, secured in real estate in Canada.

2—PERSONS NOT ENTITLED TO VOTE.

(1). Judges of every court whose appointment rests with the Governor-General,

(2). Revising-officers, returning-officers and election clerks; but a returning-officer can vote where there is a tie.

(3). Agents of candidates, counsel, attorney, solicitor, agent or clerk, who has received or expects to receive any sum of money, fee, office or place of emolument, or any promise, pledge or security for any of these.

Very stringent provisions are enacted in regard to bribery and corrupt practices at elections; and when any candidate is returned, any voter may file a petition complaining of the undue return or undue election of a member, or of no return, or of a double return or unlawful act on the part of the person returned as member; and on notice of the presentation of the petition being given to the respondent the parties can go to trial on the question, as provided by the Controverted Elections Act. These cases are tried by various courts in the different provinces, and an appeal lies therefrom to the supreme court at Ottawa.

All the elections, except in a few places, are now made returnable on one day, fixed by the Governor-General, and the various returning officers send in their returns to the clerk of the crown in chancery at Ottawa. Thither the members are summoned by proclamation in the *Canada Gazette*, at the same time as the senate is assembled. Each member sits for five years, which is the duration of each parliament, unless sooner dissolved by the Governor-General. Twenty members, reckoning the speaker, form a quorum for the transacting of business. The members themselves elect their speaker at the first sitting, and he continues in office during that parliament, unless a vacancy occurs. When a vacancy occurs in the office of speaker by death, resignation or otherwise it is filled by the house, in the same way as a speaker is originally appointed.

The speaker receives a salary of $4,000, per annum and has very important duties to perform. He presides at all meetings of the house but has no vote except when there is a tie. In his absence there was a provision that he might call on the chairman of committees to act as deputy speaker. But for some two sessions past the house following the English practice has appointed a deputy speaker who takes the chair in the speaker's absence. At the dissolution of a parliament the speaker is deemed for certain purposes to retain the position until a new speaker is chosen.

The reports of judges in respect of controverted elections are made to the speaker and he gives orders for the issue of new writs. Members who resign their seats inform the house through him and he proceeds in the same way to have the vacancy filled up, whether it be caused by death or acceptance of office, or as the case may be. It is through him that the privileges of the house and its members are claimed at the opening of each parliament, he announces and reads the message from the Governor-General, and he presents the supply bill with the usual formula shewing that the commons are the important factors of parliament in that respect. He has charge of the decorum of the house, reprimands members when necessary, and may name a member for any breach of parliamentary etiquette. He states motions and their amendments, signs votes and proceedings, receives messages from eminent persons and from the upper house, with a variety of other duties appertaining by custom to or imposed by regulations on his office. He has charge of the officers and clerks in attendance on the house, fills vacancies therein, and fixes salaries of new employees. Both speakers have to deal with the library of parliament, and during the session no person except the Governor-General, the members of the privy council and of the senate and commons, and the officers of both houses can resort thither unless under authority from one of the speakers. The house of commons is summoned by instrument, under the great seal of Canada, in the Queen's name, by the Governor-General, at the same time with the senate. Each member of the commons must take the oath of allegiance, as a senator does, before taking his seat in the house. When a vacancy occurs in the commons it is filled by the issue of a new writ, from the office of the clerk of the crown in chancery, for the election of a member for the unrepresented constituency.

The privileges, immunities and powers of the commons and its members like those of the senate and its members, are such as may be from time to time defined by the parliament of Canada, but they must never exceed those held, enjoyed and exercised by the commons of England or its members, at the time such defining act is passed in Canada. The eighteenth section of the Confederation Act being somewhat ambiguous, an amending Act was passed at Westminster in 1875 called *The Parliament of Canada Act, 1875*, to put beyond doubt that section. (a) Otherwise it may have been construed that the privileges, etc. of the senate and commons in Canada were to be those of the commons in England in the year 1867, and not the year in which any Act of parliament of Canada was passed defining such privileges, immunities and powers. No Act[1] has been passed by the parliament of Canada in reference to this matter.

There is a law and custom of parliament in England forming part of the common law of the land; the privileges of parliament which it affords are large and indefinite and properly left indefinite, like the definition of fraud so that no new case not within the line of privilege can be devised " under the pretence thereof," as Blackstone says, " to harass any refractory member and violate the freedom of parliament." Every political in-

(a) 38-39 Vic. (Imp.) cap. 38.

stitution, whether invested "with the authority to make laws or to explain and enforce them must of necessity possess all the powers requisite to ensure the purposes for which it was created." It might remove or exclude or expel a member. It can commit for contempt till the close of the existing session, but no longer.

The house of commons has the sole right of beginning the grants of aids and supplies, and of directing and limiting the ends, purposes, considerations and qualifications of such grants, without the upper house having the power to alter or change them. They can enforce at any time the standing order to prohibit their speeches and proceedings from being published.

The members themselves are privileged from arrest for forty days after every prorogation, and for forty days before the next appointed meeting, and after a dissolution for a reasonable time to return home. (b) This does not apply to treason, felony, and many other charges of a less grave nature. There is an ancient privilege of exemption from serving on juries or attending as witnesses; but in the latter case, the house gives leave if the public business will not suffer by it. There is freedom of speech and freedom from libellous attack. The privilege of franking was said to have the same limit as that of arrest. It was the right of sending a certain number of letters daily through the post office, whether the house be sitting or not. (c) Members have the right to enter their dissent or remonstrance in the journals of the house.

(b) *Eundo, Morando, et propria Redeundo.*
(c) This was denied to the Legislature of Upper Canada in 1837.

CHAPTER VI.

THE QUEEN'S PRIVY COUNCIL FOR CANADA.

Who are privy councillors and who cabinet councillors—
Oath and office and duties—Number—Portfolios—Carry
on administrative government with approval of parlia-
ment—Cabinet questions—Relation to executive and to
legislature—Privy council a peculiarly British institu-
tion.

THE privy council of Canada, as in England, is assumed
to be the past and present advisers of the crown. Privy
councillors are chosen to aid and advise in the government
of Canada, and are summoned by the Governor-General to
advise and assist him in every way that good councillors
should do. Ex-cabinet ministers since confederation, are
said to be members of the privy council, merely as honorary
members and in analogy to the English custom ; but what
is generally understood by the term is the acting ministry
for the time being. (a) This is known here and in England as the cabinet or privy council. The nominal privy
councillors who are not supporters of the ministry take no
part in the government. They are members of the privy
council not of the cabinet. They are styled " honorable "
for life and rank next after the judges of law and equity.

All the privy councillors are sworn in as such on accepting office, and are chosen for life ; that is, they are liable
to be summoned at any time to take part in forming a

(a) There are at present 31 members of the privy council who are
not members of the cabinet.

government. In order to be a member of the government
a privy councillor, if not a senator, must have a seat in the
commons. An acting minister must be in either house,
but he cannot be a member of both houses at the same
time. A member of the privy council may be a member of
the cabinet and yet have no portfolio in the government;
that is, may not be the head of any of the departments of
state, but he is equally answerable with his colleagues to
the house of commons or to the senate for the conduct of
the public affairs of the Dominion. The government as a
body is responsible for all acts of its ministers whether they
have portfolios or not.

The cabinet, or ministry, is now composed of fourteen
members; thirteen of these have charge of the different
departments into which the work of governing the country
is divided, and one is president of the council, or without a
portfolio or departmental office. The practice now prevails,
as has already been pointed out, of having two of the
cabinet ministers selected from members of the senate.
(See chapter on the senate.) The duties of the ministers
having charge of departments are laid down by Act of
parliament, and they are obliged to report annually to
parliament as to the matters under their control. This
most important part of the management of public affairs
is called administrative government and will be fully
detailed hereafter. The number of cabinet ministers since
1867 has been thirteen, but the number was increased in
1873 to fourteen, two without portfolios. Only one minister
is at present without an office.

Besides the individual duties of the ministers, the privy
council, as a body, has very important powers and duties.
It advises the Governor-General, it may be safely said,
upon all his official acts, and it, and not he, is responsible for all parliamentary enactments, all proclamations,

all orders in council, directing enquiries in public matters, taking action in unforseen emergencies, and advising in all matters done officially by the Governor-General in council and out of it. One of its members, the minister of justice, takes the place of the crown law officers in England at least for a large part of the work of advising the crown.

As advisers of the crown, they must see not only that the parliament of Canada keeps within its due limits, but that the provincial legislatures do not transgress their constitutional bounds in legislation or otherwise. They advise the Governor-General of the proper persons to be Lieutenant-Governors of the provinces and suggest their removal when the gravity of the case may require it. They are, in short, responsible for the legislation passed in parliament, or permitted, or omitted to be passed ; for the due execution of the laws, whether done under their own supervision in the department of state or otherwise : and with them rests the appointment of judges for the construction and interpretation of the laws, when enacted. In this country they are themselves relieved from any judicial functions, as there is no such thing as a judicial committee of the privy council in Canada, as a court of appeal. The occasion does not arise for similar duties to the judicial committee of the privy council in England, as the latter entertains chiefly appeals from the colonies. The judicial committee of the privy council in England determines all matters that can come judicially before the Queen ; amongst others, it decides all matters of colonial reference, and is the ultimate resort of a colonial subject, on an appeal from the laws of his own colony. The privy council in Canada can refer certain matters to the supreme court at Ottawa, as will be noticed hereafter ; but it does not form a court and has no judicial powers or duties.

The duties of the privy councillors, as defined by their oath of office, are to serve her Majesty truly and faithfully in her council ; to keep secret all matters treated, debated or resolved in the privy council from all persons outside of that body; and if the matter refer to any member of the council concerning his loyalty and fidelity, then it must not be disclosed to that member until the Queen's pleasure be known in that behalf. They must in all things faithfully, honestly and truly declare their mind and opinion to the honor and benefit of Her Majesty; and in general be vigilant, diligent and circumspect in all their doings touching the Queen's affairs, as good councillors should be. (b)

The proceedings of the privy council are secret, or supposed to be so, and the council is presided over by one of its members called the president of the council. The Governor-General is not often present; on exceptional occasions he presides. The practice was reported to England to be that the questions of state are discussed by the council and by the first minister, and reported to the Governor-General.

Complete harmony of action is required among the members of the government when what are called " cabinet questions " arise. If any member of the government fails to agree with the views of the council on such questions it is his duty to resign. On these questions the government of the day stands or falls together. Measures initiated by members of the government are not necessarily measures upon which, if the ministry are defeated in the commons, it would be their duty to resign. But if the ministry make any question, otherwise not a government measure, to be

(b) These functions of the privy council are exercised by the cabinet council; but the oath taken by each privy councillor on his accepting office would oblige him to be mindful of these duties during his life-time, his appointment lasting during that period.

such, then their defeat on that would give rise to votes of
want of confidence, which, if successful, would necessitate
a change of ministry—a new set of cabinet ministers.

The cabinet council is, therefore, a fluctuating body,
which, besides being the choice of the crown, is also the
choice of the two houses of parliament. The cabinet, on
one side, takes its origin in the two houses of parliament,
chiefly in the commons, and on the other side, it exists and
acts in the executive. It is well defined as the connecting
link between the legislative and executive authority. For,
although in theory the Queen is the executive, the privy
council or government is the real executive. The other
is a fiction perpetuated in England but none the less a
fiction. The Queen, or Governor-General in Canada, is
the executive, does every thing, it is true, but does it because the privy council advises it to be done ; and without
such advice nothing is done.

The privy council is a committee of the house of parliament, acting by its authority and empowered to carry on
the government. Its aim is to please the senate and commons. So long as it does that it cannot displease the
crown. It is the agent of the people, and when the people
are satisfied the crown is satisfied. The crown makes no
choice till the cabinet has lost the confidence of the people,
it then discovers the people's choice, and selects him
as leader—as prime minister. Our constitution does not
admit of the supposition that the crown will choose any one
not the choice of the people. This is not saying but that
the crown has certain abstract rights ; but these may be
said to be obsolete and disused in England, and without any
practical application in this country. The cabinet council,
the premier, in effect, governs the people ; and the people,
and the people only, have to say of what party or persons

the cabinet is to be composed. It is their loss or gain, and is their choice by right. The crown approves with. out interfering. (c)

When a ministry resigns, the crown stands alone with no adviser known to the constitution. Its first step taken towards the formation of a new ministry is one taken on advice. A member accepting the position of leader of a new government is by the theory of the constitution advising the Governor-General to that step. The new leader advises by accepting.

Probably the only instance in which a Governor must act on his own independent advice is when he conceives for the moment that the policy of his present advisers is not such as the country would uphold if the elective branch were dissolved and the country left to decide the question. This new ministry would, however, have to shoulder the responsibility of this extraordinary course.

This, however, may not happen, with a series of Governors, in the space of a century. His ministry for the time being, represent the people; and it is more reasonable that he should take their advice than that they take his, and the responsibility of it, at the same time. They cannot avoid the responsibility ; and they would be ridiculous and inconsistent in saying the advice was not theirs, but was the Governor's. He is not responsible to the people, but his ministry is ; and it is generally better for the people to have a Governor who will follow his advisers, than to have one looking for advisers. In the ordinary course of events, there could be no hesitancy in preferring the advice of a responsible ministry to that of an irresponsible Governor.

(c) See Chap. III. *ante* on the undoubted power of the Governor-General to dismiss one set of cabinet ministers and select another.

The people decide at the polls who is to rule them for a term of years at a time. Their choice may have been unfortunate, but there appears no way of recalling it, unless the Governor fancies he can safely dissolve the house on the strength of what he believes the public sentiment to be. This may sometimes be necessary and expedient ; but it is a dangerous experiment, and appears to be contrary to the spirit of the British constitution in modern times. The crown is satisfied at the choice the people *have* made in the last election—it does not speculate, as to what choice they may make in the next election.

The fact is, that some set of ministers must take the responsibility of every official act of the Governor-General, either the outgoing or incoming ministers, and this applies to a change of government as well as to all other acts. The moment any one accepts the leadership, he tenders advice as to the choice.

The privy council is an institution peculiar to the English form of government. There is nothing at all similar to it in the United States. The constitution of Canada has provided for its existence in the government of this country by an express section (11.), and the executive is aided and advised by it. It is probable that the 17th section which creates a parliament for Canada, would of itself have been sufficient to bring with it a privy or cabinet council, as the mode of government peculiar to the imperial parliament. It is the feature of all others that suggests the principles of the British constitution. Following the declaration as to executive power in the early part of the Act, it precedes the provisions as to a parliament. Those who drafted the Act of Union were determined that the federal side of the constitution was not to absorb the principles of a monarchy and the characteristics of parliamentary government. Government under the federal system in the

American union is not conducted by a committee of both houses, such as is the Queen's privy council ; the executive power is vested in the President of the United States, and he really holds and exercises it. He is not appointed to office as is the Governor of Canada, he does not hold it by virtue of hereditary right as does the Queen of England, he is elected by the people for a term of years ; he has large powers of veto, he has no constitutional advisers who prevent him from going wrong ; he is entrusted with large powers, and he has to bear the responsibility of using them. On all these points the government of Canada is modeled on other principles and the constitution has put at rest any controversy regarding them. The machinery and procedure of government in Canada is indisputably British ; and the existence of a privy council is one of the best evidences of that fact.

CHAPTER VII.

THE PRIVY COUNCIL.—DEPARTMENTAL ADMINISTRATION AT OTTAWA.

Ministers with portfolios—Salaries—Power of investigation— Department of justice, powers, duties, officers—Finance revenue, currency, banks—Agriculture, immigration, manufactures, patent office, copyright, statistics—Secretary of State, writs, commissions, proclamations, N. W. mounted police—Marine and fisheries, pilots, light houses, shipwrecks—Militia and defence, classes of militia, districts, exemptions, pensions.

ATTENTION will now be directed to the individual duties of ministers of the cabinet in the departmental work of government at Ottawa. The task of administering the public affairs of Canada is divided into fifteen departments, each presided over by a minister of the crown ; and each minister, by command of the Governor-General, makes an annual report to parliament of the affairs confided to his management. These reports and the other information issued by the government form the voluminous Blue Book literature—official information that is eagerly enquired for if not ready, and is very generally disregarded after it is issued. The substance of the ministers' reports is the work of the year in their departments and the manner in which they and their deputies and assistants have carried it out. Parliament and the people see how their work is being done—how the country is being governed, and if this is not to their satisfaction the task may be assigned to another set of ministers.

The following are the departments in the Dominion Government :

1. The department of justice and attorney-general.
2. The department of finance and receiver-general.
3. The department of agriculture.
4. The department of the secretary of state for Canada.
5. The department of militia and defence.
6. The department of customs.
7. The department of inland revenue.
8. The department of the interior.
9. The department of public works.
10. The department of railways and canals.
11. The post office department.
12. The department of marine and fisheries.
13. The department of public printing and stationery. (a)
14. The department of Indian affairs.
15. The department of trade and commerce.

The president of the council sometimes has no department in the public service; he presides over the meetings of the privy council.

Each minister is paid $7,000 per annum as compensation for his labor. The ministers in the different departments at Ottawa are assisted by deputies and assistants who form the civil service of Canada.

Any minister presiding over any department may appoint one or more commissioners to investigate and report upon the state and management of the business or any part of it in his department, or the official conduct of any person in his service. Very full powers are given to these commissioners who may summon any person before them to give evidence on oath or take evidence by commission for the purposes of the investigation.

(a) This department is presided over by the secretary of state, and the Indian affairs by the minister of the interior.

1. DEPARTMENT OF JUSTICE.

This department of the civil service is presided over by the minister of justice for Canada, who is appointed by the Governor-General, by commission under the great seal, and who holds office during pleasure—that is, so long as the government, of which he is a member, retains office. The minister of justice is by virtue of his office attorney-general of Canada, and in this regard he is entrusted with the same powers and charged with the same duties, which belong to the office of attorney-general for England, by law, or usage, so far as the same powers and duties are applicable to Canada; and also with such powers and duties as belonged to that office, prior to 1867, in the provinces, in order that the provisions of the Confederation Act may be carried out by the government of the Dominion.

He is the official legal adviser of the Governor-General, and the legal member of the privy council. He must see that the administration of public affairs is in accordance with law. He has the superintendence of all matters connected with the administration of justice in Canada, that do not fall within the jurisdiction of the provinces. He must advise upon the legislative Acts and proceedings of the provinces, and must advise the crown generally upon all matters of law referred to him. He advises the heads of the other departments upon all matters of law connected with their departments. He settles and approves of all instruments issued under the great seal of Canada, has the conduct and regulation of all litigation for or against the crown, or any public department, in matters within the authority and jurisdiction of the Dominion; and he may have to advise on other matters referred to him by the Governor in council. He has also the superintendence of penitentiaries and the prison system of the Dominion, and returns are made to him every year from penitentiaries, gaols, lunatic asylums and reformatories.

The Governor appoints a deputy of the minister of justice, who is charged with the performance of these departmental duties, under the minister. He has the control and management of the officers, clerks and servants of the department, who are appointed by the Governor, and he may have other powers and duties assigned him by the Governor in council. He is now assisted by the solicitor-general of Canada.

The minister of justice is a member of the treasury board.

The attorney-general of the province, and not the attorney-general of the Dominion, is the proper party to file an information when the complaint is not of an injury to property vested in the crown as representing the government of the Dominion, but of a violation of the rights of the public of the province, even though such rights are created by an Act of the parliament of the Dominion. (b)

2. THE DEPARTMENT OF FINANCE.

This department of the civil service is presided over by the minister of finance and receiver-general, appointed and holding office like the minister of justice and the other ministers of the crown.

This department has the supervision, control and direction of all matters relating to the financial affairs, public accounts, revenue and expenditure, of the Dominion, excepting such of these matters as may be assigned to other departments, as customs, etc.

The Governor-General appoints a deputy minister of finance and receiver-general, who is deputy head of the department and secretary of the treasury board. For-

(b) *Att'y-Gen.* v. *The Niagara Falls International Bridge Co'y*, 20 Gr. 34.

merly the auditor-general and an officer called the deputy inspector-general were officers of this department. A board called the treasury board, consisting of the minister of finance and receiver-general, the minister of justice, the minister of customs, the minister of inland revenue, the secretary of state of Canada, and one other minister, is a committee of the privy council on all matters mentioned as belonging to this department—finance, revenue and expenditure or public accounts; and the board may call the attention of the council to any of these matters, or the council may refer any of them to the board. The board has power to require from any public department, board or officer, or other person or party bound by law to furnish the same to the government, any account, return, statement, document, or information which the board may think necessary for the due performance of its duties. By the word revenue in this department is meant revenue of the Dominion of Canada and all branches thereof, and all public moneys, whether arising from duties of customs or other duties, or from the post office, or from tolls on canals, railways or other public works, or from penalties or forfeitures, or rents or dues, or other source whatever, and whether the money belongs to or is collected by the Dominion in trust for any province or for Great Britain. The Governor in council determines what officers are necessary in the collection of the revenue, divides up Canada into posts and districts for revenue purposes, and makes all necessary regulations for payment of and accounting for the revenue. No money is paid out of the public chest unless by cheque on some bank upon the warrant of the Governor in council, and signed by the minister of finance and receiver-general and countersigned by his deputy.

For the more complete examination of the public accounts, and for the reporting thereon, the Governor-General may, under the great seal, appoint an auditor-general of Canada, who holds office till removed by the Governor-General on the address of the senate and commons. He issues all cheques under the parliamentary appropriation, and unless in these cases no cheque of the finance minister shall issue unless upon his certificate. He certifies and reports as to the public accounts presented to parliament by the minister.

This department has to deal with banks issuing dominion notes in place of their own, and also with the issue of dominion notes, and with the currency generally.

All public moneys, from whatever source of revenue derived, shall be paid to the credit of the account of the minister of finance and receiver-general through such officers, banks or persons, and in such manner as the said minister from time to time, directs and appoints.

The denominations of money in the currency of Canada are dollars, cents and mills,—the cent being one hundredth part of a dollar, and the mill one tenth part of a cent.

The currency of Canada is such, that the British sovereign of the weight and fineness now prescribed by the laws of the United Kingdom, is equal to and passes current for four dollars eighty-six cents and two-thirds of a cent of the currency of Canada, and the half sovereign of proportionate weight and like fineness for one-half the said sum. All public accounts throughout Canada must be kept in such currency; and in any statement as to money or money value, in any indictment or legal proceeding, the same shall be stated in such currency: and in all private accounts and agreements rendered or entered into on or subsequent to the first day of July, one thousand eight hundred and seventy-one, all sums mentioned shall be understood to be in such currency, unless some other is clearly expressed, or must, from the circumstances of the case, have been intended by the parties.

. The deputy of the minister shall keep the accounts with the financial agents of the Dominion in England and with the banks paying or receiving public money, and accounts of money paid for interest on Canadian stock, debentures or other Canadian securities. He shall countersign all debentures and keep a debenture book, an interest book respecting them, and an appropriation book, and shall keep the public accounts of the Dominion, and have control and direction of its financial affairs, public accounts, revenue and expenditure under the minister. He prepares and submits to the ministers the public accounts to be laid before parliament. (c)

The Governor in council may authorize the issue of Dominion notes to a specified amount, and such Dominion notes may be of such denominational values and in such form, and signed by such persons and in such manner, by lithograph, printing or otherwise as he from time to time directs, and such notes shall be redeemable in specie on presentation at branch offices established in certain cities in Canada.

The expression " specie " means coin current by law *in Canada*, at the rates and subject to the provisions of the law in that behalf, or bullion of equal value according to its weight and fineness.

The amount of Dominion notes issued and outstanding at any time may, by order in council, founded on a report

(c) The manner of dealing with this most important part of the public affairs in the finance department is too complicated to give even a general idea of its workings within a small space. The reader must be referred to Public Accounts Audit Act, 1878, and its amendments to see the former workings of this department and the duties of the board of audit, now superseded by later provisions. See also the Act of 1887.

of the treasury board, be increased to, but shall not exceed twenty million dollars, by amounts not exceeding one million dollars at one time, and not exceeding four million dollars in any one year :

3. THE DEPARTMENT OF AGRICULTURE. (d)

This department is presided over by the minister of agriculture, who, with a deputy minister, has charge of the management and direction of the department.

The duties and powers of the minister of agriculture, extend to the execution of the laws enacted by the parliament of Canada, and of the orders of the Governor in council relating to the following subjects, which are controlled and directed by the department.

1. Agriculture.
2. Immigration and emigration.
3. Public health and quarantine.
4. The marine and immigrant hospital at Quebec.
5. Arts and manufactures.
6. The census, statistics and the registration of statistics.
7. Patents of invention.
8. Copyright.
9. Industrial designs and trade marks.
10. Experimental farm stations.

Any of these powers and duties may be assigned to other members of the privy council by the Governor in council, and the same power may also assign additional duties to the minister of agriculture than those above enumerated. The minister is bound to make his annual report to both houses of parliament within twenty-one days after the commencement of the session.

(d) See Act of 1887 D. chap. 12.

Each of the provinces has power to legislate in relation to agriculture within its own limits, and also in relation to immigration into such province. The Dominion has power to legislate, in relation to these same subjects, in all or any of the provinces; and the provincial law takes effect so long and so far only as it is not repugnant to any Act of the parliament of Canada. These two subjects of agriculture and immigration into the provinces are the only subjects in which Canada and the provinces have concurrent jurisdiction. Canada maintains immigration offices in Great Britain and in Canada. Arrangements are entered into by which the dominion and provincial governments assist each other in this particular and conferences of the delegates of both governments are convened from time to time in the office of this department. Minute statutory regulations are made in regard to immigrants, quarantine, &c.; and the Governor in council is empowered to make regulations to carry out the quarantine Act or prohibit the landing of vicious immigrants, etc. (e)

The minister of agriculture keeps a register of copyrights, in which proprietors of literary, scientific and artistic works or compositions may register the same under the copyright Act of 1875. The minister has power to make rules and regulations and prescribe forms for this purpose. The term of copyright is for twenty-eight years, and may, under certain circumstances, be renewed for fourteen years after the expiration of that time. Two copies of the work are deposited in this office, one of which is forwarded to the library of parliament. Notice that a copyright has been obtained must appear in the work itself in a prescribed form. The rules and regulations are laid down by an order of the privy council dated 7th December, 1875. (f) The regulations

(e) See duties of the High Commissioner for Canada, *infra*.
(f) See *Smiles* v *Bedford*, 1 App. Ont. 436.

as to trade-marks and designs were laid down by statute in 1879. Patents of invention and copyright may now be transferred to the secretary of state.

The minister of agriculture receives returns of criminal statistics every year up to the 30th September from the proper officers of the courts administering criminal justice, and from wardens and sheriffs and justices of the peace; and records of the same are kept in his department. He receives also such returns as to the exercise of the prerogative of mercy as are furnished by the secretary of state. These statistics and returns are abstracted and printed yearly.

The census shall be taken in 1891, and at the beginning of every tenth year thereafter. The details of the census shall be directed by the Governor in council; and this department shall prepare all forms and instructions necessary for that purpose, and examine into the returns and records, and lay before parliament such abstracts and tabular returns shewing the results of the census as accurately and fully as possible.

The minister of agriculture is, under the approval of the Governor in council, from time to time to collect, abstract, tabulate and publish the vital, agricultural, commercial, criminal and other statistics of the country; and he has all the necessary powers to provide himself with all the proper officers and assistants for that purpose. Regulations as to contagious diseases in cattle issue from this department by order of the Governor in council. See Act of 1887, D. cap. 12.

4. THE DEPARTMENT OF THE SECRETARY OF STATE OF CANADA.

This department is presided over by the secretary of state of Canada and managed under his direction. The

Governor in council may also appoint an "under secretary of state" and other necessary officers.

The duty of this minister is to have charge of the state correspondence, to keep all state records and papers not specially transferred to other departments, and to perform such other duties as may be assigned him. He is the registrar-general of Canada, and, as such, registers all instruments of summons, proclamations, commissions, letters patent, writ and other instruments issued under the great seal and all bonds, warrants of extradition, warrants for removal of prisoners, leases, releases, deeds of sale, and all other instruments requiring registration. The deputy registrar-general of Canada, may sign and certify the registration of all instruments and documents required to be registered, and may issue certified or authenticated copies of these or any records in the office which may be so required.

The department of the interior now takes charge of Indian affairs, of crown lands being the property of Canada, of ordnance and admiralty lands, and other public lands formerly entrusted to this department. The charge of the North-West mounted police was also transferred to that department, but is now in the Indian department.

The secretary of state reports annually to parliament within ten days after its commencement.

The secretary of state has charge of the state correspondence with the provinces, as there is now no secretary of state for the provinces.

The Act of 1887, cap. 12. D. must be read in connection with this department. (g)

(g) See department of public printing and stationery.

5. THE DEPARTMENT OF MARINE AND FISHERIES.

The minister of marine and fisheries has the management and direction of this public department under his control. His deputy directs and oversees the other officers and servants of the department, and has general control of its business in the absence of the minister.

The following are the matters within the control of this department, under any existing laws in reference thereto: (h)

1. Sea, coast and inland fisheries, and the management, regulation and protection thereof, and anything relating thereto; also the administration of any laws relating to pilots and pilotage, and decayed pilots' funds;

2. Beacons, buoys, lights, light-houses, and their maintenance;

3. Harbors, ports, piers and wharves, steamers and vessels belonging to the Government of Canada, except gunboats or other vessels of war;

4. Harbor commissioners and harbor masters;

5. Classification of vessels, examination of and granting of certificates to masters and mates and others in the merchant service;

6. Shipping masters and shipping officers;

7. Inspection of steamboats and boards of steamboat inspection;

8. Enquiries into causes of shipwrecks;

9. Establishment, regulation and maintenance of marine and seamen hospitals and care of distressed seamen, and

(h) See *Queen* v. *Robertson*, 6, S. C. R. 52.

generally such matters as refer to the marine and navigation of Canada.

Orders in council regulate the close seasons for fish in the different provinces, and are made on the recommendation of the minister of this department.

The Governor in council may at any time, by proclamation, transfer from this department to the department of public works the construction and repair of light houses.

1. All harbors, wharves, piers and breakwaters constructed or completed at the expense of Canada, or otherwise the property of Canada, except only such as are on or connected with canals shall be under the control and management of the minister of marine and fisheries respecting the use, maintenance and ordinary repairs thereof, the making and enforcing of regulations concerning such use, maintenance and ordinary repairs, and the collection of tolls and dues for such use ;

2. The construction and repairs, and the works connected therewith, other than maintenance and ordinary repairs, shall be under the control and direction of the minister of public works.

6. DEPARTMENT OF MILITIA AND DEFENCE.

The minister of militia and defence is charged with and responsible for the administration of militia affairs, including all matters involving expenditure, and of the fortifications, gunboats, ordnance, ammunition, arms, armories, stores, munitions, and habiliments of war belonging to Canada. He has also the initative in all militia affairs involving the expenditure of money. The Governor in council may appoint a deputy to this minister, and such other officers as may be necessary, and prescribe their duties. (i)

The Command-in-chief of the land and naval militia, and of all naval and military forces of and in Canada, is vested in the Queen, and shall be exercised and administered by Her Majesty personally, or by the Governor-General as her representative.

The militia consists of all the male inhabitants over eighteen years of age and under sixty, not exempted or disqualified by law, and being British subjects by birth or naturalization. There are four classes of militia as follows:

1. 18 and over 18, and under 30 years, who are unmarried or widowers without children. These will be called upon to serve first.

2. Those of 30 and upwards, but under 45, unmarried, or widowers, without children. These will be called after the first class.

3. Those of 18 and upwards, but under 45, who are married, or widowers with children. These are next liable to be called.

4. Those of 45 and upwards, but under 60. These are not called until the others are serving.

Her Majesty may, however, in the case of a general rising, or rebellion, require all the male inhabitants of the Dominion, capable of bearing arms, to serve in the militia.

The militia shall be divided into active and reserve militia—land force; and active and reserve militia—marine force:

(i) See *Holmes* v. *Temple*, Queb. L. R. 351

The active militia—land force—shall be composed of : —

   (*a*) Corps raised by voluntary enlistment;

   (*b*) Corps raised by ballot ;

   (*c*) Corps composed of men raised by voluntary enlistment and men balloted to serve;

The active militia—marine force—to be raised similarly, shall be composed of seamen, sailors and persons whose usual occupation is upon any steam or sailing craft, navigating the waters of Canada :

The reserve militia—land and marine—shall consist of the whole of the men who are not serving in the active militia for the time being. 46 V., c. 11, s. 6.

Canada is divided into twelve military districts :
   Ontario 4 ; Quebec 3 ; Nova Scotia, New Brunswick, Manitoba, British Columbia, Prince Edward Island, one each.

Schools of instruction are established in garrison towns in Canada ; and the staff of instructors, under the superintendence of a military officer called a commandant, is appointed by the Governor in council. The regulations for admission, etc., are laid down by order in council.

The department of militia and defence pays those on the pension list, and enquires who are entitled to pensions.

EXEMPTIONS.

The following persons only, between the ages of eighteen and sixty years, shall be exempt from enrolment and from actual services at any time :—

The judges of all the courts of justice in the Dominion of Canada ;

The clergy and ministers of all religious denominations;

The professors in every college and university and all teachers in religious orders ;

Officers and persons regularly employed in the collection or management of the revenue, or in accounting for the same ;

The warden and all officers and servants employed permanently in the penitentiaries, and the officers, keepers and guards of all public lunatic asylums ;

Persons disabled by bodily infirmity ;

The only son of a widow, being her only support ;

2. The following, though enrolled, shall be exempt from actual service at any time except in case of war, invasion or insurrection ;

Half-pay and retired officers of Her Majesty's army or navy ;

Seafaring men and sailors actually employed in their calling ;

Pilots and apprentice pilots during the season of navigation ;

Masters of public and common schools actually engaged in teaching ;

3. Any person bearing a certificate from the society of Quakers, Mennonites or Tunkers, or any inhabitant of Canada, of any religious denomination, otherwise subject to military duty, who, from the doctrines of his religion, is averse to bearing arms and refuses personal military service, shall be exempt from such service when balloted in time of peace or war, upon such conditions and under such regulations as the Governor in council may from time to time, prescribe.

CHAPTER VIII.

THE PRIVY COUNCIL—ADMINISTRATIVE GOVERNMENT.

(Continued.)

The department of customs—Inland revenue, excise, weights and measures, stamps, tolls—Interior, Indian affairs, crown lands, geological survey, N. W. mounted police— Post office, powers and duties, postal union, money orders, letters—Public works, officers, works—Railways and canals—Public printing and stationery, Queen's printer, statutes, Canada Gazette—Indian department—Trade and commerce—The high commissioner for Canada.

7. THE DEPARTMENT OF CUSTOMS. (a)

THE department of customs is presided over by the minister of customs appointed under the great seal and holding office during pleasure. The Governor-General appoints a commissioner of customs and an assistant commissioner of customs. These have certain powers and perform certain duties assigned them by the Governor-General or by the minister of customs.

This department has control and management :

1. Of the collection of the duties of customs and of matters incident thereto, and of the officers and servants employed in that service.

(a) See Act of 1887, chap 11 D. by which the departments of Customs and Inland Revenue are placed under the control of the Minister of Trade and Commerce, and the Minister of Finance. The Act is not yet in force.

The Governor-General may appoint a board of examiners for all employees in this department, and these may classify the persons employed and grant certificates accordingly.

The minister of customs reports annually to parliament on the transactions and affairs of his department within 15 days after parliament opens.

8. THE DEPARTMENT OF INLAND REVENUE.

This department is presided over by the minister of inland revenue. He is assisted by a commissioner of inland revenue who is deputy of the minister, and by an assistant commissioner, who is the inspector of inland revenue, in performing such duties as are assigned to them by the Governor-General or by the minister in charge.

This department has the control and management :—

1. Of the collection of all duties of excise ;

2. Of the collection of stamp duties and the preparation and issue of stamps and stamped paper, except postage stamps ;

3. Of internal taxes ;

4. Of standard weights and measures ;

5. Of the administration of the laws affecting the culling and measurement of timber, masts, spars, deals, staves and other articles of a like nature, and the collection of slidage and boomage dues ;

6. Of the collection of bridge and ferry tolls and rents ;

7. Of the collection of tolls on the public canals, and of matters incident thereto, and of the officers and persons employed in that service ;

Subject always to the provisions of the Acts relating to the said subjects and matters connected therewith.

The regulations as to balances and weighing machines are laid down by an order of the privy council dated 10th July, 1877. Under a previous order Canada was divided into ten districts, under the Act respecting weights and measures; four for Ontario; two for Quebec; and one for each of the other provinces, except Prince Edward Island. In this office regulations are made for the inspection, verification and testing of gas, and for analyzing food, under the Acts to prevent the adulteration of food. The weights and measures Act of 1879 provides for uniformity of weights and measures, and prescribes standards therefor as deposited in this department.

The Governor-General may appoint officers and other persons to carry out all Acts relating to the department of inland revenue, or any orders in council, or regulations made thereunder. A board of examiners may be constituted in this department, as in that of customs.

The minister reports annually to parliament, within fifteen days after the house opens.

9. THE DEPARTMENT OF THE INTERIOR.

This department of the civil service is presided over by the minister of the interior. He has the control and management of the affairs of the North-West Territories. He is the superintendent general of Indian affairs and has the control and management of their lands and property in Canada. (b) He has also the control and management of all crown lands, being the property of the Dominion, including those known as ordnance and admiralty lands, and

(b) See *Church* v. *Fenton*, 28 U. C. C. P. 384.

all other public lands not specially under the control of the public works department, the department of railways and canals, or of that of militia and defence (and excepting also marine hospitals and light houses, and land connected therewith, and St. Paul's, Sable and Portage Islands). He is substituted for the former commissioner of crown lands as regards ordnance and admiralty lands transferred to the late province of Canada and lying in Ontario and Quebec. He takes the place of the secretary of state in regard to Dominion lands, and has all the powers, attributes, functions, restrictions and duties necessary to the enforcement of the provisions of the Dominion Lands Act, R. S. C. cap. 54.

There is a deputy minister in this department who has charge, under the minister, of the performance of the departmental duties, and the control and management of the officers, agents, clerks and servants in the department.

The minister of the interior has the control and management of the geological survey of Canada, and there is a branch of the department of the interior known as the geological survey branch, which is under the control of the minister and takes charge of and conducts the geological survey of Canada.

The objects and purposes of the survey and museum are to elucidate the geology and mineralogy of Canada and to make a full and scientific examination of the various strata, soils, ores, coals, oils and mineral waters, and of its recent *fauna* and *flora*, so as to afford to the mining, metallurgical and other interests of the country, correct and full information as to its character and resources.

10. THE DEPARTMENT OF INDIAN AFFAIRS.

This department has the management, charge and direction of Indian affairs. It is presided over by the superintendent-general of Indian affairs, and the minister of the interior is at present appointed to that office. The Governor-General in council appoints a deputy superinten- dent-general and such other officers, clerks and servants as are requisite for the proper conduct and management of the department.

An Indian commissioner may be appointed for Manitoba, Keewatin, and the North-West Territories, or for one or two of these, and an Indian superintendent for British Colum- bia who may have certain duties assigned them.

The Indian Act, R. S. C. cap. 43, amends and consoli- dates the law relating to Indians. It defines who they are, what lands they hold and are entitled to, the protection the law affords them, and the disabilities they labor under. The Governor in council may, however, exempt Indians ' from any portion of the operations of the Act. The Chancellor of Ontario has recently given an elaborate judg- ment as to the position occupied by the Dominion and Ontario governments on Indian lands. The territorial jurisdiction of the Dominion is held to extend only to lands reserved for Indians. The same judgment contains a briefly sketched history of the public lands of Ontario from the time of their acquisition by the crown till they became subject to provincial legislative control. (c)

The law relating to the administration and management of the Dominion lands is amended and consolidated by an Act passed in 1879 (cap. 31); and these are under the con- trol of the minister of the interior in a branch of this department called "the Dominion lands office." This Act provides for the survey and disposal of these lands,

(c) *Regina* v. *The St. Catharines Milling and Lumber Coy.*, 10. Ont. Reports 196, affirmed in 13 Ontario appeals, and now entered on the privy council appeals.

makes regulations as to homesteads, mining and coal fields, timber lands, and licenses thereon, and for the issue of patents to these lands.

The minister of this department has charge of the North-West mounted police.

11. POST OFFICE DEPARTMENT.

There is at the seat of Government, with the other public departments, a post office department, for the superintendence and management of the postal service of Canada, under the direction of a postmaster-general.

He is appointed, like the other ministers, by commission under the great seal, and holds office, as they do, during pleasure.

He has power to appoint postmasters having permanent salaries in towns and cities.

He may also subject to the Acts in force: (d)

1. Establish and close post offices, and post routes.

2. Appoint and suspend postmasters, and other officers and servants.

3. Make mail contracts or other business as to the post office, regulate what is mailable matter as to size and weight, prohibit dangerous or improper or other articles being sent, establish rates, unless others are laid down by parliament therefor in Canada, and arrange for these outside Canada.

4. Prepare stamps, stamped envelopes, post cards, wrappers, etc., and provide for the sale of the same, establish a money order system, and make necessary regulations as to registration.

(d) This is an abridgement of the eighteen sub-sections in the Acts.

5. Establish street, letter, or pillar boxes; and generally make such regulations as he deems necessary for the due and effective working of the department.

A deputy postmaster-general is appointed by the Governor in council, who has control of the department, under the minister.

The rate of postage on letters, newspapers and periodical publications, and what are called book and parcel post, are laid down by statute, and the postmaster-general has no power over these.

The "General Post Union," formed under a treaty taking effect on the 1st of July, 1875, regulates the understanding had between Great Britain, Germany, Austro-Hungary, Belgium, Denmark, Egypt, Spain, the United States of America, France, Greece, Italy, Luxembourg, Norway, the Netherlands, Portugal, Roumania, Russia, Servia, Sweden, Switzerland and Turkey.

Postal arrangements and a money order system are arranged between Canada and the United States.

The postmaster-general has the sole and exclusive privilege of sending and delivering letters in Canada; and any person who infringes upon this privilege, except as provided, is liable to a penalty of at least $20 for every letter delivered or found in his possession. The exceptions provided are letters sent by a private friend, or by a messenger sent on purpose, on private affairs of the sender, or receiver, or sent by a private vessel to a place out of Canada, or letters brought into Canada, and immediately posted; or letters sent with goods, but without pay or return and commissions, or other papers, issuing out of a court of justice. (e)

(e) From the time any letter, packet, chattel, money or thing is deposited in the post office for the purpose of being sent by post. it shall

The postmaster-general reports very fully to parliament on the finances, receipts and expenditure of his department; what has been paid for mail transport, salaries of persons employed, incidental expenses, dead and lost letters, the transactions of the money order offices, and losses and costs under this system, and the transactions of the post office savings bank.

This report is presented to the house within ten days after the opening of the session.

DEPARTMENT OF PUBLIC WORKS.

Prior to the 20th of May, 1879, the department of public works was presided over by one minister appointed in the usual way. On that day, by proclamation, it was divided into two departments, to be presided over and managed by two members of the administration, who are designated as the minister of railways and canals, and the minister of public works.

12. DEPARTMENT OF RAILWAYS AND CANALS.

The minister in charge of this department has the management, charge and direction of all railways, and works and property appertaining or incident thereto, which immediately before the proclamation mentioned were under the management and direction of the department of public works, to the same extent and under the same provisions as they were formerly managed. Each of the two ministers

---

cease to be the property of the sender, and shall be the property of the *person* to whom it is addressed or the legal representatives of such *person*: and the postmaster-general shall not be liable to any *person* for the loss of any letter, packet or other thing sent by post; no letter, packet or other mailable matter shall, whilst in the post office or in the custody of any person employed in the Canada post office, be liable to demand, seizure or detention, under legal process against the sender thereof, or against the *person* or legal representatives of the *person* to whom it is addressed. 38 V., cap. 7, s. 37.

succeeds to all the powers and duties before vested in the minister of public works, so far as respects the works under their respective charges. In case any doubts arise as to which of them any particular branch of the public works belongs, it shall be decided by order of the Governor in council; and he may make order assigning any of the officers and employees of the former department to either of the newly constituted departments, or direct them to act in both.

The Governor in council may appoint as chief officer of the department a deputy minister of railways and canals, a secretary, one or more chief engineers; a chief architect, and other necessary officers.

The deputy has charge of the department under the minister, directs the other officers, has general control of the business of the department, and may be assigned other duties by the Governor in council.

The secretary keeps account of the moneys appropriated for and expended on each public work and building under the management of the department, keeps accounts with contractors, looks after contracts to see that they are correctly drawn up and executed, prepares certificates, reports, etc.

The chief engineer and architects prepare maps, plans and estimates, and report to the minister thereon.

13. THE DEPARTMENT OF PUBLIC WORKS.

The minister of public works presides over this department and has charge of all public works of the Dominion, except the railways and canals, assigned to the minister of railways and canals under the Act of 1879.

He has control of :

1. Works for the improvement of the navigation of any water, such as locks, dams, hydraulic works, harbour piers, etc., and works for facilitating the transmission of timber, such as slides, dams, piers, booms, and other works, except those appertaining or belonging to canals, or being incident thereto.

2. Roads and bridges, public buildings, vessels, dredges, scows, tools, implements and machinery, for the improvement of navigation, not belonging to canals.

3. Telegraph lines.

4. All other property (except that managed in the department of railways and canals) heretofore acquired, constructed, repaired, maintained, or improved at the expense of the late province of Canada, or of New Brunswick and Nova Scotia, or hereafter to be acquired by Canada.

5. Such portions of ordnance property transferred to the late provincial government of Canada by the imperial government, and afterwards placed under this department.

But any public works or property which were or will be transferred to any of the provinces mentioned, or leased or sold to municipalities, corporations, or other parties, are not within this department; nor are any public works, roads, bridges, harbours, or property which were abandoned by proclamation to the control of the municipal or local authorities.

The Governor-General may, by proclamation, declare any other works, roads, bridges, harbours, slides, light-houses, or buildings purchased or constructed at the public expense, and not assigned to the provinces, to be under the management of this department.

All land, streams, water courses, and property acquired for the use of the public works, are vested in Her Majesty; and the minister may take possession and acquire lands necessary for the public service in her name. The price and other conditions are regulated under arbitration, from which, in cases over $500, an appeal lies to the Exchequer Court of Canada.

Any work for or connected with the public defence may, by order in council, be declared within the management of this department, saving the rights of the secretary of state for war as to imperial interests.

14. THE DEPARTMENT OF PUBLIC PRINTING AND STATIONERY.

A new department was created in 1886, called "The department of public printing and stationery," and the secretary of state or some other member of the privy council presides over it.

All printing, stereotyping or electrotyping, lithography or binding work, or work of a like nature, and paper and other material therefor, required for the use of the senate and of the house of commons and of the several departments of the government of Canada—inside and outside service—must be procured or executed subject to the superintendence of this department.

This department also manages the purchase and distribution of all books and all other articles of stationery, and the distribution and sale of all books or publications issued by either of the houses of parliament or any department, and all public advertising.

The Governor in council appoints by commission the Queen's printer and controller of stationery, who is the deputy head of this department, and holds office during pleasure. There are several officers connected with the public printing establishment and stationery office.

The Queen's printer prints and publishes, under the authority of the Governor in council, the official gazette of the Dominion, known as the *Canada Gazette*. All the requisite departmental and other reports, forms, documents and other papers, all state proclamations, and all official notices, advertisements and documents relating to the Dominion of Canada and under the control of parliament, and requiring publication, must be published in the *Canada Gazette*, unless some other mode of publication is required by law.

15. THE DEPARTMENT OF TRADE AND COMMERCE.

This department was created in 1887, and is presided over by the minister of trade and commerce, a member of the privy council of Canada. His powers and duties extend to the execution of laws enacted by the parliament and of orders in council relating to trade and commerce. A proclamation of the Governor is necessary before the Act creating this department takes effect.

THE HIGH COMMISSIONER OF CANADA.

The Governor in council appoints, under the great seal an officer called "The High Commissioner for Canada." who holds office during pleasure at a salary of $10,000 per annum. He acts as representative and resident agent of Canada in the United Kingdom, and he exercises such powers, and performs such duties, as are conferred on or assigned to him by the Governor in council. He has the charge, supervision, and control of the immigration offices and agencies. He carries out instructions respecting the commercial, financial, and general interests of Canada.

The high commissioner is specially entrusted with the general supervision of all the political, material and financial interests of Canada in England. He occupies a *quasi*-diplomatic position at the court of St. James, with all the social advantages of such rank and position. (Official Correspondence, 1879.)

CHAPTER IX.

THE DISTRIBUTION OF LEGISLATIVE POWERS IN CANADA.

*Provincial and Dominion sovereignties, opinions of eminent
Canadian judges—Sovereignty in the United States,
classes in the 91st section—Classes in the 92nd section—
Education—Concurrent jurisdiction—Grouping of subjects assigned to the Dominion—Assigned to the provinces
—Disputed jurisdiction—Cases—Reserve powers, distribution of powers—Comparison with American union—
Mr. Dicey on the principle of distribution.—General
powers of parliament—The territories.*

In some respects it would have been more convenient,
and perhaps more consistent to have begun any discussion
on the constitution of Canada with the executive and legislative powers of the provinces, and having endeavoured to
define these, to proceed then with the powers of the
Dominion government. The powers of the Canadian
parliament on the one hand are subject to imperial authority, and on the other are shorn of a large part of legislative
and executive control by the powers given to the provinces.
The parliament of Canada stands midway between the
sovereignty of the British parliament and what is sometimes called the sovereignty of the local legislatures. The
accepted meaning of the term sovereignty as used by constitutional lawyers in England, is not readily adjusted
to the jurisprudence of any country governed under a purely
federal system. Among the numerous definitions of sovereignty, a simple one is given, viz., that it extends to
everything which exists in a state by its own authority, or
is introduced by its permission. A dependency cannot be
sovereign. If there were no division of governmental

power in Canada, it would nevertheless lack the essential element of sovereignty. It is maintained by many writers that a division of powers, such as there is in the United States, prevents that country in a constitutional point of view, from being a sovereign state. The convention—that political organization which represents the people, and which can be set in motion for the purpose of altering the constitution—is alone sovereign. If the central government possesses part, and the states the remainder, then in the opinion of many other writers the sovereignty is enjoyed between them, and possessed in the aggregate by both. (a) It is admitted however by all, that the central and state governments are each sovereign within their own limits,—a description, however, which falls short of the English theory of sovereign power, inasmuch as it is limited; and it is manifest if the PEOPLE of the United States can control both constitutions by the convention, that the supreme power rests with them, and them alone. In our own country it has been said judicially that, subject to imperial authority, the powers of the parliament of Canada are the general powers of a sovereign state, excepting those which have been specially conferred on the provinces. (b) The effect of imperial authority is that the Dominion parliament has no power to pass any Act, repugnant to the provisions of any Act of parliament, order, or regulation thereunder, having the force of law in England. Such an Act, if passed, would be void and inoperative, but only, however, to the extent of its repugnancy. (c)

(a) The tenth amendment to the United States constitution gives the reserved powers to the state or to the people. If sovereignty was not in the aggregate given to the central and state governments, then they do not possess it. They have no more than they received.

(b) Mr. Justice (now Chief Justice) Wilson, in *Queen* v. *Taylor*, 36 U. C. R.

(c) Imperial Act, 28 and 29 Vic. cap. 63. A colonial Act is not void merely because it is inconsistent with the royal instructions to the Governor-General.

There is at least one limitation to the provincial sovereignty, to adopt the language parallel to that of federal writers. (*d*) Another high judicial authority speaking of the provincial legislature says :

" The powers of their legislatures are not conferred on them by their own provinces, but by the people of Canada, with the consent of the sovereign power of Great Britain ; and these provinces cannot confer a sovereignty which will extend over them, and they cannot be regarded as sovereign states. " (*e*)

The limitation on the Dominion parliament by reason of imperial authority, is, however, not much more than the nominal subjection of a colony to the mother country. Assuming that no laws will be passed in Canada, repugnant to those in Great Britain, there is very little subjection in that quarter beyond the fact of paramount authority in reserve. The Act of 28 and 29 Victoria could be repealed by the British parliament, and so could the Act of Union of the following session, but unless the people of Canada so desire it, these are only speculative possibilities. The late Chief Justice Draper was of opinion that the parliament of Canada has the right to legislate on the subjects mentioned in the 91st section of the Act to the exclusion of the Imperial parliament. The exclusive authority mentioned in that section as belonging to Canada does not, he says, refer to the subordinate provincial authorities, whose powers were not then conferred on them, but refers to the matters on which the imperial parliament has renounced its right to legislate. In support of this he refers to the two constitutions given to Canada in the reign of Geo. III., which empower the colonial legislature to make laws for the

---

(*d*) The power of disallowance of a provincial statute rests solely with the government of Canada. The imperial authorities have declined to deal with a power given to the Governor-General of Canada.

(*e*) Chief Justice Hagarty, in *Leprohon* v. *Ottawa*, 2 App. Ont.

" peace, welfare, and good government" of Canada. The present constitution sets out specifically the subjects which the parliament of Canada can deal with, and which may be supposed to comprise all subjects within the " peace, order, and good government" of Canada; and in regard to these the English legislature has no concern, and has deprived itself of the right of ever interfering. (f)

The 91st section, to which the learned chief justice refers, is as follows:

" It shall be lawful for the Queen, by and with the advice and consent of the senate and house of commons, to make laws for the peace, order, and good government of Canada, in relation to all matters not coming within the classes of subjects by this Act, assigned exclusively to the legislature of the provinces; and for greater certainty, but not so as to restrict the generality of the foregoing terms of this section, it is hereby declared that (notwithstanding anything in this Act) the exclusive legislative authority of the parliament of Canada extends to all matters coming within the classes of subjects next hereinafter enumerated, that is to say :

(1). The public debt and property.

(2). The regulation of trade and commerce.

(3). The raising of money by any mode or system of taxation.

(4). The borrowing of money on the public credit.

(5). Postal service.

(6). The census and statistics.

(7). Militia, military and naval service, and defence.

(8). The fixing of and providing for the salaries and allowances of civil and other officers of the government of Canada.

(9). Beacons, buoys, lighthouses, and Sable Island.

(f) *Regina* v. *Taylor*, 36 U. C. R.   See also *Crombie* v. *Jackson*, per Wilson, J. (now C.J.)

(10). Navigation and shipping.

(11). Quarantine, and the establishment and maintenance of marine hospitals.

(12). Sea, coast and inland fisheries.

(13). Ferries between a province and any British or foreign country, or between two provinces.

(14). Currency and coinage.

(15). Banking, incorporation of banks, and the issue of paper money.

(16). Savings banks.

(17). Weights and measures.

(18). Bills of exchange and promissory notes.

(19). Interest.

(20). Legal tender.

(21). Bankruptcy and insolvency.

(22). Patents of invention and discovery.

(23). Copyrights.

(24). Indians and lands reserved for the Indians.

(25). Naturalization and aliens.

(26). Marriage and divorce.

(27). The criminal law, except the constitution of courts of criminal jurisdiction, but including the procedure in criminal matters.

(28). The establishment, maintenance and management of penitentiaries.

(29). Such classes of subjects as are expressly excepted in the enumeration of the classes of subjects by this Act assigned exclusively to the legislatures of the provinces.

And any matter coming within any of the classes of subjects enumerated in this section shall not be deemed to come within the class of matters of a local or private nature comprised in the enumeration of the classes of subjects by this Act assigned exclusively to the legislatures of the provinces.

The matters referred to in the last of these enumerated powers as expressly excepted in the provincial list of powers are comprised in three heads :

(1). The office of Lieutenant-Governor.

(2). Marine hospitals.

(3). Local public works or undertakings set out in the 10th class of subjects assigned to the provinces comprising (a) inter or extra provincial or foreign lines of steam or other ships, railways canals, telegraphs and other works and undertakings ; (b) lines of steamships between the provinces and any British or foreign country ; (c) provincial works for the advantage of Canada in more than one province.

The 92nd section is in these words :

EXCLUSIVE POWERS OF PROVINCIAL LEGISLATURES.

92. In each province the legislature may exclusively make laws in relation to matters coming within the classes of subjects next hereinafter enumerated, that is to say—

(1). The amendment from time to time, notwithstanding anything in this Act, of the constitution of the province, except as regards the office of Lieutenant-Governor.

(2). Direct taxation within the province in order to the raising of a revenue for provincial purposes.

(3). The borrowing of money on the sole credit of the provinces.

(4). The establishment and tenure of provincial offices and the appointment and payment of provincial officers.

(5). The management and sale of the public lands belonging to the province, and of the timber and wood thereon.

(6). The establishment, maintenance and management of public and reformatory prisons in and for the province.

(7). The establishment, maintenance and management of hospitals, asylums, charities, and eleemosynary institutions in and for the province, other than marine hospitals.

(8). Municipal institutions in the province.

(9). Shop, saloon, tavern, auctioneer, and other licenses, in order to the raising of a revenue for provincial, local, or municipal purpose.

(10). Local work and undertakings, other than :—

a. Lines of steam or other ships, railways, canals, telegraphs, and other works and undertakings connecting the province with any other or others of the provinces, or extending beyond the limits of the provinces :

b. Lines of steam ships between the province and any British or foreign country :

c. Such works, as, though wholly situate within the provinces, are before or after their execution declared by the parliament of Canada to be for the general advantage of Canada, or for the advantage of two or more of the provinces.

(11). The incorporation of companies with provincial objects.

(12). The solemnization of marriage in the province.

(13). Property and civil rights in the province.

(14). The administration of justice in the province, including the constitution, maintenance and organization of provincial courts, both of civil and criminal jurisdiction, and including procedure in civil matters in those courts.

(15). The imposition of punishment by fine, penalty, or imprisonment, for enforcing any law of the province made in relation to any matter coming within any of the classes of subjects enumerated in this section.

(16). Generally all matters of a merely local or private nature in the province.

The 93rd section gives to the province the exclusive right of making laws in relation to education, preserving the then existing rights and privileges of any denominational schools. Whatever powers, privileges and duties had been conferred or imposed on separate schools in Upper Canada, were extended to dissentient schools in Quebec, and provision was made for an appeal to the Governor-General in regard to these schools in any province.

The 94th section provides for the uniformity of laws in the four provinces by means of an Act of the parliament of Canada; but as the Act does not take effect "until it is adopted and enacted as law by the legislature" of the province, it is only a power by consent of the two legislatures.

The 95th section is the only other one that confers a law-making power on the Dominion parliament. The parliament of Canada and the provincial legislatures may from time to time make laws in relation to agriculture and immigration, the provincial laws taking effect so long as they are not repugnant to Acts of parliament of the Dominion. These two matters are in reality the only ones over which there is concurrent jurisdiction. The public works are sometimes said to be under concurrent jurisdiction, but the Dominion and provincial works are distinct, and each belongs to and is managed by one authority. (g)

Although there are many other powers conferred by the B. N. A. Act and by subsequent imperial legislation, all of which will be noticed presently, the foregoing classes of subjects are the basis of legislative authority for the Canadian union and for the provinces.

(g) Earl Carnarvon places the concurrent powers over these three subjects.

In glancing over the classes of subjects assigned to the government of Canada it is easy to recognize them as subjects common to all the provinces, and which are properly left to the central government, the intention being to make laws *generally* for the peace, order and good government of Canada. These may be arranged as follows:

1. To provide means to carry on the work of government.

> Raising money by taxation (3); borrowing money on public credit (4); paying salaries (8). All this in the foundation of a certain amount of public debt and property (1). (*h*)

2. Subjects obviously common to all.

> The postal service (5); the militia and defence (7); naturalization and aliens (25); the census and statistics (6); the criminal law (27); penitentiaries (28); patents of invention (22); copyright (23); currency (14); banking and paper money (15); inter or extra-provincial ferries (13); navigation and shipping (10); legal tender (20); bankruptcy (21).

3. Subjects where uniformity is desirable.

> Regulation of trade and commerce (2); savings banks (16); bills and notes (18): weights and measures (17); interest (19); care of the Indians (24); quarantine (11); marriage and divorce (26); fisheries (12).

4. Subjects where the expense should be borne in common.

> Lighthouses (9); quarantine and marine hospitals (11); the public debt (1).

(*h*) The public property is given in the third schedule to the Act. There are also the revenues and stocks mentioned in sections 102 and 107 belonging to Canada.

In section 92, if we proceed on a like classification—keeping in view that the intention was *generally* to reserve all matters of a merely local or private nature to the provinces.

1. To provide means to carry on the work of government.

> Direct taxation (2) ; borrowing money on permanent credit (3) ; paying salaries (4) ; shop, saloon and other licenses (9).

2. Subjects obviously belonging to the provinces.

> Local and private matters (16) ; property and civil rights (13) ; municipal institutions (8) ; public lands and the timber and wood on them (5) ; local public works and undertakings (10) ; the administration of justice—the courts (14) ; hospitals, asylums and charities (7) ; prisons (5) ; incorporation of companies with provincial objects (11) ; solemnization of marriage (12). (*i*)

3. Exceptional powers.

> Amendment of the provincial constitution (except as to Lieutenant-Governor) (1); enforcement of provincial powers by fine, penalty or imprisonment (15).

It might have been easy to predict that some of the subjects in the 91st section given over to Canadian control would relate clearly to subjects under provincial jurisdiction. Thus in section (1) of the former, the extent of the public property given to Canada is to be traced only by a careful survey of the schedule already referred to, and by reading it with several sections of the Act. It has been held that lands escheating to the Crown for want of heirs do not revert to Canada, but to the province wherein the lands are situate. (*j*) Again lands reserved to Indians by

---

(*i*) Education is by special sections reserved to the provinces.

(*j*) *Attorney-General* v. *Mercer*, L.R. 8 App. P. C. 176.

the 24th section are, so far as the litigation has yet gone, to be considered as owned by the province but managed by the government of Canada as trustees for the Indians. (k) The regulation of trade and commerce given in the second class of the 91st section has been opposed by the tenth and other classes in the 92nd section. (l) The right to legis-late on licenses gave rise to two enactments, one by the Ontario government and another by the Dominion govern-ment known respectively as the Crooks Act and the McCarthy Act, in which the provincial jurisdiction was upheld. (m) The jurisdiction of the provinces to a certain extent over rivers and streams was questioned several times but was finally upheld; (n) as was also the right of a local legislature to attach uniform conditions to policies of insurance. The law as to insolvency and a ratable distribution of an insol-vent's estate is one that may appear to come within property and civil rights; just as the regulation of insurance policies is close to the subject of trade and commerce.

These are some of the difficulties that arise under a sys-tem where the legislative power is divided between two enacting bodies—both claiming exclusive jurisdiction over the subject in dispute. The general legislative control of the parliament of Canada cannot be determined but by a careful elimination of the provincial jurisdiction over the general local government of the provinces. The Acts of the provincial legislature which conflict with the powers conferred specifically or generally upon the general govern-ment are *ultra vires ;* so on the other hand Acts of the Dominion parliament or government conflicting with powers

(k) *Attorney-General* v. *The St. Catharines Milling Coy.* 13. O. A. 148.

(l) *Severn* v. *The Queen,* 2 Can. S. C. 77. *Queen* v. *Taylor,* 36 U. C. 2. B. 218.

(m) *Russell* v. *The Queen*—S. C.—and *The Queen* v. *Hodge,* R. L. 9 App. (P. C.) 117.

(n) *McLaren* v. *Caldwell,* L. C. 9 App. (P. C.) 392.

conferred exclusively upon the provincial legislature would be *ultra vires*, would be acts of usurpation. This must result from each being creatures of the one power—each deriving its authority from the same source. (o)

Within their respective limits each legislature is complete, absolute and supreme. The Dominion parliament has no more authority to interfere with or regulate matters specially assigned to the provinces than the provincial legislatures to regulate matters within the jurisdiction of the Dominion parliament. (p)

It has been usual to say that the legislative powers under the 92nd section given to the provinces are enumerated powers, and that the powers in the preceding section given to the parliament of Canada are the reserve, the general powers. It has been also said that a federal law is presumably valid unless on the list assigned to the provinces; a provincial law is presumably void unless in the enumerated list. The provinces can claim nothing in the way of legislative powers except what is expressly given to them; the Dominion can claim everything except what is expressly taken away from it.

This, however true it may be, is the language of American writers with regard to the central and the state governments of their Union; and it is language that, from their point of view, cannot be objected to. Section 8 of the United States constitution begins as follows:

Congress shall have power,—

(1) To lay and collect taxes, etc."

(o) Per Chancellor Spragge in *Leprohon* v. *Ottawa*, 2 Ont. app. 524.

(p) Per Mr. Justice Burton in *Parsons* v. *The Citizen's Insurance Co.*, 4 Ont. App. 96, and see also Chief Justice Harrison in *Leprohon* v. *Ottawa*, in 40 U. C. R. 486.

And then follow sixteen other sections enumerating the powers of the government of the United States. Section (9) imposes some restrictions on congress, and the following section prohibits the states from entering into any treaty, alliance or confederation, or laying any imposts or duties except what may be necessary for executing their respective laws. This is the extent of the enumeration; and by the ninth amendment to the constitution it is not to be construed to deny or disparage others retained by the people. The tenth amendment, passed in 1791, is as follows:

The powers not delegated to the United States by the constitution, nor prohibited by it to the states are reserved to the states respectively, or to the people.

Compare the foregoing with the language of the 91st and 92nd sections of the B. N. A. Act, and there is a wide difference. Of the seventeen subjects given to the United States government six refer to the army, navy, militia and the declaration of war; commerce, currency, naturalization and the postal service form four others; while the remainder are taken up with the powers of borrowing money, collecting taxes, the promotion of science, and some necessary provisions for the maintenance of any government. There is nothing in the first draft of the constitution in regard to the states except that they were guaranteed a republican form of government.

Now, the United States government has such powers only as are to be found delegated to it by the 8th section, and its legislation is presumably valid if within its scope, and presumably void if not within it. The states can claim every subject, unless those within the 8th section, and have every power except what that section takes from them.

In the Canadian union, under the B. N. A. Act, the legislative powers are strictly not powers conceded and powers withheld; they are not enumerated as opposed to non-enumerated powers; there is no grant and reservation. The fact was the provinces agreed to divide the powers into two classes, giving one to the central government, and retaining the other class for themselves. The mother country ratified the arrangement exactly in this way, so that the legislation corresponds with the facts and circumstances that brought it about. The sixth division of the Act is as follows :

VI. DISTRIBUTION OF LEGISLATIVE POWERS.

Powers of the Parliament.

By the 91st section " the exclusive legislative authority of the parliament of Canada extends to all matters coming within the classes of subjects next hereinafter enumerated;" and then follow the 29 classes of subjects.

In the 92nd section the language is varied in this way :

Exclusive powers of provincial legislatures.

92. In each province the legislature may exclusively make laws in relation to matters coming within the classes of subjects next hereinafter enumerated, etc.,

And as in the preceding section the classes—16 in all—assigned to the provinces, follow. In the Dominion, the classes of subjects do not restrict the powers of the legislature to deal with any law necessary for the peace, order or good government of Canada; and it must be taken to be the case that the parliament of Canada can legislate in reference thereto if the case was not already met with in the provincial powers. To this extent it is correct to say that the reserve powers are in the Dominion government— that is the reserve after the two classes in sections 91 and 92 are taken into account.

Still another limitation must be put on these reserve powers. They must not refer to anything of a merely local or private nature in the provinces because clause (16) of section 92 absolutely and exclusively confers these on the provinces.

The fact is that in drafting the constitution the framers put every conceivable subject for legislative action into forty-five classes ; the provinces retained sixteen of these, being fifteen enumerated and one general sub-section to cover every unenumerated residue of jurisdiction ; while the Dominion took the remaining twenty-nine subjects with a corresponding proviso including everything over and above. the twenty-nine subjects required for the peace, order and good government of Canada. There is, if one keeps the different areas of the legislatures in view, as much in reserve for the provinces in their own sphere, as there is for the Dominion in its sphere. It is easy to see that great particularity was necessary and that such was indeed used in the adjustment of these classes. There is something in reserve in each over and above the enumerated classes ; but they may be said to exhaust very completely the respective powers of each legislature. It is like what is often seen in deeds of grant ; A conveys 100 acres of land more or less, but for greater particularity sets it out by metes and bounds shewing $99\frac{1}{2}$ acres, which may generally be accepted as the size of the lot ; though if it should happen to be more the owner could take the benefit of it. In a federal constitution the owners of legislative power look to the classes of subjects when they are favorable to themselves, and when they are not favorable they fall back on the general terms of the grant.

Under this state of facts it is not so accurate to say that the enumerated subjects are assigned to the provinces, and the non-enumerated ones to the Dominion. It is not an exactly parallel case to the reserve powers in the states of the American union. The distribution of powers that took place in Canada was intended to be some such division, as Mr. Dicey points out should be in every federation. " The details of this division vary under every different federal constitution, but the general principle on which it should rest is obvious. Whatever concerns the nation as a whole should be placed under the control of the national government. All matters which are not primarily of common interest should remain in the hands of the several states. "

And again Mr. Dicey says :

" The distribution of powers is an essential feature of federation. The object for which a federal state is formed involves a division of authority between the national Government and the separate states. The powers given to the nation form in effect so many limitations upon the authority of the separate states, and as it is not intended that the central government should have the opportunity of encroaching upon the rights retained by the states, its sphere of action necessarily becomes the object of rigorous definition. The constitution, for instance, of the United States delegates specially and closely defined powers to the executive, to the legislature, and to the judiciary of the union, or in effect to the union itself, whilst it provides that the powers " not delegated to the United States by the constitution, nor prohibited by it to the states are reserved to the states respectively or to the people. This is all the amount of division which is essential to a federal constitution. "

The enumeration of the subjects, the apparent desire to include everything in them, the use of general words in both classes, and the manifest carefulness to provide for the provinces, offer so many difficulties over and above those presented by the wording of the United States constitution. When one section enacts that the central government shall generally have the power of making laws for Canada on all subjects, with the exception of those classes of subjects reserved to the provinces, and the next section enacts that each province shall have exclusive control of all civil rights, and generally of all local matters in the province, there is certainly not wanting a large field to be claimed with equal earnestness and equal sincerity by both authorities.

Parliament has other powers besides those enumerated in section 91. It has established a general court of appeal—the Supreme Court of Canada—for all the provinces —an exchequer and maritime courts, and may establish any additional courts for the better administration of the laws of Canada. (q) It fixes the salaries of the Lieutenant-Governors, and provides for their payment, and fixes and provides salaries for nearly all the judges of Canada.

In the removal of judges the parliament can take action on addresses presented to it for that purpose. Although the appointment of the judges vests technically in the Governor-General, it is, of course, in the control of the ministry as representing parliament, and the parliament has a remedy for the removal of incompetent ones. (r) It has all necessary and proper powers with the government, for performing the obligations of Canada or any of its provinces, as part of the British Empire, towards foreign countries, arising under treaties, between the empire and such foreign countries. (s) It has in its hands the power of deciding to whom the administration of

(q) Sec, 101.
(r) Secs. 96-100.
(s) Sec. 132.

government shall be entrusted. In other words it has the power of change of ministry : for no ministry can carry on a government for any length of time unless supported by a majority in parliament. The duties and powers of an administration have already been referred to under the head of administrative government. It is noted for the present, as one of the consequential powers of parliament. Parliament, by enacting private bills, such as incorporating companies, conferring privileges, or removing restraints, etc., deals largely in legislation of a judicial character. which forms the greater bulk of its work and is of great importance to the country.

By an imperial Act passed in 1871, power was given to the parliament of Canada from time to time, to establish new provinces in any territories forming for the time being part of the Dominion, and at the time of such establishment make provision for the constitution and administration of any such province, and for the passing of laws for the peace, order and good government of such province. and for its representation in parliament. Similar power was given to deal with the government of any territory not for the time being included in any province.

CHAPTER X.

Dominion assets, public works schedule, duties, revenues, stocks—Debts, consolidated revenue fund, charges on it— Provincial assets, lands, mines, etc.

TWENTY-FIVE sections of the B. N. A. Act are taken up with the property and liabilities of the Dominion and of the provinces. These are sections 102 to 126, both included. Other sections, such as the 91st and the 92nd, containing the distribution of powers, must also be looked at in connection with this matter.

The several provinces retained all their respective public property not otherwise disposed of by the Act, allowing only the right to the Dominion to assume any lands or public property required for fortifications or for the defence of the country. (*a*) It is likely that lands assumed in this way would have to be purchased as in the case of appropriated lands. The 13th sub-section of the 92nd section gives to the provinces property and civil rights, while the 1st. sub-section of the 91st. section of the Act gives to the Dominion the public debt and property. The public works and property of each province, as enumerated in the fol-

(*a*) Section 117, Mr. Justice Burton says in the Mercer case, "I find no warrant in the Act for the assertion so frequently made that all rights of property, not expressly given to the province, pass to the Dominion. On the contrary, I take it to be clear that the provinces retained all property and rights which were previously vested in them, under the constitutional Acts then in force, except those which by the confederation Act are taken from them and transferred to the Dominion."

lowing schedule, are the property of Canada, within the meaning of this sub-section : (*b*)

(1). Canals, with lands and water power connected therewith.

(2). Public harbours.

(3). Lighthouses and piers, and Sable Island.

(4). Steamboats, dredges and public vessels.

(5). Rivers and lake improvements.

(6). Railways and railway stocks, mortgages, and other debts due by railway companies.

(7). Military roads.

(8). Custom houses, post offices, and all other public buildings, except such as the government of Canada appropriates for the use of the provincial legislatures and governments.

(9). Property transferred by the imperial government, and known as ordnance property.

(10). Armouries, drill sheds, military clothing, munitions of war, and lands set apart for general public purposes.

Canada took over all duties and revenues of the old provinces except such portions thereof as were by the Act reserved to their legislatures ; and there was formed out of them a consolidated revenue fund. (*c*) All stocks, cash, bankers' balances and securities for money belonging to each province at the time of the union, unless expressly reserved by the Act, were also placed to the credit of Canada, and went to reduce the provincial debts of the respective provinces. (*d*)

(*b*) Sec. 108.

(*c*) Sec. 102. See the able argument, by the Hon. W. Macdougall, C. B., reported specially in the Mercer Escheat case, 1881.

(*d*) Sec. 107.

Although Canada assumed the debts and liabilities of the provinces, (e) they were settled at a certain sum, and if beyond, the provinces were to pay Canada interest on the excess at 5 per centum per annum.

These sums were as follows : (f)

Ontario and Quebec, liable to Canada,
    if their debt was over.............. $65,500,000
Nova Scotia 8,000,000
New Brunswick 7,000,000

If the debts of the latter two provinces were not up to these respective amounts, they were to get the same rate of interest in half yearly payments in advance on the difference.

Canada was to pay towards the expenses of the provincial governments the following sums :

Ontario... $80,000
Quebec 70,000
Nova Scotia....................................... 60,000
New Brunswick.................................. 50,000

besides an annual grant determinable on the population, and a special grant to New Brunswick. (g)

This was the basis of the consolidated revenue fund of Canada in 1867 ; and the balance of the duties and revenues not appropriated were, along with all duties and revenues raised in accordance with special provincial powers, formed into provincial funds called the consolidated revenue fund of the province.

(e) Sec. 111.
(f) Sec. 112, 114, 115, 116, 117.   See R. S. C. cap. 46, as to additional subsidies, increasing these figures about one-eighth.
(g) Sec. 119.

The expenses of the public service of Canada are paid out of the consolidated revenue fund. The first charge on it is the costs, charges and expenses incident to its collection, management and receipt. The interest on the public provincial debts is the second; and the third is the Governor-General's salary, fixed at £10,000 sterling, or such other sum as the parliament of Canada may determine. After these payments are made, the balance is appropriated to the public service of Canada, with no particular order of preference. (h)

The Governor-General in council, unless parliament otherwise directs, orders the form and manner of all payments or discharges of liabilities, under the Act of 1867 in regard to Canada and its provinces in these matters.

These funds are each year augmented in various ways. Large sums are paid in from the customs, revenue and public land departments, by means of tariffs, excise or other duties, by the sale of lands, by fees from the post office department, and from the various other departments of state. If the receipts from these sources are in advance of the amount asked for in the supply bill, (which sets out the expenditure of the country for the fiscal year,) then there is no necessity of direct taxation, or specific grants by parliament. The ways and means used for raising the supplies form the budget of the year; and when it is considered that in Canada the supplies voted by parliament usually amount to a great many millions of dollars annually as the expenses of the government from July to July, the task which the minister has in making a satisfactory budget speech is not at all an easy one.

The provinces, besides what has been already referred to, retained "all lands, mines, minerals and royalties," and "all sums then due or payable for such lands, mines,

(h) Sec. 103, 104, 105, 106.

minerals or royalties, " subject, of course, to any trust or interest of any person or against the provinces. (*i*) All assets connected with such portions of the public debt of each province as are assumed by that province, shall belong to that province. (*j*) Canada gave up to Ontario and Quebec conjointly the following properties belonging to the late province of Canada :

Upper Canada building fund.
Lunatic asylums.
Normal school.
Court houses in ⎫
Aylmer, ⎪
Montreal, ⎬ Lower Canada.
Kamarouska, ⎭
Law society, Upper Canada.
Montreal turnpike trust.
University permanent fund.
Royal institution.
Consolidated municipal loan fund, Upper Canada.
Consolidated municipal loan fund, Lower Canada.
Agricultural society, Upper Canada.
Lower Canada legislative grant.
Quebec fire loan.
Temiscouata advance account.
Quebec turnpike trust.
Education—cast.
Building and jury fund, Lower Canada.
Municipalities fund.
Lower Canada superior education income fund.

The Dominion government has exclusive legislative authority over the lands reserved to the Indians, but it is not yet definitely settled whether or not the provinces are

(*i*) Sec. 109.   (*j*) Sec. 110.

entitled to be considered owners of unpatented lands occupied by Indians within their limits. (*k*) It has been decided that lands reverting to the crown under the doctrine of escheat come under the control of the provinces. (*l*)

The assets of the Dominion at confederation were very inconsiderable compared with the vast resources she now possesses. The addition of two colonies was not of very great importance, but the purchase by the government of Canada of the Hudson Bay territory shortly after 1867 placed a large portion of the continent at her disposal—a tract of country 1,200 miles long and 500 miles broad. (*m*) The imperial Act was passed in 1868, (32 and 33 Vic. cap. 105,) and in the following year the payment of the purchase money to the Hudson Bay Company, £300,000, was guaranteed by another imperial Act. By an order in council of the 23rd. of June, 1870, the North Western territory and Rupert's Land were admitted and became part of the Dominion.

(*k*) *Regina* v. *The St. Catharines Milling Co.*, 103 A. P. 148.

(*l*) *Mercer* v. *The Attorney-General of Ontario*, L. R. 8 App. 767.

(*m*) This purchase and the purchase of Louisiana from France by the United States of America, in 1803, may be regarded as the two largest in history.

CHAPTER XI.

PROCEDURE IN PARLIAMENT—BILLS.

*Summoning parliament—Speaker of the commons—Speech
from the throne—Business of the houses—Privileges
of members—Different stages of a bill, conferences,
how a bill becomes an Act, peculiar bills, supply,
divorce, private bills, deposits—Prorogation, dissolution.*

The Governor-General, under advice, exercises the power
of summoning parliament, proroguing it when necessary
or desirable, and dissolving it, so far as the commons is
concerned, within the period of five years from its commencement.

By section 20 of the B. N. A. Act, there must be a session
at least once in every year, so that twelve months shall not
intervene between the last sitting of the parliament in one
session and its first sitting in the next session.

The senate and commons are summoned by proclamation to attend at Ottawa on a certain day, usually in February, " for the despatch of business; to treat, do, act and
conclude upon those things which in our said parliament
of Canada, by the common council of our said Dominion,
may by the favour of God be ordained."

The parliament is opened by the Governor in person in
the senate chamber. The senators being assembled, the
speaker commands the gentleman usher of the black rod
to proceed to the commons and acquaint that house that
" it is his Excellency's pleasure that they attend him immediately in this house." The commons then proceed in

a body to the bar of the senate, and, if at the beginning of a new parliament, are instructed to choose a speaker for their house. They then return to their own house, and having chosen a speaker, are again summoned to the senate, usually on the following day, and the speaker is then presented to the Governor-General. The speaker is the official means of communication between him and the commons, and is the first commoner in the Dominion.

At the beginning of each parliament, and of each of its subsequent sessions, the Governor General opens the session with a gracious speech to both houses, which is reported to them by the speaker of the senate. This address is prepared by the ministers of the crown, and is supposed to contain the leading points of proposed legislation on the part of the government. Before it is reported, however, some bill is read *pro forma*. This is to assert the right of the parliament to proceed with their work notwithstanding the fact that the crown may not have suggested to them any legislation. Afterwards the speech is discussed in the house, and, if the policy proposed in it is acceptable, it is adopted and a reply presented to the Governor-General. The legislation of the session is then taken up. English and French may be used in the debates in both houses, and the journals of the debates are entered in these languages. The rules of the house form quite a code of its kind. Members are not limited to time in their speeches, but they are not allowed to read them, though they may use notes and may cite extracts. Nothing disrespectful of Her Majesty or the royal family is permitted. It is not proper to refer to the other house or to previous debates, or to call a member by name, or to question the meaning he puts on his own words. (*a*)

(*a*) Unless it can be established that the parliament of Canada has the power, by express grant, to adopt the *cloture*, such a power is not inherent in a colonial legislature. The fact that the houses here in Canada may

The house ordinarily meets every day at three o'clock except on Saturdays, and if sufficient members are present to form a quorum, proceeds to the despatch of business. This number, as has been remarked, is fifteen in the senate and twenty in the commons, of which number the speaker in each may be reckoned as one. Certain routine business, such as presenting and receiving petitions, and presenting reports of the different committees in the house, and motions are taken up every day as they occur, and afterwards the orders of the day, which are different every day, are read and proceeded with. A day or more in the week is usually reserved to the government, in view of the large amount of business in its hands.

Every member is privileged to bring in a motion or bill; but in the commons he must give notice of his intention to bring in a bill. When a bill is brought in the house it is read simply without discussion. On the second reading the principles of the bill are discussed. If not interrupted at this or towards the next stage, the bill is committed; that is, it is taken into consideration in a committee of the house. When the house goes into committee the speaker leaves the chair, and the mace, which represents royal authority, is put under the table. The house may then appoint any member as chairman, and the strict rules of debate observed in parliament are relaxed. There are three classes of committees :

1. Committees of the whole house ;

2. Select or special committees, which do not sit in the house, but in another room when the house is not sitting ;

3. Joint committees composed of members of both houses.

adopt the rules of the imperial parliament does not of itself bring with it all future changes in the imperial parliament. See the case of *Barton* v. *Taylor*, L. R. 11 App. Cases, 197.

In committee each clause of the bill is considered and voted upon. If the committee have not time to get through they ask leave to sit again. When ready to report, or when the committee must rise, the speaker resumes the chair and the house proceeds to business. If ready, the bill is then read a third time. The only parts usually left for a fourth reading are the preamble and title, which are always the last things considered. The bill, having gone through these different stages in the house where it originates, is sent to the other house, where it passes through the same stages as to readings. Those in favour of the bill in the senate are the " contents "; those opposing it the '' non-contents." In the commons the members vote by "ayes " and "noes." In all unprovided cases the senate follows the rules, usages and forms of the house of Lords in England, and the commons in such cases follows the English commons. The duties of the speakers have been already referred to. (b)

In case of amendments by one house to a bill sent from the other, the senate arranges *conferences* to bring about an agreement. For this purpose each house appoints its own bearers of messages. One of the clerks of either house may be a bearer from one house to another, and the master in chancery, attending the senate, is received as their messenger to the commons. Messages may also be brought up by one or more members of the commons to the senate. A committee of either house does not receive a message, from the other. The speaker takes the chair; and the message, after being received at the bar, is delivered to the speaker, who reports the same to the house—the answer is sent and received with corresponding formality. If no agreement as to amendment is arrived at, the bill is lost.

(b) See *ante*, chaps. IV. and V.

After having been passed by both houses, it only requires the assent of the Governor-General to make it an Act of parliament. When a bill passed by both houses is presented to His Excellency, he has three courses constitutionally open to him. He may assent to the bill, in the Queen's name; he may withhold the Queen's assent; or he may reserve the bill for the signification of the Queen's pleasure. The Queen's assent is seldom withheld: but not unfrequently bills are reserved for the signification of Her pleasure. The royal instructions to the Governor-General set out specifically certain bills, such as divorce, etc., which must be reserved. When the bill is assented to by the Queen's representative it becomes an Act of parliament —a part of the statute law. (c)

All bills, except the supply bill, are supposed to come from the senate to the crown. The supply bill being essentially a bill of the house of commons, is assented to specially by the Governor-General, thanking them for affording the funds necessary for carrying on the government of the country. The crown suggests the supplies; and probably if the case should arise in this country the crown would originate a bill for a general pardon in analogy to British precedent. Beyond this, all measures originate indifferently either in the senate or commons. Some bills are left to be originated in select committees, some in committees of the whole house. The public bills affect the whole Dominion—private bills affect individuals, companies, or corporations. These latter bills, before being entertained, require a deposit of $100 in the senate and $200 in the commons, and the costs of printing and translating the copies sent in. This is in order to cover

(c) The old distinction between an Act of parliament and a statute was this, that an Act of parliament was an Act of two houses and that it became a statute only when the Queen assented to it. This distinction is now forgotten or lost sight of.

the necessary expenses; and private bills must also be advertised in the *Canada Gazette*, the official journal of the government, for two months before the house opens.

When the work of the session is concluded, parliament is prorogued. The speaker of the senate is informed that the Governor-General will proceed to the senate chamber at a certain day and hour and close the session. At the proper time when the two houses are in session the commons is acquainted that it is His Excellency's pleasure that they attend him in the senate. The speaker in the commons and the members proceed to the bar of the senate and after the titles of the bills are read by the clerk in chancery, and the bills assented or reserved as the case may be, the supply bill is presented by the speaker of the commons. His Excellency replies, assents to the supply bill of the faithful commons, and declares the parliament prorogued. The session is then concluded and nothing can be done with any bill or proceeding till another session with the usual formalities has been commenced. This is the distinction between a prorogation and an adjournment —the latter simply continuing the work from day to day or to a day named, while a prorogation is from session to session. A dissolution on the other hand is the termination of the house of commons as composed of the actual members representing their constituencies. It does not affect the senate much more than a prorogation, except that it brings about a new set of members and possibly a change of ministry. A dissolution of parliament virtually means dissolving the commons.

CHAPTER XII.

CONSTITUTIONS OF THE PROVINCES.

*Less particularity in describing the provincial constitutions
than the Dominion—Comparison with U. S. constitution
—Veto—Statutory description of the provinces, executives—Ontario and Quebec, Nova Scotia and New Brunswick —Powers common to all—Disallowance—Strict
and relaxed views of the constitution, Mr. Justice
Gwynne—Chief Justice Sir William Ritchie, provincial
autonomy.*

IT will be seen from the foregoing chapters with what
particularity the Act of Union provides for the establishment, the jurisdiction, and the maintenance of the general
government of Canada.   It was a new creation, and digni-
fied in express terms with the name of a parliament, (a)
supplied with a certain amount of property and the power
to acquire the other British provinces and territories
adjoining it.   The new government undertook to watch
over the general interests of those colonies that entered
the union ; the legislative and executive control were as
sharply defined as could be without resorting to the codifi-
cation of all subjects ; while the form and composition of
the machinery of government were so detailed and comprehensive as to leave that part of it little open to conjecture.

(a) Whether any British possession in America ever had a parliament
before the Dominion of Canada got one, is a question that the reader can
find discussed elsewhere and from opposite points of view.   No plantation
or colony ever received it in so many words, although it was certainly
assumed to be reproduced under the constitutions of 1791 and 1840 in
the Canadas.

The provinces however remained; two of them closely connected in their past history and very anxious about their old position; two others not so anxious for a union, but equally tenacious of their former rights and liberties. When the representatives of these four provinces came to terms concerning the new parliament for all of them, they did not apparently assume that everything would remain as theretofore in the provinces. In that respect the Canadian and United States constitutions differ very materially. In the latter case the individual states, so far as the constitution goes, are to be guaranteed a republican form of government. (b) Renouncing their right to deal with the powers delegated to the general government they pursued their way as individual states, leaving it to the courts to say whether they and the central governments kept within their respective limits.

What took place in the Canadian union was very different from this. The powers were distributed between the general government and the state or provincial governments, with a general reservation to the central government on all subjects extending over all the provinces, and a corresponding reservation to the local governments on all domestic subjects connected with the provinces. Both these governments are liable to a veto in the exercise of their powers, but the provincial legislature is subject to the veto of the dominion government, while the dominion legislation is free from any provincial control except the common one of the courts. The veto, it is true, does not in practice extend to anything beyond the competency of the local legislature to pass any particular statute; but it is made occasionally in judicial and political language to assume the form of control over provincial affairs. This power and the supplying of an executive officer called a

(b) Sec. 4, Act IV.

Lieutenant-Governor are the two circumstances common
to all the provinces and about which the central and local
governments are always and necessarily in connection with
each other. The Lieutenant-Governor is assumed to be
the chief of each local legislature, but it was only in Ontario and Quebec that his position and duties were expressly
defined by the Act. The constitution and executive authority in Nova Scotia and New Brunswick were unaffected by
the Act and continued as they were before 1867. (c) The
same was the case with the constitution of their legislatures : (d) but the duties of their chief executive officers
were not set out in detail as was the case in Ontario and
Quebec. (e) In all the provinces the provisions as to
appropriation and tax bills, the recommendation of money
votes, the disallowance of Acts, and the signification of
pleasure on bills reserved apply equally and are the same
as in the Dominion of Canada with the substitution of one
year instead of two years in regard to the disallowance or
reservation of bills. Ontario and Quebec were not content
with retaining the constitution of their predecessors, as
was the case with the other provinces. They had inserted
in the Act of Union a number of provisions as to their
executive, the executive council, Lieutenant-Governor in
council, the great seal, the executive officers, with their
powers and duties, the summoning of their assemblies in
the Queen's name, the continuance of existing laws as to
elections, etc., the yearly session of their legislatures and a
number of details as to a speaker and the mode of voting
in the house of assembly. (f) All the provinces have equal

(c) Sec. 64.
(d) Sec. 88.
(e) Sec. 65.
(f) Secs. 63, 65, 66, 134-5-6 and 69 to 87 both included. For those
who contend that the legislatures in Ontario and Quebec are " the heirs
at law " of the old parliaments of Upper and Lower Canada, there must
be something superfluous in these sections.

control over their own constitutions, and they can amend them from time to time except as regards the office of Lieutenant-Governor. The establishment and tenure of provincial offices and the appointment and payment of provincial officers are also within their exclusive jurisdiction. (g) All articles grown, produced or manufactured in any one of them are admitted free of duty by all of the others; (h) their lands and property, as is the case with Canada, are exempt from taxation; (i) and all laws in force at the time of the union, all courts, legal commissions, powers and authorities and all officers judicial, administrative and ministerial existing at the union continued as if no union had been effected, subject to be repealed, abolished or altered by the proper authority. (j) This is the substance of the various provisions of the B. N. A. Act as regards the provinces.

If the power of disallowance of provincial legislation is strictly viewed, there is an end to a Canadian federal union. It is essential to a federation, as has been already seen, that each government should be supreme within its own limits. (k) The Dominion government has the power of disallowance of provincial statutes within one year after they are enacted. There is no limitation as to this disallowance, except that the Governor-General exercises the right on the responsibility of ministers who are elected to office by the people of the provinces. This power is not so destructive of provincial rights as it might appear from the wording of the 90th section. (l) All legislation in

(g) Sec. 92, S.S. 1 and 4.
(h) Sec. 121.
(i) Sec. 125.
(j) Sec. 129.
(k) *Ante*, page 8.
(l) Lord Carnarvon stated officially to Lord Dufferin during the vexed controversy over the New Brunswick School Act :—
"The constitution of Canada does not contemplate any interference

Canada is subject to disallowance from imperial authorities, and it was thought desirable to allow the responsibility of so grave an act to rest on the people immediately affected, and to be exercised by the local advisers of the crown, who might be expected to be more familiar with the lines of distribution between provincial and Dominion power than are the advisers of the crown in England. In the United States the supreme court is thought sufficient to keep the legislatures within their limits. In Belgium there is not any constitutional check, but with us the aggressiveness of the provinces was subject to a two-fold restraint. However, it could scarcely be expected that a power of disallowance would be held over the larger government and none over the others; and there was much force in leaving all local questions to be settled by the Canadian people themselves. After a statute of the local legislature has been enacted and disallowed for several successive sessions, the subject in dispute, as in the case of the Streams Bill of Ontario, comes before the judicial committee of the privy council in some way, and the limits of jurisdiction are thus defined. There would be less contradiction in the preamble of the Act if the sovereign authority of the Empire was held equally over the two governments, and exercised in exactly the same way. A federal union should secure to its constituent states an absolutely independent sphere of action within their assigned limits; otherwise there is no federation. (m)

With the written constitution in a way not quite in pur- suance of the history and intention of it, one may expect to have two very decided and contradictory views in regard to the provinces and the scope of provincial authority.

with provincial legislation, on a subject within the competence of the local legislature, by the Dominion parliament, or, as a consequence, by Dominion ministers."

(m) See *post* as to principles upon which the power of disallowance is exercised.

One of these emanates from the strict, literal interpretation of the B. N. A. Act, construed exactly as any other statute is construed, and with steadfast adherence to the principles of the British constitution ; the other is the result of close regard to what is understood by a federal union seen in the light of a relaxed rule of interpretation.   If the decisions of the English court of appeal had not overborne, to some extent, certain extreme views of Canadian judges and statesmen, the result would have been one party viewing the Canadian union from a federal or central standpoint, and another party regarding the union from a provincial point of view.   The advocates of these aids to discovering the meaning of our written constitution, are probably not concerned by any decision that conflicts with their own view of it; but it has become apparent within the last half-dozen years that a strictly legal interpretation is not the one congenial to the lords of the privy council.   On the other hand, the idea of a federation is not or was not allowed to have much weight in very many instances with the judges of our own courts.   To have a federal union is one thing and not impossible, and the same is, of course, true of a constitutional monarchy; but any attempt to combine both of these in one country can only end in the partial or complete extinction of one or the other.   It must be understood, both as a historical fact and as the fair reading of the B. N. A. Act, that the Canadian union is, and was intended to be, a federation.   It has all the essentials of a federal union.

The Act of union, however, recites that the federal union shall have a constitution similar in principle to a constitutional monarchy.   The difficulty then arises whether the federation is to neutralize the British principles of monarchical government or to be neutralized by them. The view taken in these pages is that in applying the principles of British government, they must be subordinated to the federation whenever their application would be fatal to the existence of a federation. This view accords with the historical fact and is not an improper rendering of the words of the statute of 1867 : a federal union with British principles, if possible, but a federal union at all events.

It is in regard to the provinces that these principles of British government have met with the greatest difficulties and opposition. The early sections of the Act of Union set out with great particularity a parliament for the Dominion—the Queen and two houses—a privy council apparently for the sole use of the Dominion ; and then follows a very large grant of legislative power, in words very like what were used in preceding constitutions, but with just such a reservation to the provinces as was necessary to the existence of a federation. Except this limit to legislative power all these sections pointed to a reproduction of a government on British principles. There is no difficulty in the central power being as monarchical as needs be. It was copied and moulded on British principles.

The question virtually arose whether or not this reproduction of a British parliament would not suffice for the provinces as well as for the Dominion, especially as there is very little in the Act to lead one to suppose that a copying of English forms and procedure was to be carried into every provincial legislature. The provinces, regarding themselves as the factors of the union, were not disposed to be relegated to the unimportant position of municipal councils, and from the beginning they asserted their co-ordinate jurisdiction and the perpetuation of their ancient prerogatives. Looking at the historical side of the case they regarded the central power as one created by themselves, having such duties and jurisdiction as they thought fit to bestow on it, and reserving to themselves whatever was too important or valuable to be given away. The central authorities, on the other hand, point to the statute and the unity in the principles of British government, and they say, " We have the sole parliament, you have no parliament; our executive is the Queen, the Queen is no part of your constitution, you are no longer colonies of the empire, you are our provinces, and the imperial government or the Queen will not notice you except through us ; you are only the provinces of a colony ; we have the power to disallow your Acts ; we provide you with Lieutenant-Governors and you have no control over us except through appeal to the paramount law of the constitution. "

It is not easy to define, in a few words, the exact position of the provinces comprising the Dominion of Canada. The strictly legal view of the Act of Union is that in 1867 three existing provinces desired to be federally united into one Dominion ; and they were so united, and formed thereafter Canada. The three provinces merged their 'existence in Canada. They were then lost sight of, and in their stead Canada appeared, and was immediately afterwards divided up into four provinces, with the power of legislating on certain limited subjects under the supervision of the parliament of Canada. The late province of Canada, with Nova Scotia and New Brunswick, voluntarily terminated its existence as a distinct portion of the British possessions or colonies. They were to be thereafter known under a new name collectively, and with a new constitution. Had the new political division one legislature only for all purposes, there would be little difficulty in defining the new situation. But the duty of legislating for all parts of the new Dominion was deemed by the framers of its constitution so great that one central parliament could not satisfactorily accomplish that task. Accordingly, in almost the very next section of the Act of 1867 uniting the three provinces into Canada, it is declared that Canada shall be

divided into four provinces, with territorial areas the same
as they had been prior to the union, with exclusive but
curtailed powers of legislation, and with their chief executive officers provided by and representing the government
of Canada.   The Act of Union divided the Canadas as they
were before 1840, and the old provinces retained their
geographical boundaries.   They were merged in the
Dominion, and then re-created and given another set of
names—Ontario, Quebec, Nova Scotia and New Brunswick.

Those who contend for a strict interpretation, insist that
there is a great difference between the present and past
position of these provinces.   Formerly they were colonies
of the empire, and possessed governors or lieutenant-
governors, who were the immediate representatives of the
crown in their provinces.   Now their chief executive officers
are members of the colonial administration staff, and are
but lieutenants of the Governor-General of Canada : the
provinces are no longer colonies, but provinces of a colony.
Under the former constitution they had, subject to imperial
authority, the right to make laws for the peace, order and
good government of their provinces ; now their legislative
power is limited to a prescribed set of subjects ; and though
they may be supreme within these constitutional limits, the
imperial authority has entrusted to the government of
Canada the control of keeping them within such limits.
Whether wisely or foolishly, the provinces have surrendered
a large portion of their rights to the determination of the
federal government at Ottawa.   Any attempted assumption
of authority beyond the rights retained by the provinces,
if not vetoed by the Governor-General, is liable to be
declared unconstitutional by the provincial or by the
Dominion courts.

Again, it is said that the lieutenant-governors, being
deputies of the Governor-General, and not of the Queen,

have no power to give the Queen's sanction to any Act of the legislature. They assent on behalf of the Governor-General. (*n*) They have not the power to do so under the written constitution; and there is certainly something anomalous in the case of the Governor-General, the Queen's deputy, disallowing an Act passed in the provincial legis-lature by the Queen's Most Excellent Majesty. An objec-tion was formerly raised in the American colonies in the corresponding case of a Governor-General who was unques-tionably the royal representative, but it was over-ruled. On the matter being referred to England an opinion was given in these words :—

" I have heard objections drawn from the style of this Act. ' It is enacted by the King's Most Excellent Majesty,' etc., but I think this objection of little weight. The King is here named in his royal and politic capacity, which, at the time of making the Act, was to this purpose residing in his Governor, who there enjoyed and exercised the func-tions of it in this province, and the personal assent was not necessary to the Act." (*o*)

" The Queen," says Mr. Justice Gwynne, " forms no part of the provincial legislatures, as she does of the Dominion parliament. * * The use of her Majesty's name by these provincial authorities is by the Act confined to the sum-moning and calling together the legislatures ; and, singular as it seems, this is by the 82nd section, rather by accident, I apprehend, than design, confined to the Lieutenant-Governors of Ontario and Quebec." (*p*)

" By the 91st section it is declared that the Acts of the Dominion parliament shall be made by the Queen, by and

(*n*) Per Draper, C.J., *in re Goodhue*, 19 Grant.

(*o*) Chalmer's Opinions.

(*p*) The case of *Lenoir* v. *Ritchie*, decided at Ottawa in 1879, contains some strong views on these points.

with the advice of the senate and commons, treating the
Queen herself as an integral part of the parliament; whilst
the 92nd section enacts that the "Legislatures" of the
respective provinces, that is, the Lieutenant-Governor and
the legislative assembly in provinces having but one house,
and the Lieutenant-Governor and the legislative council
and assembly in provinces having two houses, shall make
laws in relation to matters coming within certain enumerated classes of subjects, to which their jurisdiction is
limited. Nothing can be plainer, as it seems to me, than
that the several provinces are subordinate to the Dominion
government; and that the Queen is no party to the laws
made by those local legislatures, and that no Act of any
such legislatures can in any manner impair or affect Her
Majesty's right to the exclusive exercise of all her prerogative powers, which she continues to enjoy untrammeled,
except in so far as we are obliged to hold that, by the express terms of the British North American Act, or by
irresistible inference from what is there expressed, she has
by that Act consented to be divested of any part of such
prerogative." (q)

The foregoing will give an idea of the case from a federal
point of view; the provinces, however, have not allowed
their case to go by default. They maintain that the Act
of Union was passed at the request of the provinces and
that so far as the provinces are concerned, whatever has
not been expressly delegated to the Dominion has been reserved to themselves. Whatever the provinces had under
former constitutions they shall have unless it can be
pointed out in the Confederation Act as taken away from
them. The old constitutional Acts were not repealed. As
to land and property, everything has been retained except
what is contained in the sections and schedules of the Act.

(q) *Lenoir* v. *Ritchie*, 3 S. C. Can. 634.

It is decided that escheated land falls to the provinces, and an appeal is now pending from the decision of five eminent judges in Ontario, who hold that Indian lands belong to the provinces. The provinces retained the administration of justice, civil rights, the municipal system, the constitution of the courts and everything of a local and private nature. The scope of the legislative work assigned to the provinces is relatively of greater importance to the people than is the work allotted to the Dominion. Their powers are derived from the same source and are on the same plane —the Queen disallowing directly or secondarily dominion or provincial laws. Whatever the Dominion is, the provinces have made her such, and they could unmake her by the same process. If they withdraw their support and adhesion the structure falls to the ground.

A recurrence to the history of events leading up to confederation is not generally allowable in the legal construction of the statute. The intention is to be gathered from the words of the Act.

But the British statesmen and judges are disposed to regard the Act of Union as a compact—a treaty—and to adopt a rule of interpretation in the light of preceding events. That is favorable to the provincial view. The strict rendering of the B. N. A. Act, in regard to the executive, is somewhat shaken by the decision in the Mercer escheat case, decided since *Lenoir* v. *Ritchie*, and the tendency of the courts has been rather in favour of the provincial view of the question.

The late chief justice of the supreme court, Sir William Johnston Ritchie, says (r): " When it is claimed that a Lieutenant-Governor and council are not competent to deal with a matter, or to do an executive administrative Act

(r) *Mercer* v. *The Attorney-General of Ontario*, 5 S. C., 637.

that was within their competency before confederation, the burthen is cast on those putting forward such a claim to show clearly from the B.N.A. Act that by express language or by necessary implication the local governments have been deprived of that authority, and the power has been placed in the executive authority of the Dominion. To say that the Lieutenant-Governors because appointed by the Governor-General do not in any sense represent the Queen in the government of these provinces is, in my opinion, a fallacy; they represent the Queen as Lieutenant-Governors did before confederation, in the performance of all executive or administrative Acts now left to be performed by Lieutenant-Governors in the provinces, in the name of the Queen. "

The same learned judge says : " Special pains appear to me to have been taken to preserve the autonomy of the provinces so far as it could be consistently, with a federal union. "

CHAPTER XIII.

THE PROVINCIAL LEGISLATURES.

Lieutenant-Governors, in Ontario and Quebec, in other provinces—Former governors—Powers, dismissal, opinions of Earl Kimberley, of Sir John Macdonald, Mr. Justice Gwynne—Legislative assemblies, procedure,—Extent of disallowance, Mr. Lash's memorandum.

THE provincial legislatures are not framed on any uniform plan. The Dominion government supplies the executive officer—the Lieutenant-Governor—and the provinces by virtue of the Act of union provide the house or houses of assembly. In Ontario the legislature consists of the Lieutenant-Governor and one house — a legislative asembly. (*a*) In Quebec there are two houses—a legislative council as well as an assembly,—and the Lieutenant-Governor is also part of their legislature by the Act. (*b*) In Nova Scotia and New Brunswick the legislatures were allowed to continue as before the union, subject to the provisions of it. So far as the constitution of these legislatures is concerned, they were affected to the extent of having a Lieutenant-Governor sent them by the Dominion and not by the imperial government. The Act defines nothing as to their powers, authorities and functions beyond the recommendation as to money votes, and provisions as to assent, disallowance and reservation of bills, which are the same as the provisions for the other Lieutenant-Governors.

(*a*) Sec. 69.
(*b*) Sec. 65.

The provision of the Act as to the Lieutenant-Governor in council means "acting by and with the advice of the executive council " of the province, (c) but this is the only section in the Act that applies generally to all the lieutenant-governors except some unimportant provisions as to the oath, and tenure of office, salary, administration, etc. (d)

In Ontario and Quebec the case is different. By the 65th Sec.

" All powers, authorities, and functions which under any Act of the parliament of Great Britain, or of the parliament of the United Kingdom of Great Britain and Ireland, or of the legislature of Upper Canada, Lower Canada or Canada, were or are before or at the union vested in or exerciseable by the respective governors or lieutenant-governors of those provinces, with the advice and consent, of the respective executive councils thereof, or in conjunction with those councils, or with any number of members thereof, or by those governors or lieutenant-governors individually, shall, as far as the same are capable of being exercised after the union in relation to the government of Ontario and Quebec respectively, be vested in and shall or may be exercised by the Lieutenant-Governor of Ontario and Quebec respectively, with the advice or with the advice and consent of or in conjunction with the respective executive councils, or any members thereof, or by the Lieutenant-Governor individually, as the case requires, subject nevertheless (except with respect to such as exist under Acts of the parliament of Great Britain, or the parliament of the United Kingdom of Great Britain and Ireland) to be abolished or altered by the respective legislatures of Ontario and Quebec."

Bearing in mind the differences in the powers of the chief executive officers in Ontario and Quebec from those in the other provinces in the union, the mode of appoint-

(c) Sec. 66.
(d) Secs. 59 to 62.

ment and other particulars which are common to all may be enquired into.

The Governor in council appoints a Lieutenant-Governor for each province, by instrument under the great seal of Canada.

Under the federal system of government the chief executive officers in the province are now members of the civil service of Canada, and not as formerly, members of the civil service of England. They are neither appointed nor removed by the crown, but by the Governor-General of Canada : they are local not imperial officers. The Lieutenant-Governor is head of the legislature, or rather the legislature is composed of a Lieutenant-Governor and a house of assembly, either with or without a legislative council. He is essential to the legislature, and is chief of the executive in the provinces. His assent to all bills in behalf of the Governor-General is necessary before they become law; and he has a negative voice, probably the same as the crown, in all legislative Acts.

In 1875 the secretary of state for the colonies wrote :

· " The Lieutenant-Governors of the provinces of the Dominion, however important locally their functions may be, are a part of the colonial administration staff, and are more immediately responsible to the Governor-General in council. They do not hold commissions from the crown ; and neither in power nor privilege resemble these governors of colonies, to whom, after special consideration of their fitness, the Queen under the great seal and her own hand and signet delegates portions of her prerogatives, and issue her own instructions."

Sir John A. Macdonald, in his report as to marriage licenses in 1869, speaking of Lieutenant-Governors, says :

" They do not hold their appointment directly from the Queen, but are appointed by the Governor General in council pursuant to the 58th section of the Act. Their powers are simply those conferred on them by statute, and they have no right to deal with matters of prerogative as representatives of the sovereign."

The effect of Earl Kimberley's reply to the Dominion government in the Queen's Counsel case, 1872, would indicate that the powers of a Lieutenant-Governor since 1867 are not so great as they were formerly. He says:

" The Governor-General has now power as her Majesty's representative to appoint Queen's counsel, but a Lieutenant-Governor appointed since the union came into effect (1867) has no such power of appointment." (e)

A Lieutenant-Governor holds office during the pleasure of the Governor-General; but the usual length of his term of office is five years. (f) He cannot be removed within that period without cause assigned. This cause is to be communicated to him in writing within one month after the order for his removal is made; and shall be communicated by message to the senate and to the house of commons within one week thereafter, if the parliament is then sitting; and if not, then within one week after the commencement of the next session of the Parliament. (g) The senate and commons must be the judges as to sufficiency of the cause alleged. It appears that it is sufficient for the ministry at Ottawa that parliament has passed a censure on his con-

(e) The English law officers of the crown were of opinion in this case that the legislature of a province can confer by statute on its Lieutenant-Governor the power of appointing Queen's counsel. In *Lenoir* v. *Ritchie*, in the Supreme Court, Mr. Justice Gwynne uses this language in reference to the position of a Lieutenant-Governor : " The head of their executive government is not an officer appointed by Her Majesty, or holding any commission from her, or in any manner personally representing her, but an officer of the Dominion government appointed by the Governor-General under the advice of a council, which the Act constitutes the privy council of the Dominion."

(f) Sec. 59.

(g) Sec. 59.

duct. Whenever it is felt by the Dominion government that it is for the public interest that a Lieutenant-Governor should be displaced, then he is and ought to be removable. He has no vested right to his office for the full term ; nor does he hold office for the full term ; nor does he hold office during good behavior, like our judges. (h)   He is answerable to the Governor in council, just the same as that officer is answerable to the imperial government; and the administration of the day must take the responsibility of his removal precisely the same as of any other administrative act.   The cause may be insufficient or unreasonable ; but when the cause is assigned for his removal, and the parliament expresses itself thereon, the constitutional powers of the Governor-General to dismiss the Lieutenant-Governor of a province cannot be questioned.

The legislatures are composed of one or two houses, as the different provinces may think desirable.   In Nova Scotia and New Brunswick they were to remain as before confederation ; while many particulars are mentioned in the Act in reference to the constitutions of Ontario and Quebec.   A single house in Ontario, with 82 members, is provided by the 69th and 70th sections of the Act.   Two houses were assigned to Quebec, with 65 members in the elective assembly and 24 legislative councillors, (i) the latter to have the same qualifications as the senators of the province of Quebec, and like them to hold office for life.   The legislative assembly is called together in the Queen's name by instrument under the great seal of the province.   The limit set for each assembly was four years, and a yearly session, as is required by the parliament of Canada, is necessary in the case of these provinces.   A special provision as to the first elections

(h) Sir John A. Macdonald's memorandum to the Governor-General in the *Letellier* case.

(i) Sec. 71 to 81.

(extending also to Nova Scotia) provided for the first summoning after the union, and the provincial capitals or seats of government are given in an early section. (*j*) These are Toronto for Ontario, Quebec for Quebec, Halifax for Nova Scotia, and Fredericton for New Brunswick.

The procedure in provincial legislation is almost as intricate and elaborate as in the parliament at Ottawa. In those provinces which have no legislative council, the bills have of course to pass through the usual stages in one house only. The provisions relating to the election of a speaker originally, and on vacancies, to the duties of the speaker, the absence of the speaker, the quorum, and the manner of voting, are the same in the Ontario and Quebec legislatures as in the Canadian house of commons.

The provisions in the Act relating to appropriations and tax bills, the recommendation of money votes, the assent, allowance and reservation of bills, apply to all the provinces substituting the Lieutenant-Governor for Governor-General, and the Governor-General for the Queen. The Lieutenant-Governors, on a bill being presented to them, shall, according to their discretion, but subject to the provisions of the Act, declare that they assent thereto in the Governor-General's name, or that they withhold the Governor-General's assent, or that they reserve the bill for the signification of the Governor-General's pleasure. (*k*)

A bill reserved by the Lieutenant-Governor for the signification of the pleasure of the Governor-General in council shall not have any force unless and until, within one year from the day on which it was presented to the Lieutenant-Governor for the assent of the Governor-General, the Lieutenant-Governor signifies by speech or message to the house or houses of his legislature, or by proclamation, that it has received the assent of the Governor-General in council. Bills assented to by the Lieutenant-Governor may be annulled by the Governor-General in council within one year after an authentic copy of the Act has been sent to him.

The Governor in council in the Dominion parliament is said on very high authority to have the same controlling power over the provincial legislatures that the imperial parliament has over the Dominion. The extent of provincial subordination, however, is not to be misunderstood. Both the provinces and the Dominion have their own defined, ascertained limits ; and so long as they keep within these they can constitutionally enact what laws they please without reference to each other. The power of disallowing provincial Acts rests with the central and not with the imperial government, as in the case of disallowing Dominion Acts ; but this will always be considered a harsh exercise of power unless in cases of great and manifest necessity, or where the Act is so clearly beyond the powers of the local legislatures that the propriety of interfering would at once be recognized. (l) It will always be very difficult for the federal government to substitute its opinions instead of that of the legislative assemblies in regard to matters within their provinces without exposing itself to be reproached with threatening the independence of the provinces. (m)

Mr. Lash, Q.C., late deputy of the minister of justice, prepared a memorandum on the subject of disallowance in which, after shewing the very small number of cases in which it was exercised and how reluctantly it was done, he stated that it was the practice, before taking such an extreme course with respect to any Act, to call the attention of the provincial government to its objectionable features,

(l) Per C. J. Richards, in *Severn* v. *the Queen* 2 S. C. Reports 96.
(m) *Severn* v. *the Queen*, 2 S. C. Reports 70.

and give them an opportunity of promoting its repeal or
amendment. Occasionally however, from the very nature
of the Act itself or from the shortness of time for disallowance, it has been thought necessary to disallow it without
waiting for its repeal . . . If any Act be in its main
features, clearly beyond the powers of the provincial legislature, it would seem to be the duty of the Dominion
authorities to disallow it, unless within a limited time, it
be repealed or so amended as to remove these objectionable
features.

It is often very doubtful whether an Act be within or
beyond the powers of a provincial legislature ; and very
often Acts, which in their main provisions, are clearly valid,
contain some provision beyond the competence of the legislature.   Moreover in the character of the enactments
which may be beyond the powers of the local body, there is
often a vast difference.   Though all such provisions are
alike void, some of them may without inconvenience be
passed over without interference by the Dominion government, while to take the same course as to others might
produce serious embarrassment and confusion.   It is therefore in each particular case a question to be decided,
whether an Act though containing some void provisions,
should be disallowed or left to its operation.

In deciding as to the disallowance of an Act, the government is not confined to considering its validity in a legal
point of view.   The power of disallowance is a general one;
and in arriving at a conclusion as to its exercise, the government has undoubtedly the right to take into consideration other matters than those affecting merely the validity
of the Act.   For instance, they may and should consider
whether it affects imperial or Dominion interests.   The
same principles (among others) would apply in deciding as
to giving or withholding assent to a reserved bill.   . .

CHAPTER XIV.

THE PROVINCES—ONTARIO.

Legislature, how composed, one house, members' qualifications —Speaker, quorum, procedure—Executive council, departments—Attorney-General—Provincial secretary—Provincial treasurer, agriculture—Commissioner of crown lands—Commissioner of public works—Minister of education.

THE Lieutenant-Governor and the legislative assembly of Ontario form the legislature of this province.

The Lieutenant-Governor is appointed by the Governor-General in council, and holds office for five years, unless sooner removed for cause assigned. He is the chief officer of the executive in the provinces and the head of the legislature. The provincial legislature has no power over him or his office, although he acts only upon its advice. He is a corporation sole, and may appoint a deputy for certain purposes, such as executing marriage licenses, money warrants, and commissions under any provincial statute. As advised by the executive council of the province, he nominates such proper persons, in number not exceeding six, to the departmental offices. In his absence, illness, or other inability, the Governor-General may appoint an administrator to execute his office and functions. Acting on the advice of the executive, he summons and calls together the legislature in the Queen's name, and may dissolve the same within the four years of its duration.

The assembly is now composed of ninety members; and for the purposes of representation the province is divided up into eighty-eight electoral districts or ridings, Toronto returning three members from one district. These do not correspond to the electoral districts in Ontario which send members of parliament to the house of commons at Ottawa; and, again, neither of these divisions corresponds with the division of the province into counties for municipal or judicial purposes. Every county is a county for municipal purposes (to be noticed hereafter), and sends at least one member to the local and federal house, while sometimes two or more counties are united for judicial purposes.

Members of the local legislature require no real property qualification, and are elected for four years. No senator, privy councillor of the Dominion who is a member of the commons, nor any member of the commons, can hold a seat in this house; no person accepting or holding any office, commission or employment under the crown by provincial or dominion appointment, and to which office any salary or fee, allowance, or emolument in lieu of salary, is attached, can be a member—except those members of the executive office who are the members of the government of the province; and with these exceptions, no person accepting or holding such office, commission or employment of profit whether under provincial or dominion appointment, or under any head of a department in the provincial government, is eligible, no matter whether such profit be payable or not out of the public funds.

But any army, navy or militia officers (except militia staff officers receiving permanent salaries), and any justice of the peace, and any notary public, may, unless otherwise disqualified, be members of the legislative assembly. No public contractor is eligible to sit or vote in the house; and any disqualified person who does so shall forfeit the sum of $2,000 per day for so doing.

The house meets every year at Toronto, and is presided over by a speaker appointed by the members. Not more than twelve months must intervene between the last sitting in one session and the first sitting in the next session. (86th sec. B. N. A. Act.)

Twenty members in the house are the smallest number capable of transacting business or forming a quorum. The speaker may be one of the number. The conduct of business, the rules of debate, the regulation and management of the house, questions of proceedings, etc. are regulated by the house ; and in all unprovided cases the rules, usages and forms of the house of commons in England are followed. The provisions relating to the election of speaker, the absence of the speaker, quorum, and mode of voting, are the same in the provincial legislature of Ontario as in the house of commons for Canada. (87th sec.)

The house is not organized till the speaker is chosen ; and there is no vacancy in the office till such choice has been made and the office has been filled. In the first meeting of the assembly after a general election the speaker is elected. Before the election of speaker the clerk of the house is substituted for the speaker, but the clerk has no casting vote in case of an equality of votes for speaker. No one can vote in the election of speaker but a member of the assembly. In case the house were equally divided in the election of a speaker, no one would be appointed. (a)

The procedure as to bills, orders, etc., is as nearly similar to that in the house of commons as can be. A bill here has to pass through the same stages, though only through one assembly, there being no upper house or legislative council in this province. The Lieutenant-Governor then may assent to a bill, or dissent from it, or reserve it for the con-

(a) Opinion of the late Hon. J. H. Cameron.

sideration of the Governor-General, as has been already explained. He recommends all money votes, opens, prorogues, and dissolves the house, issues orders in council, proclamations, etc. (90th sec.)

The executive council of Ontario is composed of six members, who are appointed under the great seal of the province, and hold office during pleasure. The ministers have charge of the following offices, some one member always taking two departments. (b)

1. Attorney-General for the province.
2. A secretary and registrar of the province.
3. A treasurer of the province.
4. A commissioner of crown lands.
5. A commissioner of agriculture.
6. A commissioner of public works.
7. A minister of education.

Any of the powers and duties assigned by law to any of the officers constituting the executive council may, by order of the Lieutenant-Governor in council, be transferred to any of the other officers, by name or otherwise. No member of this council can sit or vote as a member of the commons of Canada without forfeiting his office as councillor.

The executive councillors are the administration or ministry of the province—the provincial privy council so to speak—and they form the government of the day. They must have the support of a majority in the legislative assembly. They hold office during pleasure of both the Lieutenant-Governor and the assembly; but the choice of the assembly is the choice of the Lieutenant-Governor.

(b) By Sec. 134 of the B. N. A. Act the number was placed at five with power to add others. By the following section all the " rights, powers, functions, responsibilities, or authorities " as vested in such offices before confederation, passed to the provincial executive councillors so far as these duties, etc., were not repugnant to the Act.

He has the undoubted right to dissolve the house and to dismiss ministers having a majority of the members at their back ; but he does that always at great risk to himself, and probably with serious results to his province. The procedure and line of conduct of the local legislatures has been copied so diligently from the parliaments of Canada and Great Britain, that in case a Lieutenant-Governor follows the analogous power of the crown in these places, he will content himself to follow the advice of his responsible ministers rather than attempt to find ministers supporting his own opinions. He has in fact no opinions. The ministers are the choice of the provincial members and answerable to the people—he is neither answerable to the province nor its choice. If it be a question who is to rule on any occasion, the people affected have no right to complain if the determination of it is left in the hands of their own representatives.

Assuming, therefore, that the provincial government is carried on by its executive under the advice of an executive council, the principles in regard to a change of government, the responsibility of the ministry, its relations to the executive and to the assembly, and all other matters peculiar to a privy or executive council apply equally in the provincial as well as in the dominion government. Laws are enacted and enforced. Except as otherwise provided by the Act, all laws in force in the late province of Canada, all courts of civil and criminal jurisdiction, and all legal commissions, powers and authorities, and all officers, judicial, administrative and ministerial, continue in Ontario, as well as in the other provinces, as if the union had not been made, subject to imperial legislation, to be repealed, abolished or altered by the parliament of Canada, or the legislature of the province, according as either one possesses the power. (c)

(c) Sec. 129.

DEPARTMENTAL ADMINISTRATION AT TORONTO.

The following are the departments in Ontario and a summary of the work done in them.

ATTORNEY-GENERAL'S DEPARTMENT.

There are no statutory regulations as to the duties of the attorney-general of Ontario, or the work performed in his office or department.

He is the legal adviser of the crown, and of the executive council or ministry, and also of the departments of the executive government of the province ; and all legislation for the province is conducted in his name and under his responsibility. He makes all appointments connected with the administration of justice, such as police and stipendiary magistrates, justices of the peace, county attorneys, sheriffs, and other officers of the courts, and he advises them in all matters of such administration. Hence he has to deal with cases of bail and its forfeiture, the discharge of prisoners on a *habeas corpus*, or the quashing of convictions. He considers applications for writs of error, for leave to file petitions of right, to file informations, to allow criminals as Queen's evidence, and other matters in connection with the administration of public justice. He is the proper person to complain of the violation of public rights.

He appears on behalf of the crown in civil and criminal cases ; and he is the proper officer to enforce criminal laws by prosecution in the Queen's name in courts of justice in the province. The attorney-general of this province is the officer of the crown who must be considered to be present in the courts of the province to assert the rights of the crown and those who are under its protection. (d)

(d) Mr. Justice Strong (as Vice-Chancellor) in *Attorney-General* v. *Niagara Falls Bridge Company*, 20 Chy. 34.

His duties are somewhat analogous to those of the minister of justice at Ottawa; and he has all the rights, powers, duties, functions, responsibilities and authorities which, up to 1867, were vested in or imposed on the attorney-general or solicitor-general of the province of Canada by virtue of any law, statute, or ordnance of Upper Canada or Canada, and not repugnant to the Confederation Act of that year. This also applies to the other executive officers in regard to their respective departments as mentioned hereafter, both in Ontario and Quebec.

2. THE SECRETARY AND REGISTRAR OF THE PROVINCE OF ONTARIO.

This office is under the control of the provincial secretary, but no express statute has constituted it a department. (*e*)

Reports on the asylums, prisons and public charities of the province are returned to this department every year; reports on the common gaols, prisons and reformatories; the Ontario institution for the education and instruction of the deaf and dumb, at Belleville, and a similar institution at Brantford for the blind; the hospitals of Ontario; houses of refuge, orphan and magdalene asylums; also reports relating to tavern and shop licenses.

The inspector of division courts reports to this department, and it is the provincial department of immigration.

The bonds and securities required to be given by public officers are registered in the registrar's department, and returns made also in regard to them. The other matters upon which returns are made are the following:

(*e*) Secs. 134 and 135 continue the office which succeeds to that of the secretary and registrar of the province of Canada.

The state of the fee fund, the expenses of the administration of justice, the number of marriages, births and deaths, copies of all returns from the clerks of the various municipalities as to the population, real property, assessments, income and expenditure, liabilities, assets and property of their respective corporations. A statement of the indebtedness of each municipal corporation at the close of each year is made to the Lieutenant-Governor through the provincial secretary; and a return also made to him from the sworn returns of the clerks of each municipality of the number of resident ratepayers of the different counties and cities, and such towns as are separated from counties.

Commissions under the great and privy seals are prepared and issued by this department; warrants for the removal to the asylums from the county gaols of persons found insane and dangerous; appointments to office gazetted; proclamations, letters patent, notarial certificates, commissions and marriage licenses issued; and returns of patented lands made to the different county registrars of the province.

3. THE PROVINCIAL TREASURER'S DEPARTMENT. (*f*)

All public moneys, from whatever source of revenue derived, and all moneys forming part of special funds administered by the provincial government, are paid in to the credit of the provincial treasurer. These revenues form what is called the consolidated revenue fund of Ontario; and it is on the strength of the supplies of this fund that the Lieutenant-Governor in council can invest in Dominion securities or debentures whenever any surplus is not required for the public use of the province.

(*f*) This office is continued by the 134 and 135 sections of the Act succeeding apparently to the minister of finance of the former government of Canada.

The treasurer of the province lays every year before the house a financial statement as to the assets and liabilities of the province. He reports to the Lieutenant-Governor from the sworn returns of the clerk of each municipality (except county clerks) as to the number of resident rate-payers and their indebtedness to the municipal loan fund. He also reports as to the taxable property and the resources and liabilities of each municipal corporation.

The executive government has charge of all fees and charges under the Act relating to law stamps ; and the provincial treasurer procures the necessary stamps under the Act, keeps an account of all stamps, sells the same, and allows or may allow a commission of five per cent. to those taking more than five dollars' worth.

The treasurer has also certain statutory duties in reference to the land tax in Algoma.

The moneys arising from the clergy reserves form a separate fund called " The Ontario Municipalities' Fund ; " and are paid into the provincial treasurer's office, and paid out by him under orders in council, or under the Act respecting clergy reserves, to the different municipalities in Ontario, in proportion to their resident rate-payers, pursuant to the returns already referred to.

The provincial board of health is a branch of this department, as is also the department of agriculture and arts.

5. THE DEPARTMENT OF AGRICULTURE. (*g*)

This department may be in charge of a commissioner of agriculture, but the office is for the present combined with the provincial treasurer's department.

(*g*) This office was joined in the 134th section to that of the commissioner of public works. See also section 135.

The bureau of agriculture and arts, now called the bureau of industries, is attached to this department; and the Lieutenant-Governor in council appoints a secretary, known as the secretary of the bureau of agriculture and arts, who conducts the correspondence of the department and such other business as may be assigned him by the commissioner.

The commissioner institutes enquiries and collects useful facts and statistics relating to the agricultural, mechanical and manufacturing interests of the province, and adopts measures for disseminating or publishing the same in such manner and form as he finds best adapted to promote improvement within the province, and to encourage immigration from other countries. He may appoint persons to inspect the books and accounts of any society receiving government aid, and may examine witnesses and have documents produced in reference thereto.

The societies in connection with the department are : the agricultural and arts association, all agricultural and horticultural societies, the fruit growers' association of Ontario, the entomological society of Ontario, the poultry association, the Ontario creameries' association, the bee-keepers' association, and the dairymen's associations of Ontario. These make returns to this department and supply information on questions submitted to them.

The agricultural college and model farm at Guelph, and a library and museum in connection with it, are under the control of the commissioner ; and a veterinary college is established under prescribed rules of the council of the agricultural and arts association, which also holds an annual provincial fair or exhibition.

The commissioner reports to the house of assembly, within 30 days after the opening of the session, giving a detailed account of the proceedings in his department.

4. THE DEPARTMENT OF CROWN LANDS. (*h*)

The commissioner of crown lands presides over this department, and has the management and sale of the public lands and forests belonging to the province.

An assistant commissioner, appointed by the Lieutenant-Governor in council, has charge of the department in the absence of the commissioner, or when a vacancy occurs in that office; and he performs such duties in the department as may be assigned to him by the Lieutenant-Governor in council, or the commissioner of crown lands. Other officers may also be appointed in the same manner as the assistant commissioner.

The department and office of the surveyor-general are now transferred to this department; and the commissioner exercises and performs such powers and duties as were assigned to or vested in that officer before the 17th March, 1845.

The commissioner of crown lands reports to the legislative assembly, within ten days after the meeting of the house, the proceedings, transactions and affairs of his office, during the preceding year—sales of lands, revenues of woods and forests, reports of surveys, colonization roads, free grants, etc.

The public lands of the province are under the control of this department. These are the crown lands, school lands, clergy lands, and mineral lands. The Lieutenant-Governor in council fixes the price, the terms and conditions of sale, and of settlement and payment, of the public lands; and the sales and appropriations of water lots, licenses of occupation, and all assignments and the issue and cancellation of patents, are issued, registered and

(*h*) This is a department by provincial statute, but is recognized and continued by the B. N. A. Act, secs. 134, 135.

effected by the commissioner, with other departmental business. He, or his assistant, may issue commissions, and may authorize those in the employ of the department to take affidavits in reference to the business of the department, or regarding which it is interested. He causes lists of patented lands to be forwarded to the different treasurers in the province in the month of February in each year; and also a list of lands leased or licensed, or located as free grant. He advertises, if he thinks fit, lists of public lands for sale, and furnishes such other information as may be desirable.

If a patent has issued to the wrong person through mistake in the department or has a wrong description of the land or contains any clerical error or misnomer, the commissioner, if there is no adverse claim, may direct the defective patent to be cancelled and a correct one of the same date to be issued. If a patent has issued through fraud or in error or improvidence the complaining party may institute a suit in the high court of justice and have the patent declared void. The commissioner may also cancel any sale, grant, location, lease or license if there has been fraud or imposition or violation of any of the conditions of sale, etc. by the purchaser or his assignee.

As to the free grant lands, the Lieutenant-Governor in council almost exclusively deals with these. The Act relating to free grants and homesteads does not interfere with the power of the commissioner to grant timber licenses on these lands. The free grant territory lies within the districts of Algoma and Nipissing, and certain lands lying between the Ottawa river and the Georgian Bay. (See Act of 1886 as to the Rainy river district.)

The department looks after all trespasses on public lands, and has very full statutory instructions in regard thereto. It deals with the mining lands of the province, subject to such orders in council as may be made in reference to them and under the provisions of the General Mining Act.

This department has charge of crown, municipal and mineral surveys, and contracts and repairs on colonization roads.

By an Act called the Ontario Fisheries Act 1885, the commissioner of crown lands may grant and issue fishery leases and fishing licenses under certain conditions, regulations and restrictions, but not over any lands or waters where an exclusive right of fishing already exists by law. The leases are for not more than five years and only granted to the highest bidder after public competition. The Act applies to such of the waters of any lake, river, stream or water-course wholly or partly within said province, as flow over or cover any of its crown or public lands or crown domain. (i)

A recent order in council dated 5th May, 1887, has issued under this Act.

When a claim is made by any person as heir, devisee, or assignee of the nominee of the crown, to the right to a patent, special commissioners are appointed to decide thereon. These form what is called the heir and devisee commission, which is one of the courts of law in Ontario. But now under an order in council matters of this sort are reported on by the law-clerk of the department to the commissioner who decides them without reference to the commissioners.

6. THE DEPARTMENT OF PUBLIC WORKS. (j)

This department is presided over by the commissioner of public works, appointed by commission under the great seal.

(i) See the *Queen* v. *Robertson*, 6 Supreme Court Appeals, page 52.

(j) This office is also created a department by provincial statute. See *ante*, agriculture.

The other officers, who are appointed by the Lieutenant-Governor, are an architect, an engineer, a secretary, a law-clerk, an accountant, and such others, whether their appointment be temporary or otherwise, as may be necessary. The duties of the architect, engineer, secretary, law-clerk, and accountant are laid down by statute.

The commissioner has management of the department: and it is his duty to oversee and direct the other officers and servants; and he may have other duties also assigned him by the Lieutenant-Governor in council.

The department has control of all land, streams, water-courses, and property, real and personal, heretofore or hereafter acquired for the use of public works; all canals, locks, dams, hydraulic works, harbour piers, and other works for improving the navigation of any water; all slides, dams, piers, booms, and other works for facilitating the transmission of timber; all hydraulic powers created by the construction of any public works; all roads and bridges; all public buildings; all railways and rolling stock thereon; all vessels, dredges, scows, tools, implements and machinery for the improvement of navigation; all drains and drainage works; and all property heretofore or hereafter acquired, constructed, repaired, maintained, or improved, at the expense of the province, and not under the control of the Dominion government. These are declared to be vested in Her Majesty, and under the control of this department.

Any other property, and any of these works, roads, etc., purchased or constructed at the public expense, may, by proclamation of the Lieutenant-Governor, be vested in Her Majesty, and subject to this department.

Any property not required for the use of the public works may be leased or sold, under the authority of the Lieutenant-Governor; and for the purposes of the department the commissioner may acquire and take possession of any land or real estate, streams, waters, water-courses, fences and walls, for specified purposes and under certain restrictions.

The commissioner has also the necessary powers as to drainage of land, and the construction of slides in mill-dams or embankments; and he acts under the "Ontario Drainage Act" in reference to drains within municipalities, on the request of their councils, as provided by that Act. In case any township desire to undertake such work, after the plans and estimates are submitted to the department, he can report thereon as to the investment of a portion of the public money in debentures for the construction of such drainage for the benefit of such township.

All expenses connected with the provisions for preventing riots near public works are paid through the commissioner under the statute respecting riots near public works. The sale of liquors near public works is prohibited by stringent provisions.

The commissioner of public works must within twenty-one days after the commencement of each session, make and submit to the Lieutenant-Governor an annual report on all the works under his control, shewing the state of each work, and the receipts and expenditure thereon, with such further information as may enable the assembly to judge of the working of the department.

His report includes the expenses and repairs of the government house, parliament buildings, asylums, reformatories, prisons, institutes for the blind, deaf and dumb, the agricultural college, the educational department, schools under the government control, and Osgoode Hall; also the inspection, repair and construction of lock-ups, goals, court rooms and registry offices in the districts of

Algoma, Muskoka, Nipissing and other unorganized districts.

The engineer of the department reports on the slides, dams, crib works, piers, bridges, dredging, locks and other such matters as come within this department.

The department is charged with the duty of seeing that the conditions on which aid has been granted to railways out of the provincial treasury are complied with before the funds are paid over and has a similar duty in respect to drainage works.

Where it is necessary for a provincial railway in Ontario to cross a dominion railway the company desiring to effect such crossing must procure the approval of the commissioner of public works as well as the approval of the railway committee of the privy council of Canada, and the railway companies cannot waive the provision by agreement. (k)

7. DEPARTMENT OF EDUCATION. (l)

This department consists of the executive council of the province, or a committee out of that number. One of the executive council is nominated to the office of minister of education by the Lieutenant-Governor.

The minister of education may hold any other office in the executive council, and he may be a member of the legislative assembly and sit and vote therein.

This department supersedes the council of public instruction, which was suspended on the 10th of February, 1876; and all the duties of that council are transferred to this department, with a minister instead of the chief superintendent of education at its head.

(k) *Credit Valley Ry.* v. *the G. W. Ry.*, 25 Gr. 507.

(l) This department is created by statute of the province. It is not amongst the offices mentioned in B. N. A. Act, sec. 134, 135.

It superintends the studies and regulations of high schools, the organization, government and discipline of public schools and the classification of schools and teachers. It provides for the efficiency of the normal and public schools, examines and grants certificates to teachers, defines the qualifications of inspectors and examiners, and has the approval of all text, prize and library books. The statutory duties of the minister include the distribution of the legislative grants among the different public and high schools, and the general superintendence of normal schools and the conduct of teachers. The Acts relating to public and high schools give him extensive powers in the management of this department.

Schools coming within the range of the Separate Schools Act are subject to inspection by the minister of education, and also to such regulations as may be imposed on them from time to time by the education department.

The minister may also certify regarding any proposed industrial school in cities, that it is a fit and proper one for the reception of children and the school shall thereupon be deemed a certified industrial school.

The police magistrate may send there such children as apparently are under 14 years of age if they are found begging, or receiving alms, or are found wandering without any visible means of support, and having no home, or guardian, or any lawful business, or being destitute, either as an orphan, or one whose parent is imprisoned, or whose parents are so vicious that they are under no proper control or education ; or if such children are so unmanageable that the parents or guardians cannot control them. The rules of such school are to be approved of by the minister.

The minister of education has power to decide upon all disputes and complaints laid before him, the settlement of which is not otherwise provided for by law, and upon all appeals made to him from the decision of any inspector or other school officer.

In cases in the division court, in which school inspectors, trustees, teachers or other persons under these Acts are parties, an appeal is allowed to the superior courts of law in Ontario. This exceptional proceeding is for the purpose of securing uniformity of decision in school matters. The minister has power also to submit a case to any judge of these courts for the opinion or decision of the court therein.

The minister of education is, *ex officio*, a member of the senate of the University of Toronto, which senate has the management of and superintendency over the affairs and business of the university. The Lieutenant-Governor appoints the president and all other officers, and approves of the statutes of the senate.

The Ontario society of artists, and the mechanics institutes are by an Act of 1886 transferred to the educational department.

The minister of education reports every year to the Lieutenant-Governor in council, up to the 31st of December, the actual state of the normal, model, high and public schools, and collegiate institutes, showing the expenditure and sources of revenue, with such statements and suggestions, in reference to the improvement of the schools and the school law, and promoting education, as he may deem useful and expedient.

CHAPTER XV.

THE PROVINCE OF QUEBEC AND OTHER PROVINCES—THE TERRITORIES.

Quebec, two houses, members, otherwise similar to Ontario, Judges—Adjustment between the old Canadas—Nova Scotia and New Brunswick unchanged—Manitoba created —British Columbia—Prince Edward Island—The North West Territories—Keewatin.

QUEBEC.

THE legislature of Quebec consists of a Lieutenant-Governor and two houses styled the legislative council of Quebec and the legislative assembly of Quebec. (a)

The legislative council is composed of 24 members, who were appointed by the first Lieutenant-Governor of the province in the Queen's name by instrument under the great seal of Quebec. These hold office during life, unless the legislature otherwise provides, subject to the Act of 1867. Their qualifications are the same as those of the Quebec senators, which differ from those of other senators in one respect—that is in this way : Quebec was divided into 24 electoral divisions before confederation ; and each of these sent a senator to Ottawa, and a legislative councillor to Quebec, both senators and councillors residing or having their real property qualification in the division they represented. The regulations as to vacancies in the place

(a) The constitution of the province of Quebec differs from that of Ontario only in the addition of a second house in the former province and in the different numbers of members in the assemblies.

of a legislative councillor are the same as apply to senators ; and vacant seats are filled by the Lieutenant-Governor in the same way as the first councillors were appointed. Questions as to qualifications and vacancies in the legislative council are heard and determined by that body. The Lieutenant-Governor appoints their speaker, and may remove him and appoint another. Ten members, including the speaker, are a sufficient number to constitute a meeting for the exercise of its powers. The speaker has a vote ; and when the votes are equal, the motion is declared in the negative. (b)

Every legislative councillor, before taking his seat, must take and subscribe before the Governor-General, or some one authorized by him, the oath of allegiance, and the declaration of qualification, prescribed for senators as well, and which has already been referred to under the chapter on the senate. (c)

The legislative assembly of Quebec is composed of 65 members, until altered by the legislature of the province ; and even then the second and third readings of a bill for altering the limits of certain electoral divisions cannot be presented to the Lieutenant-Governor for his assent unless with the concurrence of the majority of the members representing all these divisions, and an address presented by the assembly stating that the bill has been so passed. Those electoral districts of Quebec, specially fixed, are the counties of Pontiac, Ottawa, Argenteuil, Huntington, Missisquoi, Beauce, Shefford, Stanstead, Compton, Wolfe and Richmond, Megantic, and the town of Sherbrooke. (d)

The seat of government is at Quebec ; and the executive council is composed of the same number of ministers

(b) Secs. 72 and 80.
(c) Sec. 128.
(d) Sec. 80.

as in Ontario, except that in Quebec the speaker of the legislative council and the solicitor-general are included in the executive. In Ontario there are no offices for such persons. (*e*)

All the other provisions in the Act of 1867 relating to the constitution and legislative powers of Quebec are the same as have been set out in regard to Ontario.

The judges of the Quebec courts must be selected from the bar of that province; but when the laws relating to property and civil rights in Ontario, Nova Scotia and New Brunswick, are made uniform, the Governor-General may appoint judges for these provinces from any one of them. (*f*)

The powers, authorities and functions of the Lieutenant-Governors are the same in both provinces, except possibly in so far as the legislatures of Upper and Lower Canada, prior to 1840, may have vested their respective Governors or Lieutenant-Governors with different powers, authorities and functions. The legislature of Lower Canada was suspended at one time by Imperial Act, a circumstance which did not happen to Upper Canada; but it is unlikely that this caused any very material difference in the statutory powers of their Governors.

The Lieutenant-Governor of Quebec may, by proclamation, constitute townships in those parts of his province not already constituted, and fix the metes and bounds thereof. (*g*)

The executive government, as was seen, is carried on by the same number of members as in Ontario, except that

(*e*) Sec. 134.
(*f*) Secs. 97 and 98. Sec. 94 provides for the contingency of uniform laws, but it does not extend to Quebec.
(*g*) Sec. 144.

they have no minister of education; but they have additional officers in the persons of the solicitor-general and speaker of the legislative council. The office of agriculture and public works is under one minister, and there has been a commissioner of railways, but the office is now abolished. (h)

The officers in charge of the departments in Quebec succeed to all powers, duties, functions, etc., of those officers in the government of the late province of Canada, or of Lower Canada, in the same way as the departmental officers in Ontario do. The departmental offices in the two provinces agree in their main points, and are different chiefly in matters of detail; and it is not necessary to enter into a separate consideration of them as regards the province of Quebec.

The division and adjustment of the debts, credits, liabilities, properties and assets of Upper and Lower Canada was referred at confederation to three arbitrators, one chosen by each government of the provinces and one by the government of Canada; and the Governor-General in council may order a division of the records, books and documents of the late province of Canada between the present provinces of Ontario and Quebec. (i)

NOVA SCOTIA AND NEW BRUNSWICK.

The Act of 1867 uniting the provinces did not alter the legislatures of either Nova Scotia or New Brunswick. Subject to the provisions of this Act, they continued as they were before that date, and remain so until altered under the authority of the Act. (j) The same applies to the

(h) Quebec Statutes, 1886, cap. IV.
(i) Secs. 112-113.
(j) Sec. 88.

executive power of these provinces, which was also unchanged. (*k*)   They were restricted to legislating only on
the prescribed class of subjects assigned to the provinces
by such machinery as they always possessed.   The mode
of appointing the governors was changed—it thereafter
rested with the Governor-General of Canada.   Nothing is
said as to the powers, authorities and functions of any
Lieutenant-Governors, except those of Ontario and Quebec.
All of them recommend to their respective houses by message, appropriations, tax bills and all money votes.
They can assent to bills, disallow them, or reserve them
for the signification of the Governor-General's pleasure.

These provinces have the exceptional privilege of appointing judges to their own courts of probate. (*l*)

Nova Scotia and New Brunswick, like Quebec, have two
houses—a legislative council and a legislative assembly.
The house of assembly in Nova Scotia is composed of 38
members, and in New Brunswick of 41 members—the
legislative councils of 16 and 18 respectively. (*m*)

(*k*) Sec. 64.

(*l*) Sec. 96.

(*m*) In 1879, a measure to do away with the upper house in Nova
Scotia passed the assembly, but was rejected in the legislative council.
The assembly then presented an address to the Queen, asking that the
B. N. A. Act be amended so that new councillors might be added to carry
the measure in the other house.   The legislative councillors presented a
counter address, and the executive council a memorandum showing its
approval of the action of the assembly.   The colonial secretary replied
(25th June, 1879), declining to advise any action in the matter.   Considerable correspondence is to be found in the years 1880-81 on this
question.   The secretary of state of Canada advised the local government
that a full opportunity had not arrived in order to restore harmony
between the houses, and that the Governor-General would be glad to
submit any additional papers to the colonial secretary.   Accordingly,
Nova Scotia secured the co-operation of the other maritime provinces in
the hope of freeing themselves from their legislative councils.   The
matter was strongly urged before the Dominion government, but nothing
came of it.   In 1882, a bill in the assembly in Nova Scotia to abolish the
council was, on its second reading, defeated by 12 to 9.

The executive council in Nova Scotia is at present composed of seven members, of which only three have portfolios—that is the provincial secretary, the attorney-general and the commissioner of public works and mines.

In New Brunswick the number of the executive council is seven also; but here they have an attorney-general, a provincial secretary and receiver-general, a chief commissioner of the public works, and a solicitor-general.

MANITOBA.

By an Imperial Act passed in 1871, the parliament of Canada may from time to time establish new provinces in any territories forming for the time being part of the Dominion of Canada, but not included in any province thereof, and may at the time of such establishment make provision for the constitution and administration of any such province and for the passing of laws for the peace, order and good government of such province and for its representation in the said parliament. (n)   This Act was passed to confirm the Dominion Act, establishing the province of Manitoba.

This province and the territories hereafter mentioned were part of Rupert's Land and the North-West Territory before they were admitted into the union in 1870.   This was affected by proclamation pursuant to order in council at Ottawa.   The boundary of Manitoba was defined then, but has been altered since, in 1877, by the parliament of Canada, with the consent of the legislature of Manitoba. (o) All the provisions of the British North America Act which apply to the whole of the provinces are applicable to Mani-

(n) 34 and 35 Vic. cap. 28; see sec. 146 B. N. A. Act.

(o) The present boundaries are set out in R. S. C. chap. 47.   The eastern boundary is a line due north from the point where the western boundary of Ontario intersects the international boundary with the U. S.

toba as if it had been one of the provinces originally united by that Act. The Act admitting this province defines the qualification of voters—the duration of the assembly to be four years with a yearly session, as in Ontario, and the seat of government to be at Fort Garry, or within a mile of that place. Fort Garry is now the city of Winnipeg.

The constitution originally given to Manitoba provided for a Lieutenant-Governor and two houses, as in Quebec ; but in 1876 the legislative council was abolished by the local legislature.

The legislative assembly, which, with the Lieutenant-Governor, now forms the legislature, is composed of thirty-five members, representing the districts into which the province is divided. (p)

The executive council is composed of such persons and under such designations as shall seem fit to the Lieutenant-Governor. It at present consists of five persons—a provincial treasurer, a provincial secretary, minister of public works, the attorney-general and a minister of agriculture, statistics and health.

The provisions regarding the speaker originally, and in vacancies, the duties of speaker, the absence of speaker, and the mode of voting, are the same as in the house of commons at Ottawa. Canada assumes and defrays a large portion of the expenses of the province. Almost every year since its admission a number of Acts have been passed in the parliament of Canada applying to Manitoba ; but except as to the limits of that province (and only then by consent of the Manitoba legislature,) the parliament of Canada has no power to alter the provisions of the Act originally establishing that province. (q)

(p) Statutes of 1886, Man.

(q) The B. N. A. Act, 1871, secs. 3 and 6. The provisions as to the alteration of limits (sec. 3.) apply to all the provinces.

BRITISH COLUMBIA.

This province was admitted into the union on the 20th of July, 1871, by royal proclamation of the Queen in council.

. The constitution of its legislature is the same as that of Ontario, it being composed of a Lieutenant-Governor and one house of assembly. The executive council is at present composed of an attorney-general, a chief commissioner of lands and works, a provincial secretary, minister of mines and a minister of finance and agriculture. The legislative assembly is composed of twenty-five members.

PRINCE EDWARD ISLAND.

This province was admitted into the union on 1st of July, 1873.

The legislature is composed of a Lieutenant-Governor, a 'legislative council of 13 members, and a legislative assembly of 33 members—both houses being elected by the people.

The executive council is composed of the attorney-general the provincial secretary, treasurer and commissioner of public lands, and a commissioner of public works, with some other members without office.

The terms upon which this colony was admitted are laid down at considerable length in the order in council in that behalf. Canada became liable for the debts of the province, and the province was entitled to incur a liability of four millions of dollars in view of her isolated and exceptional condition, and as something towards the share other provinces received from Canada in reference to railways and canals. There being no revenue from crown lands in the

province the Dominion government agreed to supply her
with about $40,000 per annum in order to purchase lands
from large landed proprietors. Canada also pays a large
yearly sum towards defraying the expenses of the local
government and legislature, besides such charges as are
incident or appertaining to the general government and
allowed to the other provinces.

The constitution of the legislative and of the executive
government remained unchanged ; but all the provisions
of the Act of 1867, except those parts which in terms or by
reasonable intendment apply to only one province, or to a
part of the dominion, take effect in Prince Edward Island.

THE NORTH-WEST TERRITORIES AND THE DISTRICT OF KEEWATIN.

The territories formerly known as Rupert's Land and
the North-West Territory are, with the exception of such
portions as form the province of Manitoba and the district
of Keewatin, now called the North-West Territories.

There is a Lieutenant-Governor for the Territories appointed under the great seal of Canada and holding office
during pleasure. He administers the government under
instructions given him from time to time by the Governor in
Council or by the secretary of state of Canada. He is aided
in the administration of the territories by a council of six
persons appointed by the Governor in Council. The seat of
government is at present Regina but it may be changed
from time to time by the Governor in Council.

When the population attained certain proportions, electoral districts were formed and elections took place for a
council. This elective chamber at present has 13 members
and when it reaches the number of 21, the nominated
council ceases to exist. This body shall be constituted and

designated as the legislative assembly of the territories, and it shall sit at least once a year. The members shall hold office for two years. Bills passed by them may be approved or disapproved of, or reserved to the Governor-General. At present the Lieutenant-Governor presides over the elective council, but when the legislative assembly comes into operation the powers of the council pass to it, and it assumes the formalities of an assembly. (r)

The North-West Territories will hereafter be entitled to a representation of four members in the commons and two in the senate of Canada. (s) The provisional districts of Saskatchewan and Alberta send one member each; and Assiniboia is divided into two ridings, east and west, and each of these sends also one member.

KEEWATIN.

Keewatin was detached from the territories in 1876, but it is now somewhat different, in its southern boundary, from what it was in that year. It may shortly be described as the territory west of Hudson's Bay to a meridian line between 100 and 101 degrees of longitude west from Greenwich extending north to the limits of Canada and south to the province of Manitoba. The eastern boundary of Manitoba is a line due north from the point where the western boundary of Ontario intersects the international boundary with the United States, and this line produced north to Hudson's Bay appears to be the eastern boundary of Keewatin. As originally formed it comprised the territory lying east of Manitoba and west of Ontario, but both these provinces since 1876 have enlarged their boundaries and they now meet at the point already mentioned. (t)

(r) R. S. C. cap. 50.

(s) 50-51 Vic. D. cap. 3 and 4, R. S. C. cap. 7.

(t) The northern boundary of Ontario is yet undecided. The eastern boundary of Manitoba is not the western boundary of Ontario, except at

The Lieutenant-Governor of Manitoba is *ex officio* Lieutenant-Governor of this district ; and he, with a council of
not less than five or more than ten, administers the affairs
of the district. The council is appointed by the privy
council at Ottawa ; and all the powers it possesses are derived from orders in council there.

Provisions somewhat similar to, and in many instances the
same as those set out in the last chapter on the Government of the North-West Territories, apply to this district ;
and all laws in force in the Territories are to remain in
force in the district until otherwise altered. (*u*)

This district has no representation in the senate or in the
commons of Canada.

the point on the international boundary referred to. The province of
Ontario claims as against the Dominion government that its northern
boundary is not south of James Bay, or the most north-westerly point of
the Lake of the Woods. But no authoritative decision has been given in
the matter. The province has grounds for claiming all lands south of
those owned by the Hudson Bay Company and east of the line determined
by the judicial committee of the privy council.

(*u*) R. S. C. cap. 53.

CHAPTER XVI.

THE JUDICATURE.

Defects of written constitutions, imperfect description of boundaries to legislative powers—Position of the courts —Different sources of laws—The judicial power in the United States, in Canada, similar duties but dissimilar origin.

Under a federal system of government, as has been seen, a written constitution is a necessity. The limits of legislative control between the central and local governments must be sharply defined. The respective fields which are mapped out for the exercise of their law-making powers should be separated and fenced off with all the accuracy of language that is possible. Notwithstanding the desire to locate this distinct boundary, it has not been possible in the American or in the Canadian constitutions to do more than to express by general classification the areas intended to be covered by the different governments. To use the language of Mr. Blake, as applying to Canada, " the B. N. A. Act is a skeleton." Without resorting to the particularity of a code, the framers of the Act had to be content with a couple of pages of subjects in language necessarily imperfect, and capable as has been since seen, of more than one interpretation. The difficulties in this respect have been very great in this country, and the task of deciding upon a conflict of laws has been, and will be, by no means an easy one. It is the province and duty of the judicial department to determine the boundaries of these subjects; to say what the law is, and if two laws conflict with each other, to decide on the operation of each; so that if the law be in opposition to the constitution, and both apply to a particular case, the court must either decide the case conformably to the law, disregarding the constitution, or conformably to the constitution, disregarding the law. (a) Where the powers of the legislatures are defined and limited it is the duty of the courts to say whether or not these limits have been passed. "The right of all courts, state and national," says Mr. Justice Story, "to declare unconstitutional laws void, seems settled beyond the reach of judicial controversy." This language is as applicable in the Canadian as in the American union.

An imperial statute in 1867 gave Canada a written and defined constitution. Under this constitution two governments were endowed with large legislative powers. All the laws were to be interpreted by the courts, but interpreted so as not to conflict with the imperial laws, which must be executed before all others. Our courts, therefore, are bound to determine what laws are in force. A Canadian law which is repugnant to any imperial enactment must be declared void by the courts—a higher than Canadian power has said that it is no law at all. Again, the Dominion parliament may usurp provincial rights, or a province assume to deal with dominion matters; the courts still sitting under the constitution, the imperial enactment must refuse to accept such attempted legislation as valid law. The courts in Canada are still the Queen's courts and bound to interpret such law as is in force, and equally bound to declare that the Acts of any of our legislatures, when transcending their limits, are unconstitutional and void. The courts, so long as they are permitted to exist, are not the creatures of either the provincial or federal legis-

(a) *Marbury* v. *Madison*, 1 Cranch 177.

lature; they are of course subordinate to constitutional legislation, but they are co-ordinate and in effect superior to that which is not constitutional.

In Great Britain the legislature is the chief power in the land. There being no written constitution, no plain speaking and inflexible statute of paramount law, under which the government of the country is carried on, the constitutionality of its acts cannot be questioned by the courts in the same way as in those countries wherein there is a government with divided powers. The acts of the legislature form the law, and these acts its courts must construe without questioning their validity or testing them with the constitution. The British people speak in each legislative enactment through one parliament with plenary power; and their latest utterance is the guide for their courts, which are always subordinate to this legislature, and exist solely by its permission.

In our federal government it is the duty of the judiciary, as the appropriate means of securing to the people safety from legislative aggression, to annul all legislative action without the pale of the written constitution. In matters of conflict between the powers of the local and central legislatures, the position of the judiciary is not that of a subordinate, but of a co-ordinate branch of the government; and it must declare every act of the legislature which is repugnant to the constitution to be absolutely void. This power is not confined to any particular court, but extends to all courts both dominion and provincial. The courts are the custodians of the constitution.

These courts are also bound to declare what laws are in force in the Dominion, whether they are enacted by the parliament of the Dominion or by the local legislatures. The provincial courts are no mere local courts for the administration of the laws passed by the legislatures of the provinces in which they are organized.

The union of the provinces in 1867 did not in itself effect any alteration in these courts in this respect. The powers of the courts are ones to be exercised with the most deliberate caution. Unless it is clear that the legislature has transcended its authority, the courts will not interfere. No court can pronounce any Act of the legislature void for any supposed inequality or injustice in its operation, provided it be on a subject matter purely within the scope of legislative authority, and the provisions of the law in general.

This being, it is apprehended, the position of our judiciary in Canada, the laws to be considered necessarily refer to three sources—the imperial, the dominion and the provincial.

What is known as the common or the unwritten law of England was largely imported into all parts of the Dominion in virtue not only of British subjects bringing part of this law with them of necessity, but also by means of its express introduction by statute. The introduction of English law in these various ways brought with it the decisions of the courts in Great Britain in reference to the same : and these decisions or precedents are another source of laws. The introduction of the criminal law of England to the old province of Quebec in 1774 introduced all these sources of law at once.

In the province of Ontario a few references will show how extensively the laws of England have been adopted here.

In 1792 all the amendments made in England to the criminal law since 1774 were transferred to Upper Canada ; and in the same year the law as to property, civil rights, and trial by jury as it then stood, was declared to be the law for the province. On the establishment of the Court of Chancery, the law of England, as it stood in 1837, regarding the English Court of Chancery was, unless otherwise provided, to be in force here ; and the rights, incidents and privileges of the courts of common law in England in 1859 were transferred to our Superior Courts of law. In British Columbia the criminal law of England as it stood on the 19th of November, 1858, subject to local legislation, is the criminal law of that province.

The local legislatures may delegate to municipal or other corporations the power of making laws. This is effected by the by-laws of these bodies, which are as much the law of the land as any legislative Acts; and, as another example, may be mentioned the powers of the Governors in Council under statute regulations to promulgate orders having the force of laws.

When it is remembered that all the different sources of the laws, their application and their meaning, have to be considered and determined by the courts, it will be seen how important is the judicial department of government, and how imperious and absolute is the necessity of securing its independence. (a)　It bears the whole stress of the constitution.

Mr. Duer, writing on the constitution of the United States, says :

" Whoever attentively considers the different departments of power, must perceive that in a government in which they are separated from each other, the judiciary, from the nature of its functions, will always be the least dangerous to the political rights secured by the constitution, because it will have the least capacity to invade or injure

(a) In the United States, the judges of the supreme and inferior courts hold their offices during good behavior.

them. The executive power not only dispenses the honors, but wields the sword of the community. The legislature not only holds the public purse, but prescribes the rules by which the rights and duties of every citizen are to be enjoyed and regulated. But the judicial power has no command over the sword or the purse ;—no direction, either of the strength or the wealth of the society and can take no active resolution whatsoever. It has been truly and emphatically said to have ' neither force nor will, but merely judgment ; " (b) and even for the practical exercise of this faculty, it must depend on the protection and support of the executive arm."

There is only one section in the B. N. A. Act that refers to any court not already in existence in the provinces.

The 101st section is as follows :

The parliament of Canada may notwithstanding anything in this Act, from time to time, provide for the constitution, maintenance and organization of a general court of appeal for Canada and for the establishment of any additional courts for the better administration of the laws of Canada.

The creation of the court of appeal does not in itself give to that court any power not possessed by the courts appealed from. It would have no inherent jurisdiction, it would simply settle more authoritatively questions of law from the courts in the provinces. As a court of appeal it has no more power than is possessed by the provincial courts already in existence. Under the last part of section 101,

(b) The Federalist No. 78. When the Supreme Court cannot count upon the support of the executive, its judgments may be without force in the United States, though this could not arise under our government. There the executive force being in the President, and being a real force, the latter may if so minded refuse to carry out the law. When C. J. Marshall had delivered a judgment obnoxious to President Jefferson, the latter is reported to have said, in republican simplicity of language, "John Marshall has delivered his judgment, let him now execute it—if he can."

it could be invested with new powers and endowed with original as well as appellate jurisdiction. But if this section had been omitted from the Act, the other courts would still have the same position they now occupy. They derive no assistance and receive no new powers from the Act. They are simply made subject to an appeal court which it was hoped would take the place of an appeal to England. It does not take away any of their rights and duties and does not divert the judicial power from the Crown. The judicature in Canada as in England points to the Queen as its source. There is no change in that respect under our federal system, and the principles of the British constitution have been adhered to so far as the judicature is concerned.

In the American union the position of the judicature is very different. By the 1st section of Article III.

The judicial power of the United States shall be vested in one supreme court, and in such inferior courts as the congress may from time to time ordain and establish. The judges both of the supreme and inferior courts shall hold their offices during good behaviour; and shall at stated times receive for their services a compensation which shall not be diminished during their continuance in office.

By the United States constitution, the judicial power is vested in the supreme court just as much as the executive power is vested in the president or the legislative power is vested in the congress. Under this state of things there is no common source of power such as is the first estate under the British constitution. The three divisions of government are three co-ordinate powers—one making the laws, another interpreting them and another executing them. These powers are not only co-ordinate but they are distinctly separated in theory and in practice. In the United Kingdom they are united in theory and in practice. The

Queen acting under the advice of a prime minister is in the first instance, the legislative, the executive and the judicial power. It is not to be imagined that in the judicial department the prime minister does more than create the courts and supply them with judges and everything needful in that respect: the distinction between the two forms of government is that in the United States the judicial power is independent of the congress and the president; while in Great Britain the judicial powers and all other powers are in the control of the executive.

In the Canadian union the theory and practice follow the principles of the British constitution. The supreme court in this country has no position at all analogous to that of the United States supreme court. Here it is a court of appeal for the provinces. It has no more power to declare an act of one of the legislatures unconstitutional than has the lowest court in the land. It is co-ordinate with the legislatures just as the other courts of Her Majesty are co-ordinate. There is no judicial power vested in it or in them, they are all equally under the constitution and bound to construe all legislative and executive Acts in accordance with that supreme law. There is therefore no analogy between the origin of the judicial power in Canada and in the United States; but the exercise of judicial power in Canada is analogous to its exercise in the American union in deciding whether the legislatures have kept within their proper limits. In Canada that means in effect whether the imperial Act of 1867 is not transgressed by any statute of the Canadian legislatures. It is not the supreme court or the authority to create courts that permits when necessary such legislation to be declared void, but it is the fact that the same power that decreed the constitution, created the courts; and their duty is to see that no Canadian statute is at variance with that standard of government and of laws— the Confederation Act.

CHAPTER XVII.

THE COURTS.

The judicial committee of the privy council, composition, juris-
diction, discretion as to appeals, procedure, judgment—
The supreme court of Canada, jurisdiction, court of last
resort, sittings, practice and procedure—The exchequer
court of Canada, new constitution, jurisdiction, to follow
English practice, sittings, writs run through Canada—
The maritime court of Ontario, jurisdiction, judge,
practice.

THE JUDICIAL COMMITTEE OF THE PRIVY COUNCIL.

THIS court is the last resort of a colonial British subject
in appeal from the laws of his own colony.

The privy council in England is composed of a large
number of distinguished persons. Most of the principal
judges, the speaker of the house of commons, the Queen's
ambassadors and those formerly holding offices in the ministry, besides the archbishops and some bishops, are members of this body. One distinguished committee forms the
cabinet ; another, with which only we have to deal here,
forms a judicial committee, the functions of which are to decide
all matters that can judicially come by appeal or by complaint in the nature of appeal before the Queen, or the
Queen in council. On hearing the case argued this committee reports to the Queen in council its recommendation
for her decision.

This court is composed of such privy councillors as are or were its presidents, judges of the chief courts of equity and common law, the judges of the admiralty, of the prerogative court of Canterbury, bishops and archbishops, two retired East Indian or Colonial Judges, and two others. (a)

The committee has the ordinary powers of the superior courts in England as to witnesses, juries, process, etc.; and cases may be heard by three of its members and the lord president. The court holds three sittings in the year, generally in February, June and November, and lasting about six weeks.

The jurisdiction of the judicial committee is divided into two heads—one comprising appeals allowed by right, and the other those cases where leave to appeal is first of all necessary. The crown may, in Acts of its colonial legislatures, shut out the right to appeal—it may abrogate its prerogative. Where the right of the crown is not reserved, or where the fair construction of the colonial Act is that no appeal will lie to the privy council, then the judgment of a colonial court under the provisions of such an Act, assented to by the crown, is final. The crown, by assenting, takes away the right of appeal.

The Quebec controverted elections Act of 1875, states that the judgment of the court "shall not be susceptible of appeal;" and an appeal to the privy council was refused in a case coming under the Act. (b)

The Dominion Act establishing the supreme court at Ottawa in 1875, made its judgments final without appeal, saving any right which Her Majesty may exercise in virtue of the royal prerogative.

(a) Cox's British Commonwealth.
(b) *Theberge v. Landry*, 2 App. Cas. 102.

Lord Cairns, in constructing the section of the supreme court Act containing these words, laid down the rule that the judicial committee of the privy council would have no hesitation in a proper case of advising Her Majesty to permit an appeal from the judgment of this court. The discretion of so allowing an appeal to be heard would not be exercised where the amount involved was small, and where the issue between the parties related simply to the legal construction of a particular contract, or where no general principle was involved, or where no other cases were necessarily affected by the decision complained of. (c)

Appeals lie as a matter of right from the provinces, but, so far as colonial cases are concerned, it is said that no appeal lies in any case of felony. When the last court is reached in criminal matters the condemned has the right to sue for pardon at the foot of the throne. Formerly the pardoning power was supposed to be or was in reality, in the personal discretion of the Governor-General. (d)

Appeals to Her Majesty in her privy council are entertained from the court of appeal in Ontario. where the matter in controversy exceeds the sum or value of $4,000, and in cases relating to the taking of any annual or other rent, customary or other duty or fee, or any like demand of a general or public nature affecting future rights, no matter

---

(c) *Johnston* v. *The Minister and Trustees of St. Andrew's Church,* Montreal, 3 App. Cas. 159.

(d) The instructions as to pardon are now to this effect:

" The Governor-General is not to pardon or reprieve any offender who may be tried within the Dominion without first receiving in capital cases the advice of the privy council, and in other cases the advice of at least one minister. And in cases in which such pardon or reprieve might directly affect the interests of the empire, or of any country or place beyond the jurisdiction of the government of the Dominion, the said Governor-General shall before deciding as to either pardon or reprieve, take these interests specially into his own personal consideration in conjunction with such advice as aforesaid." Instructions to his Excellency the Marquis of Lorne.

what the amount in question may be. Beyond these no
appeals lie from the court of appeal in Ontario to the judicial committee of the privy council.

All cases of appeal are commenced by petition addressed
to Her Majesty in council ; and this is the first step in
their prosecution. Afterwards certified copies of the record
from the court appealed from are sent to England and
deposited in the council office ; and an appearance having
been entered by the respondent, each side makes up its own
case if it is allowed to be heard.

Security to the amount of $2,000 must be given in such
cases.

Earl Carnarvon, in 1874, intimated to the Governor-
General of Canada that in order to bring appeals from the
supreme court of Canada, a petition for that purpose in order
to obtain leave to appeal should be brought before the
judicial committee of the privy council, and not transmitted through the secretary of state to the Queen in council.
He also intimated as the practice, that the respondent must
enter an appearance before any answer is returned by the
judicial committee in reference to the petition.   The Governor-General hereafter is to decline transmitting applications
in a private suit to the secretary of state for the colonies,
but is to inform the petitioner what steps to take in the
matter.   The circular dispatch of Earl Carnarvon, though
directed to the practice in appeals, is an indication that the
royal prerogative as to allowing them from Canada will be
exercised on the recommendation of the judicial committee
itself.   In effect it would seem to be similar to an application to any appellate court for leave to appeal, where such
leave is necessary.

The judicial committee has unlimited powers in the way

of procedure, and is not bound by the rules in the court below.

The case is argued by senior and junior counsel, the appellant's counsel having the right to reply: and the judgment of the court is delivered by one judge only, and need not be unanimous—a majority being sufficient. (e)

The judgment, after being delivered, is reported by the committee, and submitted to the Queen in council for approval. The order made thereupon is the last proceeding in the case and the judicial rights of the parties are thereby finally determined.

THE SUPREME COURT OF CANADA.

This court is the highest court of appeal within Canada, and entertains appeals, civil and criminal, within and throughout the Dominion from the last court of resort in the provinces. By consent of the parties appeals may be directly made from a superior court, and by leave the court may hear an appeal from any decree, decretal order, or order made by a court of equity, or in an equity proceeding, or any final judgment of the superior courts, other than those of Quebec, without intermediate appeal to such last provincial court, providing the case originally commenced in such superior court. In certain cases in election petitions an appeal in the same way will lie to this court. In equity cases, and in proceedings in the nature of equity,

(e) Some years ago it was discussed in England whether a dissenting member of the committee could declare his dissent. A great deal of learning and historical research were expended on another question out of which this arose, that is, whether or not the judicial committee of the privy council is a *court* at all, or merely a *consultative* body. If a court, then each member would have the right to express a dissenting opinion or judgment; but if the usages and traditions of the privy council were to govern, then there could be no dissent. at least in expression.

an appeal will lie to this court even from orders made in the exercise of judicial discretion. The court can also hear special cases, review judgments on points reserved at the trial, on motions for a new trial, on motions to set aside an award, on applications in *habeas corpus, mandamus*, or municipal by-laws. It entertains appeals from the exchequer courts, the maritime court of Ontario, and cases under the Dominion Elections Act and the Winding-up Act.

The intention of the Act establishing the supreme and exchequer courts is that all orders, decretal orders, decrees and decisions of any superior court made in any such cause, matter or other judicial proceeding in equity, or in any action, cause, suit, matter or other judicial proceeding in the nature of a suit or proceeding in equity, are and always have been proper subjects of appeal to this court.

In Quebec cases, the appeal must always come from the Court of Queen's Bench; and the matter in controversy must be at least $2,000, unless it involves the validity of a dominion or local Act of the legislature or of any Act or ordinance of the territories or districts of Canada, or any fee of office, duty, rent, revenue, or any sum of money payable to her Majesty, or any title to any lands or tenements, or annual rents, if brought in the court mentioned.

The court has jurisdiction in criminal as well as in civil matters; but in respect of any indictable offence, no appeal is allowed, if the judgment of the lower court was unanimous in affirming the conviction.

This court of last resort in the provinces does not mean the individual judges who may be authorized to sit in these courts, but the tribunals from which the appeals are to come, or the respective courts themselves, without reference to the number of judges; provided always the court be duly constituted by the presence of a sufficient number of judges to make a legal court, whatever that number may be. (*f*) The judgment of two or even of one judge, where the courts may be constituted of these numbers respectively, is not appealable. An appeal lies only where there is a dissenting judgment in the court appealed from. (*g*)

No appeal lies to this court from the judgment of a court granting a new trial on the ground that the verdict was against the weight of evidence—that being a matter of discretion. (*h*)

The Governor-General may refer any matter to the judges of the supreme court for hearing or consideration, and they shall certify their opinion thereon to the Governor in Council; and either house of parliament may refer any private bill or petition thereto.

Controversies arising between the Dominion and the provinces, or between the provinces themselves, may, with the consent of the provinces, be determined by the supreme or the exchequer court of Canada. The province of Ontario has placed herself within this jurisdiction by enacting that the supreme court may entertain controversies between the Dominion and the provinces, and also controversies between Ontario and any other province submitting to the jurisdiction of the court. In such actions and proceedings in Ontario, where the parties thereto by their pleadings raised the question of the validity of any Dominion or provincial Act, if in the opinion of the judge the question is material, the case may be ordered by the judge, either with or without the request of the parties, to be removed to the supreme court.

(*f*) Per Mr. Justice (now Chief Justice) Sir Wm. Ritchie in *Amer* v. *The Queen*, 2 S. C. 592.

(*g*) Mr. Justice Taschereau in the same case.

(*h*) *Boak* v. *The Merchants' Marine Insurance Co.*, 1 S. C. 110.

The court, or any of its judges, has original jurisdiction in *habeas corpus* cases; and has the same power to bail, discharge or commit the prisoner as any court or judge in the provinces having jurisdiction in such matters. (*i*)

The court, or any judge, may also order the issue of a writ of *certiorari* to bring up papers or proceedings necessary with a view to any enquiry, appeal, or other proceeding before such court or judge.

The supreme court sits three times a year; on the third Tuesday of February, the first Tuesday in May, and the fourth Tuesday in October, at Ottawa, and is presided over by a chief justice and five associate judges, who hold office during good behaviour. Any five of the judges are competent to hold court in term. The judges are incapable of holding any office of emolument under the Dominion or provincial governments.

Rules in relation to appeals are laid down by order in council, and the judges of the courts can make rules and orders for the purpose of carrying out the acts establishing this court. All barristers or advocates, attorneys or solicitors in any of the provinces, shall have the right to practise as counsel, solicitors, etc., in this and in the exchequer court; and all such practitioners are officers of these courts.

A registrar and reporter of the court are appointed by the Governor in Council.

The proceedings in this court are regulated by rules approved of by the court.

The first proceedings in appeals, after the notice of appeal is given and the security perfected, is the filing of a case

---

(*i*) No appeal is allowed in any case of proceedings for or upon a writ of *habeas corpus* arising out of any claim for extradition made under any treaty. R. S. C. cap. 135, sec. 31.

stated by the parties, setting forth the judgment objected to and so much of the pleadings, evidence, affidavits and documents as may be necessary to raise the question for the decision of the court. The case must also, if possible, contain a transcript of all the opinions or reasons delivered by the judges in the courts below ; and must be accompanied by a certificate that proper security to the extent of $500 has been given by the appellant in the court appealed from.

Twenty-five copies of the case are printed in a prescribed form, and these, with certified copies of original documents, deposited with the registrar of the court. Notice of hearing is served at least a month before the next session of the court, at which time each party deposits in court copies of the *factum* or points for argument in appeal. This contains a concise statement of facts, the points of law and the arguments and authorities in the case, and is printed and distributed in the same way as the case or appeal. They are put in under seal and when deposited are exchanged with the opposite party. When the rules of court are complied with the appeals are set down for hearing, and the case is heard with not more than two counsel for each side —one only in reply. These rules do not apply to criminal appeals or to *habeas corpus* cases, in which a certified written case is all that is necessary in order to bring them before the court. In election appeals the record or the necessary part of it is printed under the direction of the registrar of the court, but each *factum* is prepared just as in ordinary cases. (*j*)

(*j*) In Ontario, a sufficient number of appeal books are printed for the court of appeal and for the supreme court at Ottawa, when the appeal is prepared in the first instance. When the judgments of the court of appeal for Ontario are given, the unsuccessful party can have these printed and added to the appeal books, making the necessary alterations in the title and index, and use this for the supreme court at Ottawa. The *factum* is prepared, but the case is entered with much less expense in printing.

THE EXCHEQUER COURT OF CANADA.

The Act of 1875 establishing the supreme and exchequer courts of Canada has, so far as the latter court is concerned, been superseded by the Act of 1887. The court of exchequer is continued under its former name but its judge is not one of the judges of the supreme court and the court is completely detached from that court. The practice and procedure of the exchequer court are regulated by the practice and procedure, so far as they are applicable in similar suits, in the high court of justice in England. The court has exclusive jurisdiction in the following matters :—

Every claim against the crown for property taken for any public purpose.

Every claim against the crown for damage to property, injuriously affected by the construction of any public work.

Every claim against the crown arising out of any death or injury to the person or to property on any public work, resulting from the negligence of any officer or servant of the crown while acting within the scope of his duties or employment.

Every claim against the crown arising under any law of Canada or any regulation made by the Governor in Council.

Every set-off, counter claim, claim for damages, whether liquidated or unliquidated, or other demand whatsoever, on the part of the crown against any person making claim against the crown.

It has concurrent jurisdiction

In all cases relating to the revenue in which it is sought to enforce any law of Canada, including actions, suits and proceedings by way of information to enforce penalties, and proceedings by way of information to information *in rem* and as well in *qui tam* suits for penalties or forfeitures as when the suit is on behalf of the crown alone.

In all cases in which it is sought at the instance of the attorney-general of Canada, to impeach or annul any patent of invention, or any patent, lease, or other instrument respecting lands.

In all cases in which demand is made or relief sought against any officer of the crown for anything done or omitted to be done in the performance of his duty as such officer.

In all other actions and suits of a civil nature at common law or equity in which the crown is plaintiff or petitioner.

The court sits at any place in Canada, and the sheriffs and coroners of the different counties are officers of this court. In Ontario a judge of the exchequer court had, in regard to the use of the court house and other buildings set apart in the county for the administration of justice, the same authority in all respects as a judge at *nisi prius*.

Execution can issue out of this court to enforce its own decrees—the writs issuing in the name of the judge, and its process runs throughout Canada.

There are the usual officers appointed for this court. (*k*)

THE MARITIME COURT OF ONTARIO.

The parliament of Canada has established a superior court of maritime jurisdiction in the province of Ontario and conferred on it all such jurisdiction as generally belongs to any existing British vice-admiralty court in similar

(*k*) This Act is not yet in force, 50-51 Vic. cap. 16.

matters within the reach of its process. It has to deal with matters of contract and of tort, proceedings *in rem* and *in personam*, arising out of or connected with navigation, shipping, trade or commerce on any river, lake, canal or inland water, of which the whole or part is in the province of Ontario. It has jurisdiction touching the ownership, possession, employment or earnings of ships. The corresponding court in the lower province is the vice-admiralty court at Quebec. (*l*)

The county judge of the County of York residing at Toronto is the judge in this court. All barristers and advocates may plead in this court and solicitors when practising therein are known as proctors of the court. The practice follows, as far as is applicable, the instance side of the high court of admiralty in England.

An appeal lies from the maritime court of Ontario to the supreme court of Canada.

(*l*) See article "Vice-admiralty jurisdiction," by Mr. Lash, Q.C. and, Mr. R. G. Cox, in the Canadian Law Times, Vol. VII, page 21.

CHAPTER XVIII.

PROVINCIAL COURTS, CIVIL PROCEDURE, OFFICERS OF THE LAW.

Procedure in civil matters belongs to the provinces—In criminal matters to the Dominion—Want of uniformity in laws and procedure as to property and civil rights, old divisions of English courts, appeal courts—Equity and common law courts, cases heard in first instance, superior and inferior courts—Object of procedure and pleadings —Writs, statements, record, issue,—Trial, verdict, execution—Officers of the law, attorneys, solicitors, counsel, notaries, sheriffs, coroners.

THE COURTS.

By the 14th sub-section of section 92 of the B. N. A. Act :

The administration of justice in the provinces, including the constitution, maintenance, and organization of provincial courts both of civil and criminal jurisdiction, and including procedure in civil matters in these courts, forms a class of subjects within the exclusive control of the provincial legislatures. The 27th sub-section of section 91 allots " the procedure in criminal matters " to the parliament of Canada. The provinces having therefore to deal with procedure in civil matters, it is to be expected that there will be great diversity in civil trials. There is not much uniformity in the provincial laws; but the framers of the Act were in hopes that the English speaking provinces might make provision for uniform laws as to property and civil rights, and they accordingly inserted a section to meet that expectation. (a)   In Quebec where the old French law—the *Coutume de Paris* is the basis of all civil matters, and where a code obtains as to procedure, with no great likelihood of any change, the Act is silent as to the prospect of uniformity or as to the prospect of the judges for that province being appointed from the bar of any other province. (b)   The remaining provinces have a system of laws and a procedure and practice founded on English law ; and it may be possible to give the unprofessional reader some idea of the courts and of the general procedure in a civil case such as obtains in England and in some of the provinces.

In all the provinces there is some ultimate court of appeal to which suitors who are not satisfied with the decisions of the superior courts of law and equity can resort for a more authoritative disposition of their cases.   This corresponds to the house of lords court in England, which hears and determines appeals from the English courts. Formerly there were three common law courts, the Queen's bench, the common pleas and the exchequer court, and one court of equity called the high court of chancery.   The exchequer court was not usually transplanted into the colonies but the other three were generally reproduced.   The colonial courts of appeal were sometimes composed of the judges of all the superior courts sitting as one court, and sometimes composed of other judges as is the present court of appeal for Ontario.   An appeal lay from these courts of ultimate authority in the province to the judicial committee in England, the ultimate authority for such matters in the empire.   The provincial courts of appeal do not as a rule entertain cases in the first instance—except some election

(a) Sec. 94.
(b) Sec. 97 and 98.

petitions ; they sit to determine appeals from lower courts.
The superior courts of law and equity in Ontario, following
the analogous legislation in England, have been merged
into one high court of justice with divisions in it named
after the time-honored nomenclature of Queen's bench,
chancery and common pleas, and with changes very important in the constitution of these courts. Formerly the
chancery court had its own special work ; equity as distinguished from law was a source of perplexity in procedure
and interposed a division of some sort in the administration
of common justice. Anciently in England the common
pleas heard civil disputes only ; the Queen's bench criminal
matters exclusively, and the exchequer court concerned
itself solely with the revenue. Many of these distinctions
have been removed, and generally each of these divisions
has now the power of any one of them. These are the
superior courts—they sit for the whole province or country,
and two or more judges sit in term, at stated times in the
year, to review cases heard in the first instance by a single
judge. The court, wherever a case is heard in the first
instance before a single judge and with or without a jury,
is properly known as the assize court, or the court of *nisi
prius.* (c)   From the fact that the criminal cases are heard
at the same time and place and the gaol emptied, this

(c) In England the court of assizes was a court of 12 judges—three
from each of the four divisions already mentioned—empowered to try
twice in the year in their respective circuits, all causes civil and criminal
in every county in England, except London and Middlesex only.   There
were six circuits, and two judges were appointed for each.   Under the
commission of assize they took the verdicts of a peculiar species of jury
called an *assize*, and summoned for the trial of landed disputes.   The
judges sat as well under four other commissions.   (1) A court of gaol
delivery.   (2) The session of the peace.   (3) The court of oyer and
terminer and (4) The court of *nisi prius*.   The first of these and the court
of oyer and terminer dealt with criminal cases, to deliver prisoners, and
to "enquire, hear and determine " all treasons, felonies and misdemeanors on indictment found at the same assize.   The session of the peace
was held four times in the year, hearing cases under authority of Acts
of parliament and the commission of the peace.   Several justices may
sit in this and in the court of oyer and terminer but there must be one

court is also called the court of *oyer and terminer* and general goal delivery.   In these courts the evidence is heard and the judgment or verdict or sentence rendered or pronounced at the time.   The courts in term sit in review of the decisions thus arrived at ; the provincial court of appeal, or the supreme court of Canada at Ottawa may review the judgments of the court in term.

Besides these courts of general jurisdiction there are county courts having to deal with local cases of less importance ; and there are also smaller courts graded down to those of justice of the peace or police magistrate who have jurisdiction over a few civil matters.   These courts are of inferior jurisdiction and they are in most cases controlled in a modified way by the superior courts.   Writs may issue out of the superior courts directing the lower courts by *mandamus* to do certain things, or by *prohibition* to refrain from taking certain steps, or by *procedendo* to continue in the prescribed course.   These extraordinary remedies are however very rarely resorted to, both because the lower courts keep within their own constitutions and duties, and the other courts will not interfere unless in the plainest cases.   The county courts and their judges also hear criminal cases of a less grave nature than those tried at the assizes—these are the quarter sessions or the general sessions of the peace or the county judge's criminal court.

of the *quorum* in each court.   This was the origin of the phrase " justices of the *quorum*," –the commission being addressed to the assize judges one *whom* would take the particular circuit.   In London and Middlesex the commission of assize directed the trial of all matters in dispute at Westminster Hall, and a writ of *nisi prius*, (unless before) was attached to the commission.   This commission called upon all suitors in the kingdom to repair thither for the disposition of these cases, *unless before* a certain day, a court for the trial would be held in the circuit towns.   The court held in the circuits in this way was the court of *nisi prius*, and it dates back to the 13th year of Edward I.   Formerly there were nine courts of common law; the same number of ecclesiastical courts ; fourteen courts of special jurisdiction ; sixteen of criminal jurisdiction ; besides equity, military and maritime courts.

But at the sessions justices of the peace may and do sit with the county judge for the disposal of offenders.

These are the courts for all purposes, and for all laws; and the provincial legislatures have control over their constitution maintenance and organization. The Dominion government controls the criminal procedure ; that will be referred to in the next chapter. A word or two may be said of procedure in civil matters ; but as it varies in all the provinces, only a few general features can be referred to.

PROCEDURE.

The procedure in any action is the mode by which the dispute between two or more parties is brought into court to be tried and settled. The case of each side is set out in what is called a pleading ; these pleadings come into court in the form of a record—which is the guide of the presiding judge as to the matter in dispute. To get the parties before the court with a full and complete statement of their claims and defences is the object of all pleadings; and it is substantially the same under every form of procedure though the practice of the courts in each particular, may be as different as can be imagined. In the old chancery procedure the plaintiff formulated all his charges and grievances against the defendants in an elaborate document called a bill of complaint, depositing one copy with the court for the hearing and serving others on the defendants. The defendants replied on oath by an equally elaborately worded answer, and if the parties were at issue they went to trial. That mode of proceeding has almost disappeared and the procedure now begins generally with a writ of summons containing the substance of the plaintiff's claim, and calling on the defendant to appear within so many days. When the appearance is entered the plaintiff files and serves a statement of claim and the defendant similarly formulates his defence. When they are at issue on questions of law or of fact, the case is tried before some judge of one of the courts and a judgment entered, upon which the successful party is entitled to get the relief which the court has afforded him. The unsuccessful litigant has generally the right to appeal. If the amount at stake is considerable or if any principle of law is involved, he can usually go to the ultimate court in his own province and then to the supreme court or to the judicial committee of the privy council in England.

The practice and procedure in bringing any case to trial, are too elaborate to admit of any generalization beyond what has been already given. The necessary parties, the proper court, the valid legal claim or defence, the language in which it is presented to the court, are some of the difficulties in the procedure of a civil case : but assuming that a plaintiff has a good claim in law and that it is not negatived by some valid objection on the part of the defendant, the action would proceed generally in the manner indicated, until the final court was reached. The successful party then obtains payment of his claim or the performance of such duty as he was entitled to either by the submission of the opposing party, or through process by the sheriff. This process is a writ either of execution to sell goods and lands, or a writ of possession, or of assistance, or as the nature of the judgment or decree or order of the court may direct.

Every person is allowed to conduct his own case in person either as plaintiff or as defendant ; to issue his own writ or appear to one issued against him ; he can prepare and file his pleadings and go into court and argue his own case. In other words he can be his own attorney or solicitor, and counsel. (d)   But no one is allowed to act thus for another

(d) It was usual to speak of an attorney in actions at law and solicitor in chancery cases ; solicitor is the term now in Ontario.

unless he is a member of the legal profession. He is then an officer of the court, and subject to its summary jurisdiction. He must be declared by some law society specially charged with that task, to be duly qualified for such duties.

The different provinces of the Dominion make their own regulations under legislative authority as to who are and who are not legally qualified practitioners, and their powers, duties and obligations. Reference will here be made to the chief officers of the law engaged in the prosecution of a suit civil or criminal, and to such persons as are entrusted with the execution of the process of the courts.

OFFICERS OF THE LAW.

In Ontario the treasurer and benchers of *The Law Society of Upper Canada* form a corporation ; and they and their successors in office regulate the government of the society, the appointment of officers, the legal education of students and the term of studentship, and the admission of applicants as barristers-at-law or as attorneys and solicitors into the law society. The benchers have the appointment of reporters to the superior courts, and fix the amount of their salaries.

No one can practise at the bar in Her Majesty's courts of law or equity in Ontario unless he has been entered and admitted into the law society under its rules as a barrister.

The attorney-general for the Dominion ranks first in precedence in the Ontario bar, then the attorney-general for the province, then previous attorney-generals according to seniority of appointment. After these solicitor-generals and such Queen's counsel as were appointed before confederation, in the same order.   Other members rank in the order of the call to the bar. (*e*)

Attorneys and solicitors are admitted into the law society under rules similar to those for barristers, and must not practise without paying an annual fee and obtaining a certificate.   They may be struck off the roll of any of the courts by a superior court judge on application being made in a proper case.   It is usual to speak of members of the legal profession as attorneys when conducting actions or suits in the common law courts, and solicitors in the chancery or insolvency courts.   In the maritime court they are styled proctors.   The profession of barrister in Ontario, though not so distinct as in England from the office of solicitor or attorney, is yet separate from the latter.   Generally barristers here are members of both professions—if indeed there can be said to be two professions in the province.   A number of solicitors, however, are not barristers, and therefore not entitled to plead in court.   On the other hand, a barrister who is not an attorney or solicitor as well, is not privileged to act in any other capacity than that of arguing in court the cases which the attorneys or solicitors prepare for him.   The judges of the superior courts are selected from barristers of at least ten years standing.   In other courts the length of time varies with the court.

In Quebec all advocates, barristers, attorneys, solicitors and proctors-at-law, form a corporation called *The Bar of the Province of Quebec.* (*f*)   A certain number of officers of each of the sections into which the corporation is divided constitutes a council with powers somewhat analogous to

(*e*) The appointment of Queen's counsel is now left to the Dominion government—that is, the provincial authorities are not in the habit of making such appointments.   See *ante* page 35.

(*f*) See Act of 1886 of Quebec, consolidating the law on this subject.

the Law Society of Upper Canada. They entertain matters, however, among the members of the profession not dealt with in Ontario by the Law Society, noticeably the pronouncing of censures, through the *Bâtonnier*, for any breach of discipline or action derogatory to the honour of the bar. Members may be suspended by this officer, subject to approval of the council. Notaries public in Quebec form a separate profession, being divided into a number of bodies corporate under Acts very similar to those relating to the bar of the province. Their duties not only embrace the certifying and protesting of documents, but includes nearly all of what is understood in English practice by conveyancing. In Ontario a notary public is appointed by the Lieutenant-Governor, and may protest bills of exchange and promissory notes ; and may draw, pass, keep and issue all deeds and contracts, charter parties, and other mercantile transactions in this province, may give certificates as to copies of instruments, and has some other undefined duties. They form no profession and are part of none, though the commission is usually granted to members of the legal profession as of course. Any person not a barrister or attorney must, however, pass an examination as to his qualification for the office before his county judge, or before some one appointed for that purpose by the Lieutenant-Governor, and produce a certificate that on examination he is found qualified for the office ; and further, that in the examiner's opinion a notary public is needed in the place where the applicant intends to carry on business. Formerly they could administer oaths or affirmations only under certain statutes ; usually the courts of Queen's Bench and Common Pleas appoint commissioners for taking affidavits for this purpose, who have power within the county in which they reside. Under the Ontario Act of 1885 (cap. 16), all notaries public now appointed or to be appointed hereafter have all the powers of commissioners to take affidavits and declarations in all courts in any part of the province. They are now officers of the high court of justice for Ontario.

Sheriffs are officers of the courts appointed by the Lieutenant-Governor under the great seal, one for each county, and hold office during pleasure. This office is one of the oldest and most honourable in the gift of the crown. Formerly he held a court for his shire or county, and the word sheriff means a *reeve* of the *shire*. He attended the King's court and looked after the peace of the county. He is yet the chief executive officer of the courts, attends the judge in circuit, summons the juries, has charge of the gaols, and executes all writs and sentences of the courts up to the execution of a criminal—the extreme penalty of the law. Where the sheriff is personally interested in a case, or where he cannot or will not execute the process of the court, the writs may be addressed to the principal coroner of the county. (g)

(g) See Office of Coroner, etc., *post.*

CHAPTER XIX.

CRIMINAL LAW AND PROCEDURE. (*a*)

THE criminal law of Canada is defined by the Acts of
the Dominion parliament construedby the common law of
England. In Quebec it is the criminal law of England as
introduced in 1763 and re-affirmed in 1775 ; in Ontario it is
the criminal law of England as it stood on the 17th September, 1792 ; in British Columbia it is the criminal law of
England as it stood on the 19th November, 1858 ; except as
the same may have been modified by the respective legis-

(*a*) Since the repeal of the insolvency laws this is the only subject where
the procedure is not regulated by the provincial laws —except Dominion
controverted election cases and such proceedings as may be in an application for a divorce before the senate. Cases relating to bills of exchange
and promissory notes, interest, legal tender or banks, are not regulated
by procedure different from the ordinary civil procedure. The jurisdiction of the maritime and exchequer courts has been referred to and also
the original jurisdiction of the supreme court of Canada.

latures of the said provinces before the same formed provinces of Canada (b). In the other provinces the law of England was introduced at different periods before confederation, though it is not so evident that its introduction was effected in the same way as in the three provinces mentioned. In Manitoba, the criminal law of Canada was introduced by various provisions since 1870.

The procedure in criminal law is directed by Acts of the Dominion parliament, and is generally uniform in its application to all the provinces ; but the Dominion Acts recognize differences in certain cases, founded generally on differences of procedure having existed before the provinces formed provinces of the union.

In criminal trials, as it is the public that is wronged, the action is said to be brought by the Queen or King against the accused. The case under our statutes is commenced either on information laid before a justice of the peace, or police magistrate, the inquisition of a coroner's jury or the presentment of a grand jury.

A criminal information, on leave being obtained, may be filed in any of the superior courts of original jurisdiction for misdemeanors only, in cases of general public importance, or, as affecting libellously upon some high public functionary or body. Informations of this latter class it is the tendency of the courts of Ontario to discourage.

A criminal information known as an information *ex officio* may be filed by the attorney-general without leave of the court against an offender in all cases of misdemeanor immediately affecting the Queen or her government. No criminal information will lie in regard to a felony or high treason. The procedure only applies to those misdemeanors

(b) Revised Statutes, D. page 138, sections 1 and 2.

upon which an indictment would lie before a justice of the peace. Leave to file a criminal information rests in the discretion of the court, and is a proceeding of an extraordinary character in criminal matters. In England it is granted when the matter complained of is of public importance, and that a speedy remedy is desired and necessary : or where some important official or superior person is the subject of grave charges : but the tendency of the courts here would seem to be to discourage the practice of granting leave for such informations. It is the only instance where proceedings are begun in a superior court of justice.

When an indictable offence is laid before a justice of the peace, if the evidence is sufficient to put the accused on his trial, the justice must either send him to gaol to await the next sitting of the court or admit him to bail.

A number of cases are also sent up to the county crown attorney or other officer from the coroners of the different counties. (*c*)

In cases where manslaughter or murder has been committed, the coroner empanels a jury, and their verdict or inquest is transmitted to the crown attorney as in the case of justices' committals. The county attorney, or whoever the proper official may be, attends with these informations and inquisitions at the next sitting of the court of competent jurisdiction and prefers them to the grand jury for their opinion as to whether or not the evidence is sufficient to put the accused on his trial.

A grand jury is composed of not less than twelve or not more than twenty-three persons selected to be grand jurors :

(*c*) In cases of murder or manslaughter upon a verdict incriminating any person by a jury empannelled by a coroner, the party charged may be tried with the same effect as on an indictment found by a grand jury against him.

and their duty is to judge whether the prisoner ought to be put on his trial or not.

In certain cases, such as perjury, subornation of perjury, conspiracy, obtaining money or other property by false pretences, keeping a gambling house, keeping a disorderly house, or any indecent assault, no presentment to or finding by the jury is made without the person making the accusation first giving a bond to prosecute or give evidence in the matter; unless the accused is committed, or is in custody, or that the indictment is preferred by the attorney or solicitor-general of the province, or by a judge competent to give such a direction or try the offence.

The grand jury judge nothing of the guilt or innocence of the accused; that is left to another jury. In the finding which the grand jury makes to the presiding judge, if in their opinion the accused ought to be put on his trial they write " true bill " on the back of the information or inquisition; and if not they write "no bill," and the accused is discharged without trial, but not properly until the court is about to rise.

The grand jury also presents a statement in reference to the state of the county jails, asylums, etc., which is called a presentment, and in this they can take notice of certain crimes and have the accused put on his trial; but such presentments are by no means necessary.

After the grand jury brings in a true bill the accused pleads guilty or not guilty; or in the event of his silence, the court can plead not guilty for him.

In capital offences the accused can object to or challenge not more than twenty jurors. In other cases of felony not more than twelve jurors, and in all other cases four jurors. These may be objected to without any reason given. Any number may be objected to on cause assigned. The crown has the right to challenge four jurors peremptorily, and has also the right to cause any juror to stand aside until the panel has been gone through, and has the same rights as the accused as to challenge for cause. In the provinces of Quebec and Manitoba there are special provisions whereby the person accused in certain cases may be tried by a jury half English and half French (d).

The accused, after the close of the case for the crown, can make full answer and defence to any indictment preferred against him, and be heard by his counsel on his behalf. But the modern practice permits the accused, in addition to the defence by counsel, to give any explanation to the court which he may think proper, and usually before counsel representing the crown has summed up the whole case.

The judge, on the finding of the jury, sentences the accused or discharges him as the case may be. From this there is no appeal. The judge may reserve any question of law to any of the superior courts. But in case the judge refuses to reserve a point of law, or could not have reserved it, a writ of error may issue so as to bring the matter under the consideration of superior courts If the conviction is bad for any cause, the whole trial is a nullity, and a new trial may be granted in such cases. In the absence of reprieve or pardon by the crown the sentence of the law is carried out by the various punishments of death, imprisonment, etc., provided by the statutes in that behalf.

The appeals to the supreme court, as well as the exercise of pardon, have been adverted to heretofore.

(d) R. S. D. cap. 168, sec. 166-67.

In cases of offences committed in a foreign state when the guilty parties have taken refuge in Canada, the extradition Act, R. S. C., governs the classes of crimes for which the two governments subject to any extradition arrangement, have agreed to hand over the offenders. These are as follows :

(1.) Murder, or attempt or conspiracy to murder ;

(2.) Manslaughter ;

(3.) Counterfeiting or uttering counterfeit money ;

(4.) Forgery ;

(5.) Larceny ;

(6.) Embezzlement ;

(7.) Obtaining money or goods under false pretences ;

(8.) Crimes against bankruptcy or insolvency law ;

(9.) Fraud by bankers, agents, trustees, directors and officers of companies, etc. ;

(10.) Rape ;

(11.) Abduction ;

(12.) Child stealing ;

(13.) Kidnapping ;

(14.) False imprisonment ;

(15.) Burglary, housebreaking or shopbreaking ;

(16.) Arson ;

(17.) Robbery ;

(18.) Threats with intent to extort ;

(19.) Perjury or subornation of perjury ;

(20.) Piracy on board or against a vessel of a foreign state ;

(21.) Criminal scuttling or destroying such a vessel at sea, or attempting or conspiring to do so :

(22.) Assault on board such vessel, with intent to destroy life or do grievous bodily harm ;

(23.) Revolt or conspiracy to revolt on board such a vessel against the authority of the master ;

(24.) Any offence under either of the following Acts and not included in any foregoing portion of this schedule ;

(a) " An Act respecting offences against the person ;"

(b) " The Larceny Act ;"

(c) " An Act respecting Forgery ;"

(d) " An Act respecting Offences relating to the Coin ;"

(e) " An Act respecting Malicious Injuries to Property ;"

(25.) Any offence which is, in the case of the principal offender, included in any foregoing portion of this schedule, and for which the fugitive criminal, though not the principal, is liable to be tried or punished as if he were the principal.

In Ontario, Quebec and Manitoba the Speedy Trials Act provides for trials without jury (and in some cases without consent) for any crimes within the jurisdiction of a court of general sessions of the peace.

The Summary Trials Act empowers certain magistrates named therein to try offenders in certain felonies and misdemeanors therein specified, by consent, without the intervention of a jury.

JUSTICES OF THE PEACE.

One of the prerogatives of the crown is, that the King or Queen is the fountain of justice. In view of this the Sovereign has charge of the peace of the realm ; and in order that peace should prevail, certain magistrates, called justices of the peace, are appointed by commission from the Queen, and the Lieutenant-Governors in council of the provinces have power to appoint such justices.

Certain other persons, from the nature of the offices they hold, are qualified by provincial statutes to discharge the duties of justices of the peace, such as mayors of cities and towns, aldermen who have qualified themselves for that purpose, and the reeves and deputy-reeves of township and village corporations. The judges of the supreme and exchequer courts of Canada, and the justices of the court of appeal and of the courts of Queen's bench and common pleas and of the court of chancery for Ontario, are sometimes said to be justices for the whole of this province; but it is usual to include them and the county court judge within his county in commissions appointing justices of the peace. The judges of the county courts are also justices of the peace; and it would appear that the members of the executive council for this province, the attorney-general for the Dominion and the provinces, and in certain cases Queen's counsel, are also justices of the peace by virtue of their office or position.

Where justices of the peace are appointed by commission by the Lieutenant-Governor they must have, besides the mental qualifications necessary for the importance of the office, some interest in land to the value of at least $1,200. (e) Unless where specially provided for, no attorney or solicitor, while practising as such, shall be a justice of the peace; and no sheriff or coroner, acting as such, shall be qualified for this position. Every justice of the peace must take a prescribed oath before fulfilling any of the duties of his office. The authority under which they act is called their commission, and was settled by all the judges in England over five hundred years ago; so that the office is a very ancient as well as a very honourable one.

Each ordinary justice of the peace has a certain district or territory within which his jurisdiction lies; beyond that

(e) This seems to apply only to Ontario.

he has no power. The duties of a justice of the peace are
of two kinds: 1st, judicial duties; and 2nd, ministerial
duties. When any person prefers a charge against another
before a justice of the peace, the latter may issue a summons or a warrant to apprehend the offender; the summons being a command to the offender on a certain day,
and is for trifling matters or disputes—the warrant being
for all serious offences, and is the constable's authority for
arresting and keeping the accused in his charge till brought
before the justice of the peace. If the summons be dis-
obeyed, the justice may issue a warrant to apprehend the
offender.

The justice may require in all cases that the person preferring a charge against another should make his statement
on oath. In the cases of perjury, etc., where a bond
conditioned on the prosecution and giving evidence is
necessary before a bill of indictment should be presented
to, or found by, a grand jury, as mentioned in this
chapter, a prosecutor desiring to prefer an indictment
representing any of these offences before one or more justices of the peace having jurisdiction in the matter, and who
may refuse to commit or bail the person accused, must
give his bond or recognizance to the justice or justices that
he will prosecute the charge or complaint; and thereupon
the justice or justices must transmit the recognizance,
information and depositions, if any, to the proper officer in
the same way as if the accused had been committed.

When a felony or misdemeanor has been committed the
charge in the affidavit is called an information, and a warrant issued. On the accused appearing before the justice,
witnesses are examined and the proceedings conducted with
the regularity of a court.

In serious cases where an indictment would lie against
the accused, the statement of the accused is taken down,

read over to him, and signed by him in the presence of the justice, and also signed by the justice himself. When all the evidence is taken, and the case argued by counsel, when such is necessary or permitted, the justice decides on the case.

If it is an offence for which the law has given the justice express power by statute to impose a fine or imprison the accused, and that there is sufficient evidence to warrant fine or imprisonment, then the justice summarily convicts the accused. This is called a summary conviction and is regulated by Act of parliament.

In these cases, if the evidence be insufficient to warrant a summary conviction, or if the justice had no authority to convict, or if for other good reasons the conviction be bad, the superior courts of law, on application being made by the accused, will quash the conviction on a *certiorari*. An appeal from a summary conviction lies to certain courts in the provinces under procedure defined by the Dominion parliament.

At the hearing of any appeal under the Act relating to summary convictions, any of the parties to the appeal may call witnesses and adduce evidence, who or which may not have been called or adduced at the original hearing.

No action will lie against a justice of the peace acting within his jurisdiction in the discharge of his duty unless he acted maliciously and without reasonable or probable cause; and no action can be brought against a justice of the peace except within six months after judgment. In all such cases of summary conviction a justice of the peace acts judicially.

But a justice of the peace has ministerial duties to perform as well as judicial ones. After hearing all the evidence in a case before him there may be sufficient to justify him in finding the accused guilty of some crime over which the justice has no power or authority to convict summarily. It may be for a crime of a serious nature, such as murder, manslaughter, or some indictable offence and over these a justice of the peace has no power. There are certain offences in which, if the accused consents, a justice of the peace or police magistrate may try the case and sentence the accused to such punishment as may be determined by the statutes in that behalf. But without such consent punishment would not be inflicted. The accused is not deprived of the benefit of a jury of his countrymen as to whether or not he is guilty of the crime charged against him.

An indictment, it will be remembered, is the test of a crime, and the evidence must be considered by a grand jury to be sufficient to put the accused on his trial. As the law at present stands the judgment of two justices of the peace is supplanted by that of a grand jury, on the sufficiency of the evidence to support an indictment. On the duties of the justice on an indictable offence being brought under his notice, they are so far judicial that in a proper case he can admit the accused to bail till the next sittings of the court. No justices shall admit to bail any one charged with treason or a capital offence ; but any two justices may bail parties charged with other felonies. Where the offence is not bailable by him his duties are purely ministerial. If the evidence supports the charge the accused must be committed to goal. The depositions and prisoner's statement are sent to the county attorney, and the case tried either at the county judges criminal court, the court of general sessions, or the court of oyer and terminer and general gaol delivery. In the two latter courts the accused has a jury to find whether the evidence points to his guilt ; in the county judge's criminal court the accused can elect to be tried without a jury. This only refers to offences for which the accused can be tried at the general sessions.

So far as summary convictions are concerned the magistrate's decision is final, unless set aside on appeal on application to quash the same. But all committals, after being disposed of by him, are tried in the courts as already mentioned. If the justice refuses to bail the person an application, even in the cases of murder, can be made to the superior courts of law; and if a proper case be made to the satisfaction of the judge, bail can be put in for his appearance.

In cases of felony one justice cannot dispose of the case, it requires two at least; but a police magistrate, county judge, or stipendiary magistrate may of himself do whatever is authorized by our criminal law to be done by two or more justices of the peace. Justices of the peace are aided and attended by constables, whose duties are to execute the commands of the justices. They may commit an offender and convey him to prison if the offence was done in their presence, but have no authority to arrest a man for an affray done out of their presence. Each justice appoints his own constables; and when necessary any two' or more justices can appoint special constables upon the oath of a credible witness that any tumult, riot or felony has taken place, or is continuing, or is to be expected to take place. A county constable is appointed by the county judge, or by the court of general sessions, and the Lieutenant-Governor may appoint one for the whole province.

In cities and towns with a population of over 5,000 inhabitants, instead of justices of the peace, a police magistrate is appointed, who has generally the same powers as two or more justices would have, and may entertain cases requiring more than one justice of the peace. The police force in the city or town attend and execute his commands, much the same as constables do those of justices of the peace. Such police magistrate holds office during pleasure; and by virtue of his appointment as such, is a justice of the peace for the city or town where he is appointed. Every other justice of the peace within the city or town where a police magistrate has been appointed ceases to have any powers to admit to bail or discharge any person, or act in any way within the judicial limits of the city or town, except at the request of the police magistrate, or during his illness or absence.

Every other justice of the peace, however, is liable to act as one of the justices of the courts of general sessions. A police magistrate so appointed, besides having the powers of two or more justices of the peace as to matters within the legislative control of this province, has jurisdiction over all prosecutions for offences against the city or town by- laws, and penalties as to refusing to accept offices therein, or to make the necessary declarations of qualification and office.

CORONERS.

Coroners are also conservators of the peace, and are said to be the only officers known to the English law charged with the investigation of crime. They are called coroners from *corona*, the Latin word for crown, because formerly they attended to the pleas of the crown. Their duties at present are mostly defined by statute law; and with the exception of acting in times in place of the sheriff of their county, are limited to inquisitions on deceased persons and as to the origin of fires.

Coroners are appointed by the Lieutenant-Governor under the great seal; one or more coroners for each county, city, town or district in the province; and hold office for life, unless they are removed for improper conduct or resign their commission. It may be besides those appointed in this way that the chief justices of the court of Queen's bench and common pleas are coroners for the whole province, in analogy of the English doctrine, that the lord chief justice of the Queen's bench is the supreme coroner in the land.

The office of coroner, like that of sheriff, is very ancient and honourable. The peace of the county in England was entrusted to these two officers when the earls gave up the wardship of the county. It thus happened that the coroner often fulfilled the duties of the sheriff; and such is the practice to this day; so that whenever the sheriff has an interest in the suit, or makes default in serving process, the writs are directed to the coroner.

This is part of the ministerial functions of coroners; and besides acting as sheriff's substitute, they can arrest persons committing an affray in their presence; and they possibly possess other magisterial powers.

But the judicial functions of a coroner are what must be considered as properly coming under criminal law. Whenever it has been made to appear to a coroner that there is reason to believe that a deceased person came to his death through violence or unfair means, or by culpable or negligent conduct of himself or others, under such circumstances as require investigation, and not through mere accident or mischance, he is to direct an inquest to be held on the body of such deceased person.

On the death of any person in any gaol, prison, house of correction, lock-up house, or house of industry, no matter from what cause, an inquest is to be held, as the crown desires to see that the inmates of these places are properly taken care of and do not die of want, or from improper treatment from the custodians or otherwise. In furtherance of this, notice must be given immediately to the coroner of the death of the prisoner.

In all cases the inquest is held upon view of the body ; and the investigation extends to the cause of the death of the person, and to an inquiry of those accessories who it appeared were absent at the time the offence, if chargeable against any one, was committed, but who procured, counselled, commanded or abetted it. In other words, it extends to principals in the crime and accessories before the fact.

To aid him in this investigation the coroner issues a warrant to summon a jury at a certain time, not being a Sunday, and at a place named in the warrant. A constable summons the jury, at least twelve in number ; and it appears that no one is exempt from serving thereon, and may be fined for non-attendance.

Witnesses can be summoned at the same time, and are examined after the coroner's court is opened and the jury sworn. The accused can have his witnesses in his own favour ; and after all the evidence is heard the coroner sums it up to the jury, explains to them what the law is on the subject, and directs them to consider of their verdict—they are judges of what the facts are. A unanimous verdict of twelve is required ; and if it is a case to come up at the assizes the witnesses may be bound to appear at the trial to give evidence, and the prosecutor to appear and prosecute.

A written statement of the finding of a jury or their verdict is called an inquisition ; and when it contains the subject matter of accusation it need not come before a grand jury at the assizes, as the information of a magistrate or of justices of the peace must. The principle in English law, that no man is to be deprived of his life unless on the unanimous verdict of twenty-four, is still regarded, the only difference being that the grand jury in this case is superseded by a coroner's jury. The party accused, if the crime charged be murder, or an accessory to murder before the fact, or manslaughter, is to be apprehended and committed to jail, but may apply to a judge of one of the superior courts for bail, if so advised.

The inquisition itself may be quashed if taken before an unauthorized person, or if the coroner or jury misconducted themselves, or for other good causes; but any technical defect or omission, of any matter unnecessary to be proved will not vitiate any inquisition. Every coroner, immediately after inquisition found by him, shall return the same, and all papers in reference thereto and to the attendance of witnesses, to the county crown attorney.

Coroners also enquire into the origin of fires, where there is reason to believe the fire was the result of culpable or negligent conduct or design, or occurred under such circumstances as require investigation. The coroner can in his discretion empannel a jury or not, unless he is required to do so in the written inquisition of an insurance agent, or of any three householders living near the fire. The inquest is conducted the same as any ordinary inquest on the body of a deceased person; but the return is made to the clerk of the peace instead of the county crown attorney. With the exception, however, of the county of York, the clerk of the peace is the same person as the county crown attorney in Ontario.

Each coroner, before the first day of January in each year, makes a return to the provincial treasurer of the list of inquests taken before him. The informations of justices of the peace and the inquisitions of coroners, as was seen, are both returned to the same officer, the crown attorney for the county. He is therefore the next officer immediately concerned in the administration of criminal justice.

The Lieutenant-Governor appoints a crown attorney for each county in the province, who holds office during pleasure. In Ontario he must be a resident in the county and a barrister of at least three years standing. He is incapacitated, either directly or indirectly, to act as counsel for any prisoner charged with treason, felony or other offence punishable under the criminal law in force. His duties are laid down by statute, and refer almost, if not altogether, to criminal matters. It is his duty to receive and examine informations, examinations, and inquisitions, and all papers connected with criminal charges which the justices of the peace and the coroners of his county are required to transmit to him.

He secures the attendance of witnesses; institutes and conducts on the part of the Crown all the criminal business at the court of general sessions and the county judge's criminal court. He advises justices of the peace upon being asked to do so; and has certain duties as to the public revenue, public health, or any matter punishable by a justice of the peace. In criminal cases at the assizes, such as for felonies and treasons, he is required to be present and assist the crown counsel; and in his absence to take charge of the criminal business of the court. (*f*)

(*f*) The greater portion of this chapter applies more particularly to Ontario. It was not intended by the writer to give undue prominence to any province, but it was hoped that an outline of the legislation of any one might be useful to all.

CHAPTER XX.

THE PEOPLE—SUBJECTS, ALIENS, DENIZENS.

Who is a subject—Who an alien—Residents, domicile capacity of alien, subjects by birth, by naturalization, oath of residence, of allegiance—Denizens—Titles under confederation, governors, privy councillors, senators, speakers, provincial councillors—Rank of the foregoing, judges, bishops, army and nary officers, retired judges.

WE have hitherto considered the rulers, or governing powers of the people of the Dominion of Canada; we will now devote a small space to the ruled or governed—the people—whether subjects or aliens.

A subject is defined to be one who is under the protection of, and owes allegiance to, the sovereign or ruling power in the state. By British subjects are meant such as are born within the dominions of the Crown of England, or under the allegiance of the Queen. There are many persons residing within the dominions of the Crown who are not subjects of Her Majesty; and on the other hand there are many residing in foreign countries who are British subjects. All residents who are not subjects, and all non-residents not British subjects, are aliens. Of the former class may be mentioned all those who belong to other countries, and who have not renounced their allegiance thereto, or rather who have not taken the oath of allegiance and become naturalized here. Foreign consuls and other representatives of foreign nations, though resident here, are not British subjects. Nor are those such who are simply domiciled here as travellers or agents. In the same way our consuls and representatives abroad are yet British subjects, though non-residents ; and so are all British-born subjects who, living abroad, have not renounced their British nationality. Children born out of the dominions of the crown, whose father and mother were at the time of their birth in allegiance with the Queen, are subjects ; and the children of all natural-born subjects, no matter where born, are also subjects of her Majesty. In other words, the second generation of children from British parents are subjects ; but it is doubtful if this extends to the third generation. If the grand-father by the father's side was a British subject, the grand-children would be British subjects also, according to Blackstone. Out of ten of the most eminent lawyers in England, five were of opinion in a case since Blackstone's time against the right of one whose grand-father had been born out of the British dominions to inherit land in England ; and the other five were of a contrary opinion.

In Canada real and personal property of any description may be taken, acquired, held and disposed of by an alien in the same manner, in all respects as by a natural British subject ; and a title to real and personal property of any description may be derived through, from, or in succession to an alien, in the same manner in all respects, as through, from, or in succession to a natural-born British subject. (a)

An alien has only such rights as are expressly given to him, and unless naturalized he cannot hold an office or exercise any municipal, parliamentary or other franchise. Aliens in Ontario enjoy all the privileges in regard to Acts relating to building societies and joint stock companies for supplying cities, towns and villages with gas and water.

(a) R. S. C. cap. 113, sec. 3.

But an alien cannot serve as a juryman in a court, nor is he entitled to be the owner of a British ship.

Every child born within the dominions of the crown is a British subject for all purposes, and while resident therein cannot by any act of his divest himself of such a character. But a British-born subject, if a subject of another state at the time of his birth (as may be the case with ambassadors' children), can cease to be a British subject by making certain declarations prescribed by the Imperial Statutes of 1870 and 1872 in reference to these matters. Any subject, if under no disability, may voluntarily become naturalized in a foreign state, and thus cease to be a British subject. This is expatriation.

An alien may become a British subject by naturalization and in other ways.

Every alien-born woman becomes naturalized by marrying a British natural-born or naturalized subject.

Every other alien who comes to reside in the Dominion of Canada with intent to settle therein, and remains for three years, can, by taking the oaths of residence and allegiance, become a naturalized citizen. (b)

The following are the oaths of residence and allegiance :

OATH OF RESIDENCE.

" I, A. B., do swear (or, being person allowed by law to affirm in judicial cases, do affirm) that in the period of—— years preceding this date, I have resided three (or five as the case may be) years in the Dominion of Canada with intent to settle therein, without having been during such three years (or five years as the case may be) a stated resident in any foreign country. So help me God."

(b) See Naturalization Act, R. S. C. cap. 113.

OATH OF ALLEGIANCE.

" I. A. B., do sincerely promise and swear (*or, being a person allowed by law do affirm in judicial cases*, do affirm) that I will be faithful and bear true allegiance to Her Majesty Queen Victoria, (or reigning sovereign for the time being) as lawful Sovereign of the United Kingdom of Great Britain and Ireland, and of the Dominion of Canada, dependent on and belonging to the said Kingdom, and that I will defend her to the utmost of my power against all traitorous conspiracies or attempts whatever which shall be made against Her Person, Crown and Dignity; and that I will do my utmost endeavour to disclose and make known to Her Majesty, Her Heirs or Successors, all treasons or traitorous conspiracies and attempts which I shall know to be against Her or any of them ; and all this I do swear (or affirm) without any equivocation, mental evasion, or secret reservation. So help me God."

The oaths can be administered by a judge or justice of the peace; and a certificate is granted and filed in court, after which, if no objection is sustained as to its validity the alien becomes a British subject as much as if he or she was born in Canada, subject to some exceptions in the English Act relating to naturalization. (*c*) Every alien who had a settled place of abode in either of the provinces of Ontario, Quebec, Nova Scotia or New Brunswick before the 1st of July, 1867, and who is still a resident of the same, is deemed to be a British subject for all purposes, provided in the case of males, he takes the prescribed oath of residence. Any person who, being within the Dominion prior to the 1st of January, 1868, took the necessary oaths of allegiance and residence also became naturalized.

There seems to be no difference between the rights and privileges of a natural-born subject and a naturalized subject. In England at one time the latter could not be

(*c*) 33 Vic. cap. 14, Imp. Act.

a privy councillor or member of parliament, or hold any of
the great offices of state ; but he is now entitled to all political and other rights, powers and privileges, and is subject
to all obligations to which a natural-born British subject
is entitled or subject.   In case a naturalized British subject
returns to his own country, he loses the character of British subject unless he renounces his original nationality in
pursuance of the laws of the state, or in pursuance of a
treaty to that effect.

The certificate of naturalization granted in the United
Kingdom confers no rights or privileges upon an alien in
Canada. (d)

Besides subjects and aliens there is a third class called
denizens, who, by means of letters patent from the crown,
enjoy certain rights of citizenship as long as they remain
within the Dominion.   It is a sort of middle state between
subject and alien.   In England a denizen cannot hold any
high office of state, and can neither inherit nor devise land,
and only take by purchase.   In Canada, whatever significance the term may have, a denizen must at least have
equal powers and rights as to real estate with an alien ;
and he has, no doubt, the additional rights of voting and
holding such offices as his patent allows him.   The exist-
tence of such persons is contemplated at all events, as
there is mention made of denizens in some of the statutes.

The consideration as to whether any person is a subject
or not becomes material in relation to certain offences
against the crown.   None but a subject can be found guilty
of treason ; or rather what is treason in a subject may be
no more than a felony in a foreigner.   The general law as
to what offences are to be adjudged treason, as laid down
in the 25th year of King Edward III., is the law on the

(d) Earl Carnarvon's Circular Despatch to the Colonies, Sept., 1874.

question here ; and is set out in an Act relating to the security of the crown, 31 Vic., cap. 69 (1868) D.

The regulations as to titles and procedure in Canada are inserted here, and may be found useful for reference :

TITLES UNDER CONFEDERATION.

1. The Governor-General of Canada to be styled "His Excellency."

2. The Lieutenant-Governors of the provinces to be styled "His Honour."

3. The privy councillors of Canada to be styled "Honourable," and for life.

4. Senators of Canada to be "Honourable," but only during office, and the title not to be continued afterwards.

5. Executive councillors of the province to be styled "Honourable," but only while in office, and the title not to be continued afterwards.

6. Legislative councillors in the provinces not in future to have that title ; but gentlemen who were legislative councillors at the time of the union, to retain their title of "Honourable" for life.

7. The president of the legislative council in the provinces to be styled "Honourable" during office.

8. The speakers of the house of assembly in the provinces to be styled "Honourable" during office.

TABLE OF PRECEDENCE WITHIN THE DOMINION OF CANADA. (e)

1. The Governor-General, or officer administering the Government.

2. Senior officer commanding Her Majesty's troops within the Dominion, if of the rank of general; and officer commanding Her Majesty's naval forces on the British North American Station, if of the rank of an admiral. Their own relative rank to be determined by the Queen's regulations on this subject.

3. The Lieutenant-Governor of Ontario.

4.   "   "   Quebec.

5.   "   "   Nova Scotia. .

6.   "   "   New Brunswick.

7. Archbishops and bishops according to seniority.

8. Members of the cabinet according to seniority.

9. The speaker of the senate.

10. The chief justice of the Supreme Court of Canada.

11. The chief judges of the courts of law and equity, according to seniority.

12. Members of the privy council, not of the cabinet.

13. General officers of Her Majesty's army serving in the Dominion, and officers of the rank of admiral in the royal navy, serving on the British North American Station, not being in the chief command; the relative rank of such officers to be determined by Her Majesty's regulations.

(e) See Orders in Council, 43 Vic. (D) xxii.

14. The officers commanding Her Majesty's troops in the Dominion, if of the rank of colonel or inferior rank, and the officer commanding Her Majesty's naval forces on the British North American Station, if of equivalent rank; their relative rank to be ascertained by the Queen's regulations.

15. Members of the senate.

16. Speaker of the house of commons.

17. Puisne judges of the Supreme Court of Canada according to seniority.

18. Puisne judges of courts of law and equity according to seniority.

19. Members of the house of commons.

20. Members of the executive council (provincial) within their province.

21. Speaker of the legislative council within his province.

22. Members of the legislative council within their province.

23. Speaker of the legislative assembly within his province.

24. Members of the legislative assembly within their province.

Retired judges of whatever court take precedence next after the present judges of their respective courts.

The regulations respecting the precedence of naval officers, the subject of salutes, or of the precedence to be given to lieutenant-governors within their provinces or at the seat of government, accompany the orders in council to be found in the Dominion statutes of 1880. (*f*)

(*f*) The different orders of *nobility* in England—dukes, marquises, earls, viscounts, and barons—have been referred to in the Chapter on the Senate (page 45). There are also several degrees of the *commonalty*. The first name in dignity after the nobility is—

(1) Knight of the order of *St. George* or of the *Garter*,—instituted by Edward III.

(2) Knight *Banneret*, a military distinction.

(3) Baronets.—A title of inheritance created by letters patent and descendible usually to male issue.

(4) Knights *of the Bath*—an order instituted by Henry IV. and revived by George I. and so called from the ceremony of bathing the night before their creation.

(5) Knights *Bachelors*—the most ancient, though the lowest order of knighthood.

These are all the names of dignity in the United Kingdom—*Esquires* and *gentlemen* as Sir Edward Coke says being only names of worship. Any one having an office under the Crown is legally an esquire, just as gentleman is "given to those who study the laws of the realm, who study in the universities, who profess the liberal sciences, and in short, who can live idly and without manual labour, and will bear the port charge and countenance of a gentleman." A yeoman was one that had free land of forty shillings by the year, and was qualified to serve on juries and to vote for knights of the shire. *Tradesmen, artificers*, and *labourers*, formed the rest of the commonalty.

CHAPTER XXI.

THE PEOPLE, THEIR RIGHTS.

*Representation, franchise, suffrage, basis of representation—
Qualifications in the Dominion and the provinces—
Ontario—Public meetings, how called, riot act—Petitions,
when necessary, how prepared, how presented—The
press, libel, civil and criminal, Ontario Act, retractation
—Commissions of enquiry—Local government, municipalities, townships, counties, villages, towns, cities,
bye-laws, control of the courts — Religious freedom,
equality of all denominations, no established church, the
Church of England, the Roman Catholic Church, public
worship protected, statutes, Christianity part of the law
of the land.*

REPRESENTATION.

The privilege of taking part in the government of one's
country by being represented in parliament, or represented
in the legislatures or municipalities which make our laws,
is one of the most valued rights of a free people. The right
of the citizens to have a voice in every matter that affects
their liberties is called their franchise. But to have a voice
or vote in such matters is not accorded to every body.
Certain qualifications are necessary, and these qualifications
differ both in the provinces and in the Dominion.

Where every citizen is entitled to vote it is called universal suffrage—voting being the right of suffrage. (a)

The system of representation which prevails in Canada, from the highest delegate of the people in the commons down through the provincial and municipal elections, is based on divisions of the population ; though territory or certain areas of land are so connected with this that the latter are represented as well. While it is true that every acre of land is represented, the manner of its being so represented is arrived at with regard to the number of people. Numbers of people possessing no land qualification are represented by virtue of the income tax, or as in Ontario, under the Farmers' Sons Act. While it is strictly true that our system of representation regards both population and territory, the real basis is the population. The territory is an accident of the voters, and in itself is not entitled to representation. The third way, or representation by class representation, though much discussed in other countries cannot be said to enter into the idea of the Canadian or English system.

The 215 members in the house of commons represent the provinces and territories comprising the Dominion of Canada. Each province and the territories are divided up into constituencies or ridings having regard to the population and areas therein. Originally the *number* of divisions into which the provinces were divided up for electing members to their legislatures was the same as for the Dominion elections; though the *areas* of these divisions were generally different. The qualifications of voters were the same in the provincial and Dominion elections up to a few years ago, so that anyone entitled to vote for a member of

(a) In the 41st section of the B. N. A. Act every male subject aged 21 years or upwards, being a householder in Algoma was until the parliament otherwise provided, entitled to vote for a member of the commons.

his provincial legislature could vote for a member of the house of commons in that province. The parliament of Canada by recent legislation created new electoral divisions for members of the commons and assigned the necessary qualifications of voters. These have already been referred to. (b) The representation and areas are now generally different in the provinces from those of the Dominion.

It would be beside the scope of this little work to attempt any exact epitome of the qualifications necessary for voters in the different provinces, and what offices and positions disqualify persons from voting. The law in Ontario may be given and it will not be found very different from what obtains in the other provinces.

In this province the persons not admitted to vote are : 1. All judges of any of our courts, and all clerks of the peace, county attorneys, registrars, sheriffs, deputy sheriffs, and deputy clerks of the crown. 2. All agents for the sale of crown lands. 3. All officers of the customs of the Dominion, and all officers employed in the collection of any duties payable to Her Majesty in the nature of duties of excise; and 4. All postmasters in towns or cities. Any of these persons voting shall forfeit $2,000, and his vote is null and void. 5. No returning officer, election clerk, or paid election agent, shall be entitled to vote; but this does not apply to the deputy returning officers or poll clerks, who are paid under the provisions of Art. 6. Lastly, no woman can vote at any parliamentary election.

Subject to these exceptions every person being of the full age of 21 years and a subject of Her Majesty by birth or naturalization, if duly entered in the list of voters to be used at the pending election, and if not otherwise by law

(b) See chapter V. in the House of Commons.

prevented from voting, is entitled to vote for members for the legislative assembly of Ontario.

1. In order to entitle a person to be entered on the voters' lists, he must be interested in *real property* as owner, tenant, or occupant, to the extent of $200 in cities and towns and $100 in incorporated villages or townships. If he ceases to have such interest he may still have a vote, provided his name is entered in the revised assessment roll, and that he is a resident of the electoral district.

In regard to the value of the property if vested in joint owners, if there is sufficient when divided to give each a vote, each has one ; if not, none of the owners has a vote. And so if three persons in a city are jointly assessed for $600, each has a vote ; if assessed for $500, none of them can vote.

2. Persons who have resided continuously in the local municipality since the completion of its last revised assessment roll and who, being assessed on an *income* of $250 at least, have paid their last year's taxes, are entitled to vote.

3. *Farmers' sons* resident on their father's or mother's farm for twelve months prior to the return of the assessment roll, and who are rated for an amount sufficient to qualify them, can vote. Where there are a number of sons the provisions as to one or more voting are somewhat similar to those affecting joint owners of real estate, except that the division of the property enures to qualifying as many of the parties in the order of their age as the value of the property or the number of the sons will permit of.

4. All *Indians*, or persons part Indian, if duly enfranchised and possessing the same qualifications as other persons in their electoral districts, are entitled to vote.

5. In Algoma, Parry Sound, and some other exceptional

places, every male person being twenty-one years of age, a
naturalized subject and not otherwise disqualified, and who,
at the time of the election, is the owner of real estate where
he tenders his vote, to the value of $200 or who is and has
been for the preceding six months a resident householder,
is entitled to vote.

PUBLIC MEETINGS.

Public opinion is frequently expressed through the med-
ium of public meetings, which, so long as they remain
orderly, are privileged to discuss almost any subject. It is
the undoubted right of subjects to meet together in a
peaceable and orderly manner for the consideration and
discussion of matters of public interest, or for making
known their views to Her Majesty or her representative in
the Dominion or in the provinces, either in approbation or
condemnation of public matters.

Public meetings, in order to be entitled to the recognition of the law, must be called by certain persons and in
a particular way.

In any city or town, on the requisition of any twelve
citizens entitled to vote for members of the local legislature,
a meeting may be called by the sheriff or by the mayor or
other chief municipal officer, which is a public meeting
under the Act and entitled to the protection accorded to
such meeting. The requisitionists must have a property
qualification in the town or city in which the meeting is to
be called, and their property must be within the particular
district, ward, or parish, within which the meeting is to be
held. Two resident justices of the peace appear also to
have the power to call public meetings. The notice or
summons calling together a public meeting must issue three
days before the meeting ; must set forth the names of the

requisitionists, or at least 12 of them ; must state that the meeting is called in conformity with the provisions of the Act ; and that the meeting and all persons attending the same are to take notice of that fact, and govern themselves accordingly.

Whoever calls such meeting, at least in Ontario, must remain ; and whether presiding over it or not, help to preserve the peace thereat. Special constables may be appointed, and the military force, if necessary, brought to his assistance. Should a meeting of 12 or more persons become disorderly, the mayor, sheriff, magistrate, justice of the peace, or other officer may read the proclamation set out in what is commonly called the Riot Act ; and if, after the lapse of an hour, the persons do not disperse, he may forcibly break up the meeting, using the civil and military assistance as has been mentioned. The original of our Act relating to riots and riotous assemblies was passed in England in the reign of King George I. The Canadian Act is 31 Victoria cap. 70 (1868), and the proclamation to be read before using any violent measures is as follows :

" Our Sovereign Lady the Queen chargeth and commandeth all persons being assembled immediately to disperse themselves, and peaceably to depart to their habitations or to their lawful business, upon the pains contained in the Act respecting the riots and riotous assemblies. God save the Queen."

Such persons not obeying the command to disperse are guilty of felony and liable to be imprisoned in the penetentiary for life, or for any term not less than two years, or liable to be otherwise imprisoned for any term less than two years.

Powers are given to justices of the peace, sheriffs, mayors and others, to apprehend the offenders who do not disperse within one hour after the proclamation is read; and persons engaged in suppressing the riot are justified even if the death of the rioter ensue from his resistance. Any persons opposing with force and arms any peace officer or others engaged in suppressing a riot, or any persons preventing the making of the proclamation, are guilty of felony and liable to the same punishment as the rioters themselves.

The revised statutes of Canada, cap. 152, contain the authority for preserving the peace at public meetings.

PETITIONS.

Petitioning is another mode of expressing public opinion, and by it persons or classes may be heard in parliament or elsewhere when they conceive that their views are not fully set out by their representatives. It is about the only way of being heard that is left to those who are not voters. If no channel were left to the people, except through their representatives, it might well happen that the minority would never be heard except in the disorders of riot or revolution. A class may be interfered with or the legislation may be too slow or too far in advance of the interests of the people. In these and many other instances petitioning is resorted to.

Every person, whether an elector or not, may petition parliament or the local legislature; but the petition must be presented by a member of the house, who is responsible for its containing no impertinent or improper matter.

Petitions must be fairly written or printed; and in the senate three of the petitioners names must appear on the sheet containing the petition. Petitions from corporations must be duly authenticated by their corporate seal. Petitions signed by persons representing public meetings are received as from the persons whose names are affixed to the petition.

A member presenting a petition in the commons must endorse his name thereon, and confine his remarks to a statement of the parties from whom the petition comes, the number of signatures attached, and the material allegations it contains.   Petitions are laid on the table by direction of the speaker without debate in reference thereto ; but if required, the clerk may read them, and if they complain of any personal grievance requiring an immediate remedy the matter may be at once discussed.   There does not appear to be any Canadian legislation as to petitions to parliament ; but the fact that those presenting them are responsible for their propriety sufficiently insures their being consistent with the dignity of parliament.   It is probable that the English Act for the prevention of tumultuous petitioning to parliament is in force in Canada.

THE PRESS.

The press is perhaps the greatest means of expressing public opinion.   In Canada its liberty is not restrained by any state censorship, and any person feeling that he has been wronged in the public press may apply to the courts for damages in a civil action, or proceed to have the offending party arrested and tried for a misdemeanor.

Libel as a *crime* is governed by a uniform law in the Dominion, and is punishable by fine or imprisonment or both.

Any person publishing, or threatening to publish, any libel upon any other, or directly or indirectly threatening to print or publish, or abstain from so doing, or offering to prevent the same with intent to extort any money or security for money, or any valuable thing, or with intent to induce any person to confer upon or procure for any person any appointment or office of profit or trust, is guilty of a misdemeanor, and liable to a fine not exceeding $600, or to imprisonment with hard labour for any period less than two years, or liable to both, as the court may award.

Whoever maliciously publishes any defamatory libel, knowing it to be false, may be fined any sum less than $400, or imprisoned, as in the other cases, or both. Other defamatory libels are punished by imprisonment of one year or less, with a fine not exceeding $200. The truth of any libelous matter is no defence, unless it was for the public benefit that it should be published. (c)

Libel as a *civil* action is not uniformly defined, but is left to be determined by the provincial legislatures. The punishment then is the amount of damage supposed to be suffered by the aggrieved party, which amount is found by a jury. In the criminal actions the jury simply finds whether or not the accused is guilty of the charge preferred against him : in the civil action the jury finds generally if there was a libel; and if so, what damage was sustained by the plaintiff. (d)

COMMISSIONS OF ENQUIRY.

Besides matters which are brought into public notice by means of the press, of public meetings, and of petitions, the Governor in council has the right to institute commissions of enquiry into public matters concerning any matter connected with the good government of Canada, or the conduct of any part of the public business. The com-

(c) See R. S. C. cap. 163 as to libel as a crime.

(d) The legislature of Ontario passed an Act last session (50 Vict. cap. 9) as to the law of libel. By it no action lies until the plaintiff gives the defendant notice in writing of the statements complained of, so as to allow him to publish a retractation in the next regular issue of his paper or within three days from the notice.

missioners appointed in this way may have conferred on them the power of summoning before them any party or witness, and requiring them to give evidence on oath or in writing, and to produce all documents and things requisite for the full investigation of the matters into which they are appointed to examine. These commissioners may also have the same power given them as is vested in any court of law in civil cases to compel the attendance of witnesses. (e)

Similar powers are given to the Lieutenant-Governor of Ontario and of some other provinces as to commissions of enquiry.

LOCAL ADMINISTRATIVE GOVERNMENT.

The provinces are generally divided into municipal corporations having large powers of directing their own domestic concerns. While the legislature controls the corporations, these latter have ascertained rights in the exercise of which, within legitimate limits, they are free to manage their own local affairs.

The division of the Canadas into townships and counties dates back a long period. Alterations were frequently made in counties for electoral or judicial purposes; but as to municipal corporations embracing a certain area, few changes appear to have been made in those counties definitely bounded in the first Crown survey. New townships are frequently laid out in unsettled districts, and occasionally alterations made. In Ontario certain limits are prescribed for villages desiring incorporation, and the population must be at least 750 persons. In the same way towns must have 2,000 and cities 15,000 inhabitants. These do not become incorporated by the fact of having so

(e) R. S. C. cap. 114.

many inhabitants. A charter of incorporation is granted them by the Lieutenant-Governor creating them cities, towns, or villages, as the case may be. Until incorporated they belong to the county or township.

The local affairs of these different corporations are managed by a council, which is the municipal legislature; and the limits of its enactments or by-laws are prescribed by the Acts of the local legislature relating to municipal corporations. Their by-laws are very comprehensive, and in Ontario include the obtaining of such real and personal property for the use of the corporation as it may require : the appointment of necessary officers, giving aid to agricultural or other kindred societies or incorporated mechanics' institutes, aiding manufacturing establishments, road companies, and also charities and indigent persons, taking the census of the municipality, regulating the driving on roads and bridges, the egress from public buildings, and very extensive powers as to drainage. They can also impose fines up to $50 for neglect of duty or breach of these by-laws, and may distrain and sell the goods of the offender and if necessary inflict reasonable punishment by imprisonment not exceeding 21 days.

The powers of each of the different municipal corporations of cities, counties, towns and townships are very minutely set out in the Acts relating to municipal institutions. The different municipal corporations are composed of aldermen or councillors or reeves and their deputies, with a presiding officer who is the mayor, warden or reeve as the case may be. These bodies form the local administration of their municipalities, are elected for one year at a time, and must have certain property qualifications. They have certain specified powers, a regular system of procedure, and in some cases an executive. They are restrained by the superior courts when their by-laws are in excess of their powers, and these courts compel them to exercise their powers in proper cases if they refuse to do so. The provincial legislatures grant them their powers, but commit the proper execution of them to the controlling care of the courts.

It is an admitted principle of colonial legislation that all religious denominations are on a legal equality. This is declared by statute to be a fundamental principle of the civil policy of Ontario. In the language of the Act "the free exercise and enjoyment of religious profession and worship, without discrimination or preference, provided the same be not made an excuse for acts of licentiousness or a justification of practices inconsistent with the peace and safety of the province, is by the constitution and laws of this province allowed to all Her Majesty's subjects within the same." No rectories of the Church of England can be hereafter created out of the clergy reserve or the public domain; and "no tithes can be claimed, demanded or received by any rector, vicar or other ecclesiastical person of the protestant church within Ontario." There seem to be some provisions respecting these matters in the statutes in Nova Scotia.

There is no church established by law in Canada or in any of the provinces of Canada and there is no connection between the church and the state here as there is in England. The Church of England in the colonies is simply a voluntary association, and on the same footing with other religious bodies. (*f*) The Roman Catholic Church enjoys freedom and its members are secured in the liberty of professing their religion in the same way as other denomina-

(*f*) In re Bishop of Natal 3 Moore P. C. N. S. 115.

tions by the general law, and also by the treaty of Paris, 1763, and by the Imperial Act of 1774 (14 Geo. III. cap. 83,) subject only to the supremacy of the Crown of England. The extent of this supremacy is declared in a statute passed in the first year of the reign of Queen Elizabeth. (*g*)

While the different forms of Christianity are thus on the same footing, the laws further recognize that Christianity itself is part of the law of the land. (*h*)   At the same time the law protects every form of worship.   Every one who by threats or force, unlawfully obstructs or prevents, or endeavours to obstruct or prevent, any clergyman or other minister from celebrating divine service or officiating in any church or other place used for divine worship is guilty of a misdemeanor and liable to be imprisoned for any term less than two years : any person wilfully disturbing any persons met for religious worship, or for any moral, social or benevolent purpose, is also guilty of a misdemeanor and may be imprisoned for a month or fined up to the sum of twenty dollars. (*i*)

(*g*) The clause in the treaty, "so far as the laws of Great Britain permit," meant subject to the King's supremacy.   See Part II.

(*h*) *Pringle v. the Corporation of Napanee* 43, Q. B. 285.

(*i*) R. S. C. cap. 156.

GOVERNMENT IN CANADA.

PART II.

FORMER GOVERNMENTS IN CANADA AND IN THE PROVINCES.

INTRODUCTION.

THE aim of a constitutional history is to give an account of the way in which the people of any country have governed themselves. This assumes that the people do govern themselves, that they form a nation, and that they are possessed of sovereign power. None but a self-ruling people can, in strictness, have a constitution or a constitutional history, because the meaning of the term constitution is the agreement or understanding whereby the whole people—the rulers and the ruled—choose to govern themselves. It must not be supposed by the student that the rulers are distinct from the people generally—they are that portion of the community which the other members entrust with the common government of all; and it is the distinguishing feature of a limited or constitutional government that no one, not even the sovereign or chief magistrate, is exempt from obedience to the general laws of the land. In a colony or dependency with a constitutional form of government, this agreement or understanding, besides being the choice of the people, must be sanctioned or permitted by the mother country.

The Dominion of Canada is a dependency of Great Britain, and is made up of a number of colonies and possessions of that country in North America. The colonies were acquired chiefly by cession from France; the territories or possessions came through discoevry or the ventures of British subjects. Each of these, under its own form of government, has a separate history down to its admission into the Canadian union. That union took place in the year 1867, but it then only included three colonies; it now embraces, excepting Newfoundland, nearly all British North America—one half the northern continent. A constitutional history of Canada is strictly the history of Canadian government since the date of the union.

The union of 1867 appears very like the addition of colonies and possessions to the old province of Canada. The province was itself a union of the provinces of Upper and Lower Canada. Originally it was one province and called Quebec. It was the chief of the British possessions around the St. Lawrence, its governors had precedence over all other governors in adjoining colonies, and in time of disturbance they took charge of and were captains-general of all the forces. Canada as part of new France has a history reaching back into the early years of the seventeenth century; and it was the head-quarters of French authority along the great lakes and the Mississippi. For many reasons, therefore, the new Dominion was called Canada, though it cannot be denied that in a federation it is highly desirable that no one of the constituent states should have the semblance of any real or imaginary superiority. The unfortunate choice of a name in the neighbouring republic has been often deplored by American writers, though it has not prevented other republics from following their example. The prominence necessarily given to the Canadas in any historical sketch may be referred to their relative importance ; but in any account of their modes of government it is due rather to the number of changes that have taken place in their constitutions. The manner of governing Canada for more than a century past has been no small concern to Canadian and British statesmen. If a consideration of these changes occupy the larger space in the succeeding pages, it is not with any intention to disregard the importance of the other provinces. The Maritime Provinces have perhaps less eventful histories, because they have been less restless than their western neighbours. From a point of view of general history the North Western Territories are extremely interesting, but prior to 1870 they had no constitutional history.

It is proposed in the following pages to outline the different modes of government in the provinces before their admission into the union, with a word or two on such matters before confederation as properly fall under the range of constitutional history. This will not be much more than a record of changes of imperial charters that popularly are regarded in the light of that species of history. This year (1887) is the centenary of the United States constitution, and the amendments to the original document can be comprised in less than two pages of an ordinary book. These changes and the decisions of the supreme court of that country are the basis and the substance of the United States constitutional history. So it is and will be in this country, though the amendments are effected in a different way and the judicial interpretations may come from any of our courts. In both countries there is of necessity a written constitution, as there must be in every federation ; and its history is not so much the steady growth of political changes, as occasional abrupt turns by organic amendments.

In the United Kingdom of Great Britain and Ireland there is no necessity for one of that character. In fact there would be no object gained by committing it to writing, because it might be altered or repealed at the next session of the British Parliament. In the same way each session may add something to it. It has a steady growth or has the means of such. The British constitution is therefore made up of certain recognized principles of government not necessarily in any statute but regarded by the people as essential elements of its government. The Magna Charta, the Petition of Rights, the Act of Succession are some of the great landmarks of the British constitution ; and these and all other parts of it have to be discovered in the history of the people and in the laws of the land. There is not one fundamental principle of government that the British legislature is unable to amend or repeal ; but these principles hold good until they are amended or repealed.

In Canada we have had our constitutions *en bloc*, so to speak ; a reference to these is desirable to a right understanding of the present or latest one, and it is to this species of history, by whatever name it may be called that the reader's attention will now be directed.

CHAPTER I.

EARLY DIVISIONS OF THE CONTINENT—CANADA.

*Three claimants of the continent, England east of the Mis-
sissippi, France west of it and north of the lakes, Spain
to the south and west—Treaties, Ryswick, Utrecht, Aix-
la-Chapelle, Paris, 1763, Versailles, 1783—Boundaries
—French regime, Seven Years' war, fall of Quebec, of
Montreal, capitulations—Military government, 1759 to
1763.*

THE North American continent from its discovery was
claimed by several European nations, but chiefly by the
French and the English. The French owned all north of
the River and Gulf of St. Lawrence and of the great lakes,
and also Michigan, Ohio, and the territory lying westward
of the Mississippi river as far south as New Orleans. The
English owned everything to the south and east of this
somewhat indefinite boundary except Florida, which was
owned by the Spaniards. The British possessions were
originally by royal grant divided into two provinces, North
and South Virginia, but afterwards they were subdivided
until they numbered thirteen. These were the old thirteen
colonies that declared their independence in the year 1776.
The western boundary of these English colonies was conveniently placed at the Mississippi river, though the early

maps are not very uniform on that point; the northern boundary, where the great lakes interposed no natural barrier, was not so readily accepted : the boundary on the north-east was changed several times. (*a*)

The circumstances which led to the conquest of Canada by the British in the last years of the reign of George II and the formal cession of the country in the subsequent reign are matters of general history, and not so obviously within the range of that species of history which has for its object the noting of changes in the manner of our government. Nevertheless there is a Canada before the cession of 1763, and a Canada thereafter; the one French—the other English; there are the contending owners, France and England, and the terms of their settlement.

From the discovery of Canada by Cartier in 1534 down to the end of the sixteenth century, there is nothing of any special interest. There was a formal taking possession of the country in the name of France. Champlain was appointed first Governor by Condè under Louis XIII. His

(*a*) The 45th parallel of latitude was adopted for nearly one-half of the distance from the St. Lawrence to the seaboard, through what was then Massachusetts; after that "the high lands dividing the waters falling into the Atlantic from those emptying themselves into the St. Lawrence" were taken as sufficient to indicate the limits of both countries. The boundaries of the British provinces were not altered by the war of 1812-14 between England and the United States, which was terminated by the treaty of Ghent in 1814. The difficulty of determining the boundary in the east, where the 45th parallel was no longer considered as a guide, gave rise to a good deal of negotiation between the contending parties. In 1827 it was referred to the King of the Netherlands whose award was deemed highly unfavourable to the United States. That power refused to accept it. Afterwards, when fresh difficulties arose in 1842, Lord Ashburton and Daniel Webster were appointed commissioners to define the boundary. This is known as the Ashburton treaty. It recognized the 45th parallel to the high lands in New Hampshire as the northern boundary of New York and Vermont States, and traced out the line between New Hampshire and Maine to the south and east of Lower Canada and New Brunswick. Beginning at the Pacific in the west the 49th parallel was adopted to the Lake of the Woods, and from that the central line of the lakes and river St. Lawrence to complete the boundary to the 45th parallel.

French subjects numbered sixty. In 1629, by the fortunes of war, Canada passed into the hands of the British, who, three years later, returned it to the original owners. (*b*)

Cardinal Richelieu then took the infant colony in charge and the company of the One Hundred Associates was formed. This company was replaced in 1663 by a royal government and the change is one by which some interest is awakened, because it established an order of things which subsisted till the cession in 1760, a period of nearly 100 years. Louis XIV. was ruler in France and Colbert his minister. The hundred associates, reduced by more than one half, were superseded by a royal government under a supreme council. The royal government was constituted similarly to the parliament of Paris, the principal functionaries being appointed by the king and responsible to him.

The colony was practically ruled, however, by a triumvirate composed of the governor, the bishop and the royal intendant. There were a number of councillors varying from five to seven, and then to twelve, with an attorney-general and a chief clerk.

This sovereign or supreme council had charge of all the affairs and business of Canada, formed a court of appeal, collected the revenues, but had no power to levy taxes except with the king's permission. The country was divided for judicial and other purposes into three divisions, which are still maintained, viz., Quebec, Montreal and Three Rivers.

M. de Mesy was the first governor and Monseigneur Laval the first bishop.

The royal government was acceptable to the inhabitants

b) This was by the treaty of St. Germain-en-Laye, 1632.

of Quebec and they lived happily under it. It was suited,
and justly so, to Frenchmen and to Roman Catholics, and
one of the great causes of discontent, after the cession,
was that it was not and could not be suitable or acceptable
to Englishmen or to Protestants. At its basis for land
tenure were the feudal laws of the preceding centuries; the
Coutume de Paris, the ancient laws of France, were its
guide in legal matters; and the Catholic religion, as the
religion of the inhabitants, was recognized by the law of
the land.

The earliest treaty between France and England affecting American territory is that of St. Germain-en-Laye,
1632. The English in 1629 made a descent on Quebec
and kept it for three years. They then gave it back,
Canada, New France and Acadia, without limits; and it is
a peculiarity of all the treaties down to the Treaty of Paris,
1763, that the boundaries were not assigned.

After the Treaty of St. Germain-en-Laye, we find, in
1670, the Charter of Charles II. granting territory to the
Hudson Bay Company; but this did not include any lands
then "possessed by the subjects of any other Christian
Prince or State." The treaty of Ryswick was concluded
twenty-seven years after the date of this charter, and by
it the forts and factories of Hudson Bay were restored to
the French—these having been taken from them by the
English in the preceding wars. Whatever territory that
might embrace was given back again to the English by
the treaty of Utrecht in 1713,—"the bay and straits of
Hudson, together with all lands, seas, coasts, rivers, and
places situate in the bay and straits and which belong
thereto." The treaty of Ryswick has an assertion on the
part of the French that the Kennebec is the eastern
boundary between them and Massachusetts; the slice of
territory between that river and the St. Croix is now

within the United States. The entire eastern coast, Nova Scotia, Cape Breton, St. John (now Prince Edward Island), Newfoundland, Labrador and Hudson Bay remained to the French by the treaty.

By the treaty to Utrecht, Nova Scotia, then called Acadia, according to its ancient limits, together with the whole of Newfoundland, was given up to England. The French retained some reservations as to the English fisheries in Newfoundland, and the English secured the fur trade of the Hudson Bay.

The treaty of Aix la Chapelle in 1749 restored Cape Breton with the islands of St. Pierre and Michelon to France. Three years prior to this Cape Breton had been taken by the English colonists. It is the only other treaty down to the great treaty of 1763 that is taken up with the shuffling of territory between these two powers.

In 1756 the seven years' war began in Europe, and it could not be expected that the colonists of France and England in America would be unaffected by it. The English colonists met at Albany to adopt a line of common defence ; the French under the Marquis de Vaudreuil were equally active in opposing them.

Thus the war began in the colonies, and after a protracted struggle, in which success now leaned to one side and now to another, the chief strongholds of the French were taken by the English, first Quebec and subsequently Montreal.

On the 18th of September, 1759, Admiral Saunders, General Townshead and M. de Ramezay signed the articles of capitulation of Quebec. The principal terms were as follows :—" The land forces, marines, and sailors of the garrison to be accorded the honours of war, and to be conveyed in British ships to the nearest port of France ; the property of the inhabitants, as well as that of the officers, both of those present and absent, to be inviolate and their customary privileges to be preserved ; the free exercise of the Roman Catholic religion to be permitted, and safeguards granted to all religious persons, including the Bishop, until the possession of Canada should be decided between the Kings of England and France, and guards to be posted at the churches, convents, and principal habitations ; the sick and wounded of both sides to be equally cared for, and the physicians and attendants upon them to have every facility and assistance in the discharge of their duties ; the artillery and public stores to be faithfully given up, and a proper inventory taken." (c)

After the fall of Quebec the war continued for a whole year. On the 8th of September, 1760, Montreal capitulated to General Amherst. The capitulation was signed by him and M. de Vaudreuil, the French Governor, and contains fifty-five articles.

The first ten of these refer to the possession of the city, the disposition of the troops, the magazines and munitions of war and the care of the sick. The next sixteen are taken up chiefly with the governors and officers of the French King and their conduct to France. The twenty-seventh and the seven following artcles refer to religion and the religious communities. (d)

Articles 27 and 28 are as follows :—

Article 27.—The free exercise of the Catholic, Apostolic and Roman religion shall subsist entire, in such

(c) Miles' History of Canada gives this summary. Vol. I.. page 420.

(d) It is somewhat remarkable that in the surrender of Champlain to Sir David Kirkt in 1629, the terms of capitulation at Quebec and Montreal in 1759-60, the treaty of Paris in 1763, the Quebec Act in 1774, and the Constitutional Act of 1791, there should be assurances for freedom of worship.

manner that all the states and people of the towns and country places and distant posts shall continue to assemble in the churches, and to frequent the sacraments as heretofore, without being molested in any manner, directly or indirectly. These people shall be obliged by the English government to pay to the priests the tithes and all the taxes they were used to pay, under the government of his most christian majesty.

Answer.—Granted, as to the free exercise of their religion. The obligation of paying the tithes to the priests will depend on the king's pleasure.

Article 28.—The chapter, priests, cures, and missionaries shall continue, with an entire liberty, the exercise and functions in the parishes of the towns and country.

Answer.—Granted.

The remaining articles are devoted chiefly to different classes of people—French, Canadians, Acadians, Indians and others ; and except the 42nd article are not of great importance.

In this article it was desired by the French commander that " the French and Canadian inhabitants should continue to be governed according to the custom of Paris and the laws and usages established for this country." The reply to this was that they should become subjects to the king, which reply Attorney-General Maseres interpreted to mean that these subjects were put on the same footing as English subjects generally. Fortunately for the peace of Canada, General Murray interpreted it in a much more liberal sense. Attorney-General Thurlow in reporting on the state of Canada refers to the capitulation in these terms : —

" On the 8th of September, 1760, the country capitulated in terms which gave to your Majesty all that belonged to the French king, and preserved all their property, real and personal, in the fullest extent, not only to private individuals, but to the corporation of the West India company, and to the missionaries, priests, canons, convents, etc., with liberty to dispose of it by sale if they should want to leave the country. The free exercise of their religion by the laity, and of their function by the clergy was also reserved.

" There are those who think that the law of England, in all its branches, is actually established, and in force in Quebec. * * Others are of opinion that the Canadian laws are unrepealed. * * Others again have thought that the effect of the above mentioned proclamation [17th October, 1763] and the acts which followed upon it, was to introduce the criminal laws of England and to confirm the civil law of Canada. In this number were two persons of great authority and esteem : Mr. Yorke and Mr. De Grey, then attorney and solicitor-general, as I recollect from their report of the 14th of April, 1766. * * There is not, they observe, a maxim of the common law more certain than that a conquered people retain their ancient customs till the conqueror shall declare new laws. To change at once the laws and manners of a settled country must be attended with hardships and violence. * * It is the more material that this policy should be pursued in Canada, because it is a great and ancient colony, being settled and much cultivated by French subjects who now inhabit it to the number of eighty or one hundred thousand."

Although Quebec and Montreal surrendered in this way, it by no means followed that Canada had definitely changed masters. The fate of Canada depended upon the termination of the war in Europe. The articles of surrender were the *interim* terms for the adjustment of an international difficulty, the result of which no one could confidently predict. The capitulations were to govern in the meantime, and both of them refer to the possible contingency of Canada remaining a French colony. (e)

Canada was thus dealt with as between two commanders on the field of battle. The consequent occupation was military not diplomatic. In the same year France and Spain entered into a secret alliance to make war on England, and it was not till 1763 that the definitive treaty was signed that effectually disposed of Canada.

In the interval very little alteration was made in the political complexion of affairs. General Amherst, who was the first English Governor General, recognized the division of the province into three districts, and left General Murray in command at Quebec, General Gage at Montreal, and Colonel Burton at Three Rivers. The " new subjects," as the French were called, were tranquil under a state of things which differed only slightly from their former state. Both English and French regarded the military rule as a violation of the terms of capitulation which insured to them the rights of British subjects, "rights. by which their persons were not to be disposed of by any but their natural judges with their own consent."

"It fell out," says Garneau, " that when they hoped to enjoy legality under peaceful sway, they saw their tribunals abolished, their judges expelled, and their whole social organization upset, to make room for the most insupportable of all tyranny, that of courts martial. Nothing did more to isolate the government and alienate the people from it than this conduct, long since repudiated by the law and customs of nations. Yet the colony

(e) The treaty that finally adjusted the differences of the French and English is called a definitive treaty.

remained four years under martial law. This epoch in our annals is designated as the "reign of the soldiery."(f)

The military rule continued in effect until after the publication of the treaty of Paris and was abolished by a royal proclamation dated 17th October, 1763—an important state document which will be discussed in connection with the treaty itself.

(f) Garneau's History of Canada. Vol. II., page 309.

CHAPTER II.

THE TREATY OF PARIS.—1763 TO 1774.

*4th section of the treaty—Clause as to religious freedom,
opinions—Royal proclamation of 1763, islands given to
Nova Scotia, to Newfoundland—Assembly promised—
Governors, laws, courts, commissions—Petition for an
assembly, politics in England when Quebec Act was
submitted.*

By the treaty of Paris, 1763, the seven years' war was
ended and the disputes of western Europe adjusted. By
it also the war between the English and French colonists
in America was terminated.

The treaty was concluded on the 10th of February, 1763,
and signed by the representatives of England, France
and Spain: Portugal assented to it. The fourth section is
as follows:

"His most Christian Majesty renounces all pretensions
which he has heretofore formed, or might form, to Nova
Scotia or Acadia, in all its parts, and guarantees the
whole of it, and all its dependencies, to the King of Great
Britain.

"Moreover his most Christian Majesty cedes and guarantees to his said Britannic Majesty, in full right, Canada,
with all its dependencies, as well as the island of Cape
Breton, and all the other islands and coasts in the Gulf
and River of St. Lawrence, and, in general, every thing that

depends on the said countries, lands, islands and coasts, with the sovereignty, property, possession, and all rights acquired by treaty or otherwise, which the most Christian King and the crown of France have had, till now, over the said countries, islands, lands, places, coasts, and their inhabitants, so that the most Christian King cedes and makes over the whole to the said King, and to the crown of Great Britain, and that in the most ample manner and form, without restriction, and without any liberty to depart from the said guaranty, under any pretence, or to disturb Great Britain in the possession above mentioned.

" His Britannic Majesty, on his side, agrees to grant the liberty of the Catholic religion to the inhabitants of Canada : he will consequently give the most effectual orders, that his new Roman Catholic subjects may profess the worship of their religion, according to the rites of the Romish church, as far as the laws of Great Britain permit.

" His Britannic Majesty further agrees, that the French inhabitants, or others, who had been the subjects of the most Christian King in Canada, may retire with all safety and freedom wherever they shall think proper, and may sell their estates, provided it be to subjects of his Britannic Majesty, and bring away their effects, as well as their persons, without being restrained in their emigration, under any pretence whatsoever, except that of debts, or of criminal prosecutions : the term limited for this emigration shall be fixed to the space of eighteen months, to be computed from the day of the exchange of the ratification of the present treaty."

This treaty superseded the terms of the capitulation at Montreal, and is to be regarded as of binding authority for all time to come, so long as the law and honour of nations are to be observed. (a)

(a) It is an essential principle of the law of nations that no power can be released from the engagements of treaties, or modify their stipulations except with the consent of the contracting parties amicably obtained. This principle was recognized by Russia, Austria, Germany, Great Britain, Italy and Turkey at the conference in London in 1871.

The last article, XXVI. reads :

"Their sacred Britannic, most Christian and Catholic, and most faithful Majesties promise to observe sincerely and *bonâ fide* all the articles contained and settled in the present treaty ; and they will not suffer the same to be infringed directly or indirectly by their respective subjects ; and the same high contracting parties generally and reciprocally guarantee to each other all the stipulations of the present treaty."

No comment is necessary here on the 4th section except as to the exercise of religious liberty involved in the last paragraph with the condition "as far as the laws of Great Britain permit." What is the meaning of this restriction ?

In 1763 these laws did not permit of any exercise of the Roman Catholic religion in England. The question was : did these laws apply to a colony? Could it be fairly assumed that the contracting parties had adopted a provision rendering itself nugatory by the fulness of its exception ?

Opinions were given by three attorney-generals, several officers of the crown and others that none of the penal statutes in force in England at that time applied to colonies or to the Catholics in Canada, and that nothing affected them except the 1st Act of Elizabeth, chap. 1, commonly known as the Act of Supremacy. This was the only statute applying to the colonies or outlying divisions of the crown.

Attorney-General Maseres, writing about ten years after the treaty says :

"Two senses may be put upon these words, ' as far as the laws of Great Britain permit.' They may either be supposed to mean that the Canadians shall be at liberty to

profess the worship of the Roman Catholic religion as far
as the laws of Great Britain permit that worship to be
professed in England itself, or that they shall be at liberty
to profess that worship as far as the laws of England
permit it to be professed in the.outlying dominions of the
crown of Great Britain that are not parcel of the realm,
such as Minorca, Senegal, the West India Islands, and the
colonies of North America. The former of these senses I
acknowledge to be too narrow to be put upon these words,
because it would in a great measure destroy the grant of
the liberty of professing the worship of the Romish religion
which these words were only intended to qualify and
restrain ; because in England itself the laws do not permit
the worship of the Romish religion to be professed in any
degree.

" We must therefore have recourse to the latter sense
above mentioned and suppose these words to mean that
the Canadians should have the liberty of professing the
worship of their religion as far as the laws of England
permit it to be professed in the outlying dominions of the
crown that lie without the realm. . . .

" Now, upon making this enquiry we shall find that
though most of the penal and disqualifying statutes passed
against the professors of the Romish religion relate only
to England and Wales, yet the Act of the first of Queen
Elizabeth, cap. 1, which is entitled '*An Act to restore to
the crown the ancient jurisdiction over the state ecclesiastical
and spiritual and abolishing all foreign powers repugnant to
the same,*' which is commonly called the Act of Supremacy,
does expressly relate to all the Queen's dominions as well
as to the realm of England, and is even extended by
positive words to such countries and places as should at
any future time become subject to the crown of England."

He then sets out the effect of this statute of Elizabeth, and adds in conclusion that " the British Nation is bound by that article to grant to the Canadians the liberty of professing the worship of the Roman Catholic religion only so far as is consistent with that statute. (b)

So much as to this part of the treaty ; the boundaries of Canada will be referred to later on.

By a royal proclamation dated at St. James Court, October 7th 1763, the American acquisitions were divided into four distinct and separate governments, Quebec, East Florida, West Florida and Grenada, and the boundaries of each were defined. (c)   The government of Newfoundland was enlarged so that the coast of Labrador and the adjacent islands " from the river St. John's to Hudson Straits, together with the islands of Anticosti and Madeleine and all the smaller islands lying upon the said coast" were placed under the care and inspection of its governor.

Under this proclamation also " the islands of St. John and Cape Breton or Isle Royal with the lesser islands adjacent thereto " were annexed to the government of Nova Scotia.

It is afterwards promised in the proclamation that as soon as the state and circumstances of the said colonies will admit thereof, the governors will summon and call general assemblies in the same manner and form as the other American colonies, with power to make laws for the "public peace, welfare and good government" of the inhabitants, as near as may be agreeable to the laws of

(b) See Cavendish's debates on the Quebec Act and opinions of Lord Thurlow and Lord Loughborough in the Maseres collection.

(c) All the lands and territories not included within the limits of Quebec and the Floridas or within the limits of the Hudson Bay Company and other lands to the west or north-west were reserved for the use of the Indians.

England. In the meantime all colonists could confide in the royal protection for the enjoyment of the benefits of the laws of the realm of England.

Then followed directions as to the establishing of courts of judicature and public justice for hearing civil and criminal cases, according to law and equity and as near as may be agreeable to the laws of England with the right of appeal to the privy council.

On the 21st of November following, Major General Murray was appointed Captain General and Governor in chief of Quebec province in America and all the territories depending on it, to hold office during pleasure with very elaborate instructions. Lieutenant-Governors were appointed at Montreal and Three Rivers and power given as in the proclamations to summon a general assembly of the freeholders and planters at their discretion.

It is not necessary to consider the terms of this commission as no assembly was called.

General Murray issued a proclamation intimating that in all legal procedure affecting the tenure of land and succession to property, the laws and customs which had been in use under the French domination were to be followed. (d)

The Governor-General was also appointed vice-admiral of Quebec, a title still retained, and a lengthy commission on that point issued on the 19th of March, 1764.

By an ordinance of the 17th September 1764, it was declared that in the supreme court sitting at Quebec His Britannic Majesty was present in the person of his chief justice and had full power to determine all civil and

(d) Garneau's Canada, Vol. III, 317. The writer has not seen the text of this proclamation.

criminal cases agreeable to the laws of England, and to the ordinances of this province.

On the 3rd of February 1766, William Hey was appointed chief justice, and in September of the same year Francis Maseres was named attorney-general in the room of George Suckling.

In looking through these and other commissions, especially one to Captain Schlasser as justice of the peace, reference is made to administration of the laws of England and of Canada, and this uncertainty of what law was in force became at length the real difficulty between the French and English inhabitants.

In criminal proceedings the Canadians as well as the English universally supposed the laws of England to be in force. " No others are ever mentioned or thought of and the Canadians seem to be very well satisfied with them."

A report on the state of the law in Quebec and suggestions were made by attorney-general Maseres in 1769 to Sir Guy Carleton, who rejected the report and sent in one prepared from other sources. Chief Justice Hey also reported on the difficulties.

In 1773, no council being summoned in pursuance of the promise made in 1763, the English subjects petitioned the English government and a draft Act was prepared, which, however, is not now deserving of consideration as the government refused to pass it. The Quebec Act was passed in its place.

During these ten years prior to the Quebec Act several other offices were filled; a receiver general was appointed in 1765, and a license to preach and perform divine service according to the ceremonies of the Church of England was granted in 1768 to Rev. Mr. DeMontmollin. There were besides these some other commissions.

Before describing the Quebec Act, it may be well to regard the starting point of our constitutional history with more immediate reference to English politics and the great statesmen who figured in the councils of the nation at this time. The student of constitutional history in Canada must keep his eye on the events of history in England as well as in his own country—at least since the reign of George III. These events are often as necessary to be considered as the events in our own country.

During the reigns of the first two Georges, England had been engaged in many wars, and the general result was far from gratifying to the English people. No great minister had been found to fill the place of Horace Walpole. George II. in 1759 reluctantly placed Wm. Pitt in charge of foreign affairs. He it was who conducted the war in Canada to a successful issue ; but the treaty of Paris was concluded under the Grenville ministry which came in after the resignation of Lord Bute, Pitt's successor. These, with Lord Rockingham and Lord North, Mr. Fox and Mr. Wilkes are names famous then and in later times. Pitt espoused the cause of the colonists whom the Grenville ministry taxed.

Grenville and Bute were concerned in the notable proceedings for libel against John Wilkes and his newspaper the "North Briton." Rockingham professed in opposition a policy towards the Americans, which if sincere was a prudent and wise one. North's name appears very soon in our history, Edmund Burke and Charles James Fox figure in the debates, and Camden, Mansfield, and Campbell in the decisions of the court.

This was the period too of some important constitutional questions in England. In the first year of the reign of

George III. it was held that the tenure of office of the judges was not dependent on the life of the sovereign who appointed them, but that they held office during good conduct.

Another very important principle was admitted when Grenville, on assuming office, was held responsible for every act or circumstance which led to his appointment. "This principle," says Mr. Younge in his constitutional history, "was established in the fullest manner in 1834, when Sir Robert Peel admitted his entire responsibility for dismissal of Lord Melbourne by King William IV., though it was notorious that he was in Italy at the time and had not been consulted in the matter."

The Wilkes case already referred to is most instructive in the law of criminal libel and among other things is authority in the language of Lord Campbell " that privilege of parliament should not be permitted to interfere with the criminal law of the country." General warrants since this trial have been considered illegal.

Later on, when Lord Rockingham became minister a second time in 1789, a resolution was passed that expulsion does not incapacitate a member from immediate re-election.

One good resulting from these agitations of the powers of the commons was the publication of the debates in full. In 1771, the house enquired into the unfairness of reports and many printers were imprisoned for presuming to make known the proceedings. After a time the government ceased punishing and silently acquiesced in the publication while retaining a standing order to deal with the question as might be necessary.

It was in such times and with these men as rulers, that England assumed the management of Canada and its dependencies.

CHAPTER III.

THE QUEBEC ACT.—1774 TO 1791.

*Petitions for the bill, Mr. Maseres, reports of the debates—
Boundaries of Quebec—Provisions as to religious wor-
ship, civil law of Canada to prevail, criminal law of
England in force—Feeling in the other colonies in
America—Government by advising council, no assembly
—Establishment of courts, habeas corpus—Sir Guy
Carleton, commissions issued, division of Western
Canada, discontent under the government, preparations
for a change in mode of government.*

ATTORNEY-GENERAL (afterwards Baron) Maseres prepared
a draft Act for the government of Canada, but it was
deemed unsuitable to the needs of the people by the Governor, Sir Guy Carleton, and was disregarded by the British
ministry. It was framed on a narrow and injudicious plan
practically excluding every Frenchman from having any
share in the government. There were at this time about
70,000 inhabitants in the colony, of whom possibly not
500 were Englishmen. (*a*)   It was unreasonable to suppose
that the rights of the ancient subjects could be entirely
disregarded. The British ministers had no lack of material
for the Quebec Act.   A number of petitions were sent from

(*a*) The actual number given is 360.

Quebec by the French and English inhabitants, and one by the London Board of Trade. Lord North assumed the charge of the bill in the commons and the Earl of Dartmouth in the Lords. The debates on the passage of the bill are reported in a volume of 300 pages and named Sir Henry Cavendish's Report. (b) Sir Guy Carleton was examined in reference to the subject of the bill, as was also Chief Justice Hey and one Dr. Marriott. Lord Loughborough (the solicitor-general), Mr. Charles Fox, Lord North, Edmund Burke and many others took part in the discussion. The bill was carried by a large majority— 319 to 65—and became law on the 1st of May, 1775.

It begins by reciting the treaty of Paris, 1763, and the proclamation of the same year, with the defect in the latter as to the narrow boundaries of Quebec. The boundaries as set out in the proclamation, extend from the river St. John on the Labrador coast to the south side of Lake Nipissing, then towards Lake Champlain and the 45th parallel of latitude along the highlands to the Bay of Chaleurs and across the St. Lawrence west of Anticosti to the place of beginning. The extended limits are given as follows :

"All the territories, islands, and countries in North America, belonging to the crown of Great Britain, bounded on the south by a line from the bay of Chaleurs, along the high lands which divide the rivers that empty themselves into the river St. Lawrence from those which fall into the sea, to a point in forty-five degrees of northern latitude, on the eastern bank of the river Connecticut, keeping the same latitude directly west, through the lake Champlain, until, in the same latitude, it meets the river St. Lawrence ; from thence up the eastern bank of the said river to the

(b) The genuineness of these reports has been questioned, but apparently without any foundation.

lake Ontario; thence through the lake Ontario, and the river commonly called Niagara; and thence along by the eastern and south-eastern bank of lake Erie, following the said bank, until the same shall be intersected by the northern boundary, granted by the charter of the province of Pennsylvania, in case the same shall be so intersected ; and from thence along the said northern and western boundaries of the said province, until the said western boundary strike the Ohio ; but in case the said bank of the said lake shall not be found to be intersected, then following the said bank until it shall arrive at that point of the said bank which shall be nearest to the northwestern angle of the said province of Pennsylvania, and thence, by a right line, to the said northwestern angle of the said province; and thence along the western boundary of the said province, until it strike the river Ohio; and along the bank of the said river westward, to the banks of the Mississippi, and northwards to the southern boundary of the territory granted to the merchants-adventurers of England, trading to Hudson's Bay ; and also all such territories, islands, and countries, which have, since the 10th February, 1763, been made part of the government of Newfoundland, be, and they are hereby, during His Majesty's pleasure, annexed to, and made part and parcel of the province of Quebec, as created and established by the said royal proclamation of the 7th of October, 1763."

The Act then repealed the proclamation of 1763 and all commissions and ordinances thereunder, referring at the same time to the fact that the civil government so estab-lished was inapplicable to the state and circumstances of the province.

It then enacts " That His Majesty's subjects professing the religion of the Church of Rome of and in the said province of Quebec may have, hold and enjoy the free exer-cise of the religion of the Church of Rome subject to the King's supremacy declared and established in the first year of the reign of Queen Elizabeth, and the clergy of the said church may hold, receive and enjoy their accustomed dues and rights with respect to such persons only as shall profess the said religion.

" Provided, nevertheless, that it shall be lawful for His Majesty, his heirs and successors to make such provision out of the rest of the accustomed dues and rights for the encouragement of the Protestant religion, and for the maintenance and support of a Protestant clergy within the said province, as he or they shall, from time to time, think necessary and expedient."

Then follows an oath in substitution of the oath required for Catholics under the Act of Elizabeth, and which is virtually the present oath of allegiance. The statute imposed no insuperable difficulty; it required all priests and other ecclesiastical persons to take the oath, but, in the event of their refusing, it annexed no penalty beyond the deprivation of their benefices or other spiritual promotions.

The next section goes on to confirm all His Majesty's subjects (the religious orders and communities only excepted) in their property and possessions and in all their civil rights, regarding which all controversies should be decided by the laws of Canada.

The criminal law of England, as well in the description and quality of the offence as in the method of prosecution and trial and the punishments and forfeiture thereby inflicted, was continued in the province.

The Act then recited that it would be inexpedient at that time to summon an assembly and so made provision for a council not exceeding 23 or less than 17 which might make ordinances with the consent of the Governor ; depriving it however of any authority to levy taxes except for roads or public buildings.

A few unimportant provisions followed as to the passing and approbation of these ordinances, with an express clause that no ordinance respecting religion was to be in force without His Majesty's approbation. There was also a saving clause as to the right of the crown to establish civil, criminal and ecclesiastical courts.

The Act closes with a declaration that all Acts of parliament in reference to the trade and commerce of the American plantations are in force in the province of Quebec.

This Act was passed in June 1774, but the revocation and annulling of the commissions and ordinances under the royal proclamation were not to take effect till the 1st of May, 1775.

It will be seen that the Act was framed largely to meet the wishes of the French Canadians. It was directly opposed to a number of petitions from the English inhabitants of Quebec and their friends in London. It was opposed also to the arguments, reports and letters of Mr. Maseres, who had left Canada in 1769, and who was the warm though injudicious advocate of the cause of the minority in Canada. (c)

A few months after the Quebec Act was passed the first symptoms of the American revolution appeared ; the Act itself was pointed at by the other colonists as an indication of the injustice of the mother country.

The principal features of the Quebec Act are the enlarging of the boundaries of that province, the re-introduction of French or Canadian law and the recognition of the Catholic Church. The criminal law of England was retained. No assembly was granted, but in its stead an advising council. The province of Quebec as enlarged by this Act included not only Ontario and Quebec as they now exist but five

(c) The reader will find a full account of "The proceedings of the British and other Protestant inhabitants of the province of Quebec in North America, in order to obtain a House of Assembly in the province" in a book so entitled, a copy of which is in the Toronto Public Library

states of the American union and part of a sixth viz., Ohio,
Indiana, Illinois, Michigan, Wisconsin and that portion of
Minnesota north of the Mississippi river and east of the
meridian line passing through the source of that river,
probably the 95th degree of longitude west from Greenwich. (d)

The other features of the Act, especially as regards the
civil law, were fruitful sources of discontent in the province.

In 1775 the American congress addressed a proclamation
to the Canadians asking them to seize the favorable
opportunity presented to them "to play their part in the
glorious conquest of American independence." Delegates,
among whom was the celebrated Dr. Franklin, were sent
as commissioners to incite the people against their new
rulers and to join in the revolution. " The Canadians
could not but remember," says Garneau, speaking of
Franklin, " how eager he was to stimulate the British
people to make a conquest of their country some 15 years
before. He soon perceived that the quest he was sent on
would prove bootless."

The council on account of the war did no business in
1776, but there was a session with closed doors in the
following year; twenty-three members were present, fifteen
English and eight Canadians, and was taken up chiefly
with applications on personal business.

The first ordinance passed under the Quebec Act is
dated February 1777; it establishes the civil courts of
judicature in the province of Quebec. The province is
divided into two great districts named Montreal and

(d) As settled by the judicial committee of the privy council in the
Ontario Boundary Case.

Quebec and a court of common pleas established in each. An appeal lay from these courts to the court of appeal, which was composed of the Governor in council or chief justice presiding, and at least five members of the executive council. An appeal lay from this court to the privy council in England. Other ordinances regulate the procedure in the courts, the establishment of a court of king's bench for criminal justice, and matters varying from the regulation of the rate of interest, the conduct of sales, the weight of bread and the sale of liquors, to the provincial currency and the formation of a militia.

In 1776, a difficulty arose between C. J. Livius and Governor Carleton which led to the resignation of the former. The question was as to the constitution of the privy council and the irregularity of proceedings in the province. The result was that after addresses and petitions the chief justice, though exonerated, refused to return to Canada.

One effect of the American revolution was an Act passed in the eighteenth year of Geo. III., and which is sufficiently indicated by its title. It was "an Act for removing all doubts and apprehensions concerning taxation by the parliament of Great Britain in any of the colonies, provinces, and plantations in North America and the West Indies; and for repealing so much of an Act made in the seventh year of the reign of his present Majesty, as imposes a duty on tea imported from Great Britain into any colony or plantation in America, or relates thereto."

In 1778 Sir Guy Carleton, feeling aggrieved at not being appointed to the place accorded to General Burgoyne in the colonial command, retired and was succeeded by General Haldimand. He was enjoined by his commission to proclaim in the colony the writ of Habeas Corpus, and he was forbidden even in time of trouble to confine any subject without the advice and approbation of the legislative council. But Haldimand was an old soldier imperious and severe, and believed he could maintain obedience only by inflexible rigour, and the result was that he imprisoned citizens by the hundreds without distinction and whether they were innocent or guilty. (e) His last official act was in 1785 to publish an ordinance under authority of an Imperial Act of the previous year introducing the writ of Habeas Corpus such as it is in England, and it is in virtue of this that the Act is still in force. The term of office of this military governor was not without some points of interest. He caused a census to be taken in which the population in 1784 is put down at 113,032. He had a dispute with an ancient subject Du Calvet, as his predecessor had with a former chief justice, and a violent and acrimonious controversy about the administration of justice. (f)

In 1786, General Carleton under the title of Lord Dorchester returned to Canada as Governor-General, and shortly afterwards took the title of vice-admiral which is still retained. He appointed committees of enquiry into the state of the laws of commerce, of police and of education; and the information received in this way laid the foundation of the Constitutional Act of a few years later. The Governor turned his attention to the western part of his province. What is now the province of Ontario had received a large accession to its numbers by the influx of the New England loyalists. In 1788, he divided

(e) So it is stated by several writers; some say that the first Act of Henry Hamilton, the successor of Haldimand, was the publication of the introduction of Habeas Corpus.

(f) For a very fair epitome of Du Calvet's propositions see Doutre and Lareau's History of the French law. Garneau is very full on the same subject.

the country into five districts which may be roughly set
down as follows :

From Lancaster west to Gananoque,	LUNENBURG.
West of this to the river Trent,	MECHLENBURG.
West of this as far as Long Point, on Lake Erie,	NASSAU.
All the remaining part of what is now the province of Ontario,	HESSE.
South of the St. Lawrence and east of Cape Chat.	GASPE.

The Council during the ten years since his last term of
office had been of little account, and all parties were now
looking to England for a constitutional form of government.
The *Habeas Corpus* Act had been a great step in introducing
English law, but a large majority of the council presented
an address to the King, praying that he would maintain
intact the Quebec Act. This was in 1784, and the English
government thought the country was not yet in a fit state to
elect members to a popular assembly.

The people, however, proceeded from petitions to demands,
and the most conflicting views reached London as to what
was the best form of government for Canada. The British
ministry directed Lord Dorchester to collect information
and report on the state of the colony. As may be expected,
this was not obtained without great difference of opinion.
There were reports on the administration of justice, on
trade, on the manner of holding landed property, on education and on other subjects. There was a difference of
opinion between the chief justice and a former attorney-
general, M. Maseres, as to whether the English laws were
in force, though the chief justice found himself in a
minority. The view was presented that the English laws
generally were not binding under the statutes.

The reports of the several committees were sent to the ministry in England, though it was over two years before the Act was taken into consideration.

In 1789, Lord Grenville, as colonial minister, sent out a draft constitution to Lord Dorchester in order to get his advice and suggestions.

The Governor reported against the division of the province of Quebec, but, as will be seen, the English ministry deemed it advisable to separate the two races.

The Quebec Act, as a charter of government, was in force about sixteen years; the next change was the Constitutional Act of 1791.

CHAPTER IV.

THE DIVIDED CANADAS.—1791 TO 1841.

Petitions preceding this Act, Mr. Lymberger's desire to repeal Quebec Act, for a new constitution, for one province— English population, disappointment—King's message, principal parts of the Act, division into Upper and Lower Canada, legislative council and legislative assembly for each, courts, tenure of land, reservation of certain bills, clergy reserves—Provisions for Protestant clergy, for Roman Catholic clergy, tithes—Discontent, councillors, governors, suspension of constitution in Lower Canada, rebellion—Reports, Lord Durham.

WHAT Mr. Maseres did for his friends in 1774 Mr. Adam Lymberger did for his in 1791. This gentleman was the agent for the English colonists and appeared in their behalf before the bar of the house of commons. When the bill was introduced, he desired a repeal of the Quebec Act; he opposed a division of the province and he asked for a new constitution "unclogged and unembarrassed with any laws prior to it." He considered that the French Canadians being over thirty years under British rule had an opportunity to acquire more of the customs and manners of his constituents, and that therefore having studied the English constitution and its laws they were able to appreciate them. He put forward with great eloquence the claims of the loyalists of 1785. He considered it the duty of the government, in kindness to its subjects to weed out gently and by degrees, certain prejudices of the French Canadians. He insinuated that the government was formerly misled by the French Canadians and their petitions when the Quebec Act was passed, and having glanced at the uncertainty of the laws in force, requested the introduction of the laws of England with some variations that occurred to him as being best for all parties. In fact he supplied to Mr. Fox and others of the opposition a great part of their arguments as far as they opposed the bill.

Compared with the opposition used against the passing of the Quebec Act he was consistent and reasonable. The English colonists had increased to about 100,000—the French numbered 225,000,—so that it was not the claims of a few hundreds he was putting forward. He did not ask, as the Maseres party did, that the French should be excluded from all offices and all representation in the assembly and council. He objected to two legislatures and to the division of the provinces, though it was specially asked that the common law of England should be the rule in what was afterwards Upper Canada, in case a division were made. The chief object was undoubtedly to get a repeal of the Quebec Act and of all the laws under it.

It cannot be said that Mr. Lymberger was successful. Mr. Pitt's government divided the province—it did not repeal the Quebec Act, it gave no new constitution, but allowed each province to deal with that question within its own boundaries. In February 1791, the King sent a message to the house of commons to the effect that a division of the province of Quebec was for the benefit of his subjects, and that one part be named Upper and the other Lower Canada; he recommended a permanent appropriation of lands for the support and maintenance of a Protestant clergy, "and it is His Majesty's desire that such provision may be made with respect to all future grants of land within the said provinces respectively, as may best conduce to the same object," consenting that the house may make regulations therefor.

The bill was presented within a few days of the message and in the month of March the petitions against it were heard and the discussion upon it took place. The Bill passed into law on the 10th of June 1791, and is entitled " An Act to repeal certain parts of an Act passed in the 14th year of His Majesty's reign entitled 'an Act for making more effectual provision for the government of the province of Quebec, in North America,' and to make further provision for the government of the said province."

The preamble of the Act recites that the Quebec Act was in many respects inapplicable to the present condition and circumstances of the province and that further provision was necessary for its good government and prosperity.

It then repealed that portion of the Act relating to the appointment of a council having power to make ordinances for " the peace, welfare and good government of the province," and proceeded to provide a legislative council and a legislative assembly for Upper and Lower Canada. This occupies thirty sections of the Act. Upper Canada was provided with a legislative assembly of sixteen elected members and seven councillors nominated by the crown. The corresponding members in the eastern province were fifty elected and fifteen nominated members. (a)   The population was about 150,000 of whom about four-fifths were of French origin residing in Lower Canada, and one fifth English in Upper Canada.

(a) There is a provision in the Act having in view the creation of an aristocracy, but it was never attempted to be put in practice.

After describing the form of government in this way, provincial courts of appeal were constituted—these being composed of the Governor and executive council until otherwise altered by the legislature. The English tenure of land in free and common socage was to apply to Upper Canada and might be extended to the other province. Bills of the local legislatures respecting ecclesiastical rights and waste lands of the crown were to go to England before being assented to.

The recommendation in the King's message and the consequent legislation thereon in relation to the reservation of lands for the support of a Protestant clergy and the endowment of rectories gave rise to the Clergy Reserves. These reserves were to be equal in value to the one-seventh part of the secular lands, and the rents arising from them were to be devoted exclusively to the maintenance and support of a Protestant clergy. (b) This reservation was abolished in 1840 and the provisions as to parsonages and incumbencies were repealed in 1851.

Provision was made in regard to the Roman Catholic clergy, continuing and enforcing "their accustomed dues and rights with respect to such persons only as should profess the said religion," as declared in the Quebec Act, and in pursuance of the instructions to Sir Guy Carleton and Sir Frederick Hamilton, two of the previous Governors. The instructions were to protect Protestants from being liable to pay tithes for the support of the Roman Catholic clergy. The Act of 1791 applied their tithes to their own clergy. Tithes were enforceable in Upper as well as in Lower

(b) Besides this aid to the Church of England, the legislature of Upper Canada for some years previous to the rebellion in 1837 gave assistance both for the erection of churches and the support of ministers to the Roman Catholics, the Presbyterians and the Methodists.

Canada. (c) The provincial legislatures had control over them, but bills in reference thereto were reserved for the King's pleasure.

The new constitution went into force on the 26th of December, 1791, and in the following May by a proclamation of Alured Clark, administrator, the old province of Quebec ceased to exist, and in its place appeared Upper and Lower Canada. (d) The proclamation divided each section into districts and counties, and fixed the number of those who would be called for the first time to represent the electors in the legislative assemblies.

After the elections the new representatives met, those for Upper Canada at Newark, now Niagara, on the 18th of September, 1792, and those for Lower Canada on the 17th of December following at Quebec. Governor Simcoe presided in Upper Canada. In both provinces a speaker was appointed and the usages and formalities of the English parliament adopted as nearly as might be. In the eastern province the question of race arose at once in the choice of

(c) Mention is made of tithes for the Roman Catholic clergy in Glengarry and in Sandwich. They were abolished in Upper Canada by 2 Geo. I. cap. 32. In the very early part of the French *régime* tithes were the one-thirteenth of all revenue derived from labour and from the natural products of the soil, forests and waters ; but for more than two hundred years the tithes have been the one-twenty-sixth part and are restricted to growing produce. It is somewhat singular that the word *dixmes* or *tithes* should be used for these fractions.

(d) The dividing line was fixed by an order of the King in council dated in August, 1791, and is as follows:
"Commencing at a stone boundary on the north bank of Lake St. Francis, at the cove west of the Point au Baudet, in the limit between the township of Lancaster and the seigniory of New Longueil ; running along the said limit in the direction of north, 34 degrees west to the westermost angle of the said seigniory of New Longueil; thence along the north-west boundary of the seigniory of Vaudreuil, running north 25 degrees east, until it strikes the Ottawa river ; to ascend the said river into Lake Temiscaming ; and from the head of the said lake by a line drawn due north until it strikes the boundary line of Hudson's Bay ; including all the territory to the westward and southward of the said line, to the utmost extent of the country commonly called or known by the name of Canada."

a speaker and of the language of the house, and it resulted in a compromise, the adoption of both languages. M. Panet was the speaker at Quebec, Mr. McDonell at Newark. The seat of government in Upper Canada remained at Newark for three years, and in 1799 it was removed to York.

Mr. Miles writing of the Act of 1791 says :

" The first 15 or 16 years' experience of the new constitution was rather encouraging as those concerned in working it out during that period exerted themselves in keeping out of sight the causes of discord. Through the accession of officers of the army and disbanded soldiers, as well as the influx of immigrants from the British Isles, the population increased rapidly, especially in Upper Canada, where it exceeded 80,000 in the year 1805. But, as has been already mentioned, the constitution of 1791 did not secure the extinction of former causes of dissension, while it introduced new elements of discord. In each province there was created an irresponsible body, which the Governor or Lieutenant-Governor was empowered to establish under the title of an *executive council*, and which was in fact, constituted by the selection chiefly of members of the legislative council. Some were judges and men receiving salaries as public officers. In Lower Canada in addition to the fact that legislative councillors and paid public officials formed the great majority of the executive council, natives of the province were very seldom admitted, nor, as respects religion, were the Roman Catholics represented, although a seat was conferred on the chief protestant ecclesiastic while the members of his communion did not form one-twentieth part of the population. These circumstances, so opposite in principle to the policy of representative government which has since prevailed in Canada, gave much offence to the majority of the inhabitants and rendered harmony impossible. Former feelings of animosity were revived."

In Lower Canada, also, the popular representation resulted generally in the exclusion of Englishmen; the legislature and executive councils as generally excluded Frenchmen. The governors had the councillors on their side and had the popular party against them. In this state of affairs as early as 1806 it became almost impossible to govern the province. The war of 1812-14 turned the attention of all parties to the external enemies; but after it was settled, (e) the former difficulties presented themselves and new causes of strife were introduced.

It was soon evident that, notwithstanding the ample machinery of government provided by the Act, the people were not in possession of the controlling power. The power was centred practically in the governors and their executives. In the eastern province the disputes between the elected and the nominated branches of the legislature began early; but the sister province had grievances that culminated about the same time and in the same way—in rebellion. The struggle in both was for the same objects—for responsible government—for liberty to enact laws in accord with the popular wish—for restraining the power of irresponsible governors. (f)

(e) By the treaty of Ghent, signed December 24, 1814.

(f) As regards the privileges of the Houses of Parliament or Assemblies under the constitutional Act of 1791, a few cases appear. In 1812, Mr. McDonell, member for Glengarry, complained of a breach of privilege inasmuch as that the Deputy Clerk of the Crown issued a writ to have him arrested; freedom from arrest of a member was claimed. The offending attorney was dismissed from office but was almost immediately reinstated.

In the same season Mr. Nichol was arrested under the speaker's warrant and committed to gaol, but the Chief Justice had him set at liberty. The Assembly then turned its attention again against the Chief Justice and gave vent to its feelings by petitions to the throne, which the Admiral Major-General Brock assured them would be laid before the Prince Regent.

No other encroachments on the privileges of the members arose till 1828, when the Adjutant-General of the Militia and the superintendent

The various governors had resorted to the constitutional remedy of dissolving the legislatures when their proceedings were distasteful to them. The result was that they rendered themselves and their councillors extremely unpopular. 87,000 persons petitioned for the removal of Lord Dalhousie : 24,000 signatures were sent for the removal of Sir John Colborne. In 1834, ninety-two resolutions were sent from the lower province, with the effect that a commission was appointed to report on the affairs of that province. In 1838 a high commissioner was sent from England to the upper province. This was Lord Durham, whose report is one of the features of our constitutional history. (*g*) The outcome of these reports was that the two provinces, after a separation of half a century were again united. The population at that time may be roughly set down at one million almost equally divided in race and religion.

of Indian affairs put themselves in contempt by not appearing before the Bar of the House. Both of these were found guilty, and warrants were issued for their arrest, under which they remained three days in prison when the prorogation of the House set them at liberty. Sir Peregrine Maitland, in official language declared that on all future occasions if the propriety of this proceeding is confirmed by His Majesty, "no one will be more ready than himself to recognize the privilege in question and to enforce its observance by all whom it is his duty to control." Henry John Boulton, Solicitor-General, fell under the displeasure of the House in refusing to answer certain questions put to him by a committee. He was admonished and discharged

In the following year Mr. (afterwards Sir) Allan McNab having refused to answer certain questions was committed to gaol. This case was brought into the Courts and Chief Justice Robinson upheld the committal.

The Legislature of the Lower Province was not behindhand in asserting like powers and privileges. As early as the second year of the Constitution a like case to that of Mr. McDonell as to freedom from arrest arose in the case of Mr. John Young. He was arrested and reported the indignity to the House of Assembly. The House declared that the arrest of one of its members was a direct violation of one of its undoubted rights : apology was demanded from the sheriff and inserted in the journals of the Assembly. The sheriff and his bailiff appeared at the Bar of the House and satisfied the wounded honor of Mr. Young.

In a subsequent session certain members objected to serving on a jury panel, and the House absolved them from it. They expelled one member who was convicted of the crime of conspiracy, and another charged with perjury. The Legislative Council was held by the court to have the right to commit for publication of libellous matter.

(*g*) Mr. Mills has said of it that "it laid the foundation of the political success and social prosperity not only of Canada but of all the other important colonies."

CHAPTER V.

THE UNITED CANADAS, OTHER COLONIES.—1840 TO 1867.

Lord Durham's report, recommendations—Act of Union, one legislature, two houses, legislative council, legislative assembly, duration, speakers—Governors, powers, laws continued—Amendments, elective councillors, seat of government—Former governments in Nova Scotia, in New Brunswick, in Prince Edward Island, in British Columbia—Conventions at Charlottetown, at Quebec—Confederation.

THE year 1841 marks the beginning of representative government in Canada. The Act of Union passed in the preceding year was founded on the report of Lord Durham, and it not only established a new order of things for Canada, but also served as a model for colonial government generally. It recommended that as far as possible the colonists should be allowed to govern themselves, that they should make and execute their own laws, that the provinces should be united, and that the races and districts should be represented in one legislature. It looked forward to a complete system of municipal institutions and to the independence of the judges. All provincial officers except the Governor should be responsible to the people and all questions of internal government dealt with by the local legislature. Trade, foreign relations, the disposal of the public lands and the constitution of the country he recommended should be left to imperial management; the law as it stood in regard to clergy reserves should be repealed. The prospect of a union of the other provinces was foreshadowed, but it was a legislative rather than a federal union. Though all the recommendations of the distinguished commissioner were not carried into effect by the subsequent Act of Union, it embodied the chief features of the report.

The Imperial Act, 3 and 4 Vict., cap. 35, came into force in 1841 and declared that the provinces of Upper and Lower Canada should by virtue of a proclamation form one province to be called Canada. One legislative council and an assembly were constituted, to be called " The Legislative Council and Assembly of Canada"; and within the province her Majesty, by and with the advice and consent of this body, was empowered to make laws for the peace, welfare and good government of the same, such laws not being repugnant to such portions of former constitutional Acts as remained unrepealed.

Legislative councillors, not fewer than twenty, were to be appointed. They were required to be of the full age of twenty-one years and natural born or naturalized subjects of her Majesty. They held office for life. Provision was made for vacancies by resignation, absence, adhesion to a foreign state, bankruptcy, etc., leaving the trial of any question on these points to the Governor and the council. The Governor appointed the speaker and might remove him and appoint another. Ten members, including the speaker, formed a quorum, and when the voices were equal the speaker had a casting vote. The assembly was summoned by instrument under the great seal in the Queen's name.

The legislative assembly was composed of an equal number of representatives from Upper and Lower Canada—

forty-two from each province. Power was given to alter
the representation by a two-thirds vote in each house. The
qualifications of a member were limited to property in freehold land to the value of five hundred pounds over and
above any charges on it, and provision was made in regard
to elections, vacancies, etc. Every assembly continued for
four years, unless sooner dissolved, and a yearly session,
as obtains at present in the Dominion parliament, was
necessary. The members elected their own speaker and
twenty members, including the speaker, formed a quorum
for the exercise of the powers of the assembly. He had a
casting vote as the speaker of the other chamber.

The powers, authorities and functions of former governors
so far as they were not repugnant to the Act, were vested
in the governor with the executive council, or in the governor alone where "the advice, consent, or concurrence of
the executive council is not required." All existing laws
were to remain in force until altered ; and all courts of justice, commissions, powers and authorities of officers, judicial, administrative or ministerial were continued as if the
Act had not been passed.

This is the substance of the Act, as far as it need be
referred to. A clause requiring that all writs, proclamations and instruments for summoning or proroguing the
assembly, or writs or summons in relation to elections and
other public documents should be in English was subsequently
repealed in 1848. The only substantial addition to the
Act was passed in 1854, by which power was given to the
legislature of Canada to alter the constitution of the legislative council so as to make it elective, and to repeal or
vary the property qualification of members of the assembly.
In pursuance of this statute, the provinces were divided
into 48 electoral districts with one representative councillor
for each, twelve to retire at the end of every two years.

The seat of government was, up to 1844, part of the time in Toronto and part in Kingston; it was located afterwards in Montreal, but in 1849 the assembly sat alternately in Toronto and Quebec until the provinces were united in 1867. Lord Sydenham was the first Governor-General under the Union Act and Lord Monck the last. (a)

The other provinces may be conveniently referred to in this place. The Treaty of Utrecht signed in 1713 has already come under the attention of the reader. By it Nova Scotia was formally ceded by France to England. It was called Acadia by its former owners and included New Brunswick until the year 1784. Cape Breton remained a possession of France after the Treaty of Utrecht, but came under British rule by the Treaty of Paris in 1763. Three years later it was annexed to the government of Nova Scotia, but together with New Brunswick was separated from it in the same year. In 1820 it again returned to its former partner and remained a part of it until confederation.

Nova Scotia during the first half century of British rule contented itself with a Lieutenant-Governor and a council, but in 1758 a constitution was granted to it and a legislative assembly of 22 members provided for. This form of government lasted until the year 1838 when a separation was effected between the legislative and the executive authorities. After a lapse of ten years, a limit was placed to the number composing the assembly—38 being allowed; and under this form of government the people of Nova Scotia entered the union in 1867.

New Brunswick after her separation from Nova Scotia in 1784, was governed by a Lieutenant-Governor with a

(a) Lord Monck was also the first Governor-General of the Dominion of Canada. The Governors after Lord Sydenham were Sir Charles Bagot, Lord Metcalf, Lord Cathcart, Lord Elgin and Sir E. W. Head.

council of 12 members possessing legislative as well as executive functions. In 1832 this anomaly was removed and New Brunswick entered the union in the same way as her sister province.

Prince Edward Island was known as St. John under the French rule; the English took possession of it in 1758. By the Treaty of Paris it fell to the English and was assigned to the government of Nova Scotia, where it remained until 1769. It then separated from that province and so remained up to the date of its admission into the union in 1873. It was provided with a constitution and has had a government similar to that of the other maritime provinces. (b)

British Columbia and Vancouver's Island were formerly part of the Hudson Bay Territory. The latter in 1848 was assigned to the company for ten years, and about the end of that time it and the mainland were taken away from the Hudson Bay Company and formed into separate colonies. In 1866 they were united under one administration. Previously in 1863 a royal governor was sent out and a government formed, one half of the advising council being composed of government officials and the other half elected by the people of the colony.

Manitoba and the North-West Territories had no separate political existence before forming part of Canada. They were portions of Prince Rupert's Land ceded to Canada by the home government.

(b) The Governor of Canada was Captain General of British America, but did not interfere with the administration of the other colonies. These were presided over by what were called lieutenant-governors, though they were governors in everything but name, being commanders-in-chief within their provinces and taking precedence next after the Governor of Canada.

The project of uniting the colonies of British North America is one that dates back to the first years of the century. It was not unheard of before Lord Durham's time. In 1800, 1814, 1822 and 1825 there were projects of a union and the idea revived in 1857. Nova Scotia took the first legislative step by a resolution in 1861. A conference of the maritime provinces was arranged early in 1864, and towards the end of the year delegates from the Canadas joined the eastern delegates at a convention in Charlottetown. Newfoundland was not represented. It was arranged that another convention should be called by the Governor-General and this was done in the following month. The Quebec convention as it is called assembled in the city on the 10th of October 1864. It was composed of twelve delegates from the Canadas, seven from New Brunswick, five from Nova Scotia, seven from Prince Edward Island and two from Newfoundland. After eighteen days debate with closed doors seventy-two resolutions were adopted and these were submitted to the different legislatures in 1865. The Canadian legislature adopted the resolutions by a vote of about three to one in each house ; but the other provinces did not respond so readily and two of them did not agree to them at all. New Brunswick and Nova Scotia however in 1866 resolved that it was desirable that a confederation should take place and so preparations were made for the passing of an imperial Act to give effect to these resolutions.

Delegates from the three provinces assembled at London in December 1866 and arranged for the final terms of the union. The Earl of Carnarvon introduced the Bill in the Lords on the 7th of February, and on the 28th of the following month, it had passed both houses and received Her Majesty's assent. On the 22nd of May a royal proclamation was issued by which the new constitution of

Canada was to take effect on the day named therein. That was the first of July 1867, and thenceforth CANADA as at present governed began her latest phase of existence. The object of the past part of this volume is to describe that constitution and the government that prevails under it.

It is the sixth change that has taken place for the old colony of Canada since 1760 :

1. Military government of General Murray...... 1760-1764

2. Civil government by governor and council... 1764-1774

3. Government under the Quebec Act............ 1774-1791

4. Government under the Constitutional Act... 1791-1841

5. Government under the Union Act.............. 1841-1867

6. Government under the B. N. A. Act.......... 1867

CHAPTER VI.

CONCLUSION.

THE constitution under which we in Canada live and are governed is a new departure in the history of colonial government. We have glanced over the various experiments made by the provinces now composing the Dominion of Canada in the solution of satisfactory government; and they are generally seen to be composed of a governor, a legislative council and a legislative assembly for each colony or province. Most of these colonial possessions were heretofore outlying fragments of the empire, with no cohesion and no nationality, with nothing in common except the tie to the mother country. The scheme of uniting the provinces had been long in contemplation. It was felt that at least everything which they had in common might well be decided in one central legislature; and that if one body could not direct all the affairs of the different provinces, it could manage such interests as were not antagonistic.

There was at hand as evidence of the success or at least the possibility of a federacy, the example of a great and prosperous republic, where each state managed its own local concerns, but delegated certain powers to a central government, to be held and exercised by them in trust for the whole union. There were, on the other hand, the traditions of the government of Great Britain, which are the inheritance of her present and past colonies. The present

constitution is the result—the unintentional result, perhaps—of a federal system somewhat analogous to that of
the United States, so far as the distribution of legislative
power is concerned, and yet very different from it in the
underlying principle of its constitution. Like the states
of the Union, the provinces of the Dominion are united for
some purposes and separated for others. There is a
federacy—a union for matters of general and, one might
say, national interest; there is a separation for matters of
local or internal interest.

The fact that the constitution of Canada provides one
central government for all the provinces and a local one
for each of them, as in the United States, and also that the
constitution is in principle similar to that of Great Britain,
makes the study of the government in each of these
countries necessary to the Canadian student. (a)

Canada, considered in point of territory, has a good deal
of similarity to the United States; and it cannot be said
that in copying the constitution of that country to the
extent that she has done, any mistake was committed.
Local concerns in a large country are managed most satisfactorily by local administration.

It is true that Canada, with a population somewhat
exceeding that of the city of London, has a system of
governments as elaborate as that of the United States for
a population of ten times that number. We have a central
government with powers largely in advance, comparatively
speaking, of that at Washington; and we have provincial
governments which, even if their limits are narrowly hedged
in, are yet each year asserting the necessity of their existence by volumes of statutory enactments. If this leg-

(a) The full text of the United States Constitution is given in the
Appendix.

islation be all necessary, and it must be assumed that it is, the central government might sit at Ottawa all the year through and not do one-half of it at all—and probably not do a tenth of it sufficiently. A house of over 200 members is cumbrous machinery for legislating on any subjects, but totally inadequate for the local concerns of remote provinces. The provinces are too scattered and their interests too diverse to admit of the possibility of legislating for all the ordinary means of two houses of parliament. The members may understand the legislation proposed or needed for their own province; but they could not be expected to fully understand and be interested in the legislation needed a thousand miles off.

A little consideration will show that the people of the Dominion cannot be legislated for in the same way as five or six millions of people may be in a thickly settled or confined district. There is a strip of the broadest part of the continent extending from ocean to ocean. There are different modes of life among its inhabitants—in Nova Scotia, in Manitoba, in British Columbia—each requiring special local legislation; different customs, races and religions even in the twin provinces of Ontario and Quebec, different features everywhere.

The complex system of government that obtains amongst us must therefore be regarded as a necessity : we have the territory if we have not the population to justify its existence. It is some consolation, however, that when our provinces and territories number a great many millions more than they do at present, the constitution supplies ample machinery for their government.

THE END.

APPENDIX.

———

CONSTITUTION OF THE UNITED STATES.

The Constitution framed for the United States of America, by a Convention of Deputies from the States of New Hampshire, Massachusetts, Connecticut, New York, New Jersey, Pennsylvania, Delaware, Maryland, Virginia, North Carolina, South Carolina, and Georgia, at a session begun May 25th and ended September 17, 1887.

We, the people of the United States, in order to form a more perfect Union, establish justice, insure domestic tranquillity, provide for the common defence, promote the general welfare, and secure the blessings of liberty to ourselves and our posterity, do ordain and establish this Constitution for the United States of America.

ARTICLE I.

SECTION I.

All Legislative powers herein granted shall be vested in a Congress of the United States, which shall consist of a Senate and House of Representatives.

SECTION II.

1. The House of Representatives shall be composed of members chosen every second year, by the people of the several States; and the electors in each State shall have the qualifications requisite for electors of the most numerous branch of the State Legislature.

2. No person shall be a Representative who shall not have attained to the age of twenty-five years, and been seven years a citizen of the United States, and who shall not, when elected, be an inhabitant of that State in which he shall be chosen.

3. Representatives and direct taxes shall be apportioned among the several States which may be included within this Union, according to their respective numbers, which shall be determined by adding to the whole number of free persons, including those bound to service for a term of years, and excluding Indians not taxed, three fifths of all other persons. The actual enumeration shall be made within three years after the first meeting of the Congress of the United States; and, within every subsequent term of ten years, in such manner as they shall by law direct. The

number of Representatives shall not exceed one for every thirty thousand ; but each State shall have at least one Representative; and, until such enumeration shall be made, the State of New Hampshire shall be entitled to choose three ; Massachusetts, eight ; Rhode Island and Providence Plantations, one; Connecticut, five; New York, six ; New Jersey, four ; Pennsylvania, eight ; Delaware, one ; Maryland, six ; Virginia, ten ; North Carolina, five ; South Carolina, five ; and Georgia, three.

4. When vacancies happen in the representation from any State, the executive authority thereof shall issue writs of election to fill such vacancies.

5. The House of Representatives shall choose their speaker and other officers, and shall have the sole power of impeachment.

SECTION III.

1. The Senate of the United States shall be composed of two Senators from each State, chosen by the Legislature thereof, for six years; and each Senator shall have one vote.

2. Immediately after they shall be assembled, in consequence of the first election, they shall be divided, as equally as may be, into three classes. The seats of the Senators of the first class shall be vacated at the expiration of the second year ; of the second class, at the expiration of the fourth year ; and of the third class, at the expiration of the sixth year; so that one third may be chosen every second year. And if vacancies happen, by resignation or otherwise, during the recess of the Legislature of any State, the Executive thereof may make temporarily appointment until the next meeting of the Legislature, which shall then fill such vacancies.

3. No person shall be a Senator who shall not have attained to the age of thirty years, and been nine years a citizen of the United States, and who shall not, when elected be an inhabitant of that State for which he shall be chosen.

4. The Vice-President of the United States shall be President of the Senate, but shall have no vote unless they be equally divided.

5. The Senate shall choose their other officers, and also a President pro-tempore in the absence of the Vice-President, or when he shall exercise the office of President of the United States.

6. The Senate shall have the sole power to try all impeachments. When sitting for that purpose, they shall be on oath or affirmation. When the President of the United States is tried, the Chief Justice shall preside ; and no person shall be convicted without the concurrence of two thirds of the members present.

7. Judgment, in cases of impeachment, shall not extend further than to removal from office, and disqualification to hold and enjoy any office of honor, trust, or profit under the United States. But the party convicted shall, nevertheless, be liable and subject to indictment, trial, judgment and punishment, according to law.

SECTION IV.

1. The times, places, and manner of holding elections for Senators and Representatives shall be prescribed in each State by the Legislature

thereof; but the Congress may, at any time, by law, make or alter such regulations, except as to the places of choosing Senators.

2. The Congress shall assemble at least once in every year; and such meetings shall be held on the first Monday in December, unless they shall, by law, appoint a different day.

SECTION V.

1. Each House shall be the judge of the elections, returns, and qualifications of its own members; and a majority of each shall be considered a quorum to do business; but a smaller number may adjourn from day to day, and may be authorized to compel the attendance of absent members, in such manner and under such penalties as each House may provide.

2. Each House may determine the rules of its proceedings; punish its members for disorderly behaviour; and with the concurrence of two thirds, expel a member.

3. Each House shall keep a journal of its proceedings and from time to time publish the same, except such parts as may in their judgment require secrecy; and the yeas and nays of the members of either House on any question shall, at the desire of one fifth of those present, be entered on the journal.

4. Neither House, during the session of Congress, shall, without the consent of the other, adjourn for more than three days, nor to any other place than that in which the two Houses shall be sitting.

SECTION VI.

1. The Senators and Representatives shall receive a compensation for their services, to be ascertained by law, and paid out of the treasury of the United States. They shall, in all cases except treason, felony, and breach of the peace, be privileged from arrest during their attendance at the session of their respective Houses, and in going to and returning from the same: for any speech or debate in either House, they shall not be questioned in any other place.

2. No Senator or Representative shall, during the time for which he was elected, be appointed to any civil office, under the authority of the United States, which shall have been created, or the emoluments whereof shall have been increased, during such time; and no person holding any office under the United States shall be a member of either house during his continuance in office.

SECTION VII.

1. All bills for raising revenue shall originate in the House of Representatives; but the Senate may propose or concur with amendments, as on other bills.

2. Every bill which shall have passed the House of Representatives and the Senate shall, before it becomes law, be presented to the President of the United States. If he approve it, he shall sign it; but if not, he shall return it, with his objections, to that house in which it shall have originated, who shall enter the objections at large on their journal, and proceed to reconsider it. If after such reconsideration, two thirds of that house shall agree to pass the bill, it shall be sent, together with the objections, to the other House, by which it shall likewise be reconsidered: and, if approved by two thirds of that House, it shall become a law.

But in all such cases the votes of both Houses shall be determined by yeas and nays ; and the names of the persons voting for and against the bill, shall be entered on the journal of each House respectively. If any bill shall not be returned by the President within ten days (Sundays excepted) after it shall have been presented to him, the same shall be a law in like manner as if he had signed it, unless the Congress by their adjournment, prevent its return ; in which case it shall not be a law.

3. Every order, resolution, or vote to which the concurrence of the Senate and House of Representatives may be necessary, (except on a question of adjournment,) shall be presented to the President of the United States, and, before the same shall take effect, shall be approved by him, or being disapproved by him, shall be re-passed by two thirds of the Senate and House of Representatives, according to the rules and limitations prescribed in the case of a bill.

SECTION VIII.

The Congress shall have power,

1. To lay and collect taxes, duties, imposts, and excises to pay the debts and provide for the common defence and general welfare of the United States ; but all duties, imposts, and excises shall be uniform throughout the United States :

2. To borrow money on the credit of the United States :

3. To regulate commerce with foreign nations, and among the several States, and with the Indian tribes :

4. To establish a uniform rule of naturalization, and uniform laws on the subject of bankruptcies throughout the United States :

5. To coin money, regulate the value thereof, and of foreign coin, and fix the standard of weights and measures :

6. To provide for the punishment of counterfeiting the securities and current coin of the United States :

7. To establish post-offices and post-roads :

8. To promote the progress of science and useful arts, by securing, for limited times, to authors and inventors, the exclusive right to their respective writings and discoveries :

9. To constitute tribunals inferior to the Supreme Court :

10. To define and punish piracies and felonies committed on the high seas, and offences against the law of nations :

11. To declare war, grant letters of marque and reprisal, and make rules concerning captures on land and water :

12. To raise and support armies ; but no appropriation of money for that use shall be for a longer term than two years :

13. To provide and maintain a navy :

14. To make rules for the government and regulation of the land and naval forces :

15. To provide for calling forth the militia to execute the laws of the Union, suppress insurrections, and repel invasions :

16. To provide for organizing, arming, and disciplining the militia, and for governing such part of them as may be employed in the service of the United States, reserving to the States respectively the appointment of the officers, and the authority of training the militia according to the discipline prescribed by Congress.

17. To exercise exclusive legislation, in all cases whatsoever, over such District (not exceeding ten miles square) as may, by cession of particular States, and the acceptance of Congress, become the seat of the government of the United States; and to exercise like authority over all places purchased by the consent of the Legislature of the State in which the same shall be, for the erection of forts, magazines, arsenals, dockyards, and other needful buildings; and,

18. To make all laws which shall be necessary and proper for carrying into execution the foregoing powers, and all other powers vested by this Constitution in the Government of the United States, or in any department or officer thereof.

SECTION IX.

1. The migration or importation of such persons as any of the States now existing shall think proper to admit, shall not be prohibited by the Congress prior to the year one thousand eight hundred and eight; but a tax or duty may be imposed on such importation, not exceeding ten dollars for each person.

2. The privilege of the writ of *habeas corpus* shall not be suspended, unless when, in cases of rebellion or invasion, the public safety may require it.

3. No bill of attainder or *ex post facto* law shall be passed.

4. No capitation or other direct tax shall be laid, unless in proportion to the census or enumeration hereinbefore directed to be taken.

5. No tax or duty shall be laid on articles exported from any State.

6. No preference shall be given by any regulation of commerce or revenue to the ports of one State over those of another; nor shall vessels bound to, or from one State, be obliged to enter, clear, or pay duties in another.

7. No money shall be drawn from the treasury but in consequence of appropriations made by law; and a regular statement and account of the receipts and expenditures of all public money shall be published from time to time.

8. No title of nobility shall be granted by the United States; and no person holding any office of profit or trust under them shall, without the consent of the Congress, accept of any present emolument, office, or title of any kind whatever, from any king, prince, or foreign State.

SECTION X.

1. No State shall enter into any treaty, alliance, or confederation; grant letters of marque and reprisal; coin money; emit bills of credit; make any thing but gold and silver coin a tender in payment of debts; pass any bill of attainder, *ex post facto* law, or law impairing the obligation of contracts; or grant any title of nobility.

2. No State shall, without the consent of the Congress, lay any imposts or duties on imports or exports, except what may be absolutely necessary

for executing its inspection laws; and the net produce of all duties and imposts, laid by any State on imports or exports, shall be for the use of the treasury of the United States: and all such laws shall be subject to the revision and control of the Congress.

3. No State shall, without the consent of Congress, lay any duty of tonnage, keep troops or ships of war in time of peace, enter into any agreement or compact with another State, or with a foreign power, or engage in war, unless actually invaded or in such imminent danger as will not admit of delay.

ARTICLE II.

SECTION I.

1. The Executive power shall be vested in a President of the United States of America. He shall hold his office during the term of four years, and together with the Vice-President, chosen for the same term, be elected as follows:

2. Each State shall appoint, in such manner as the Legislature thereof may direct, a number of Electors, equal to the whole number of senators and representatives to which the State may be entitled in the Congress; but no senator or representative, or person holding any office of trust or profit under the United States, shall be appointed an elector.

3. The Electors shall meet in their respective States, and vote by ballot for two persons, of whom one at least shall not be an inhabitant of the same State with themselves. And they shall make a list of all the persons voted for, and of the number of votes for each; which list they shall sign and certify, and transmit sealed to the seat of the Government of the United States, directed to the President of the Senate. The President of the Senate shall, in the presence of the Senate and House of Representatives, open all the certificates, and the votes shall then be counted. The person having the greatest number of votes shall be the President, if such number be a majority of the whole number of Electors appointed; and if there be more than one who have such majority, and have an equal number or votes, then the House of Representatives shall immediately chose by ballot one of them for President; and if no person have a majority, then from the five highest on the list the said House shall in like manner choose the President. But in choosing the President the votes shall be taken by States, the representation from each state having one vote; a quorum for this purpose shall consist of a member or members from two-thirds of the States, and a majority of all the States shall be necessary to a choice. In every case, after the choice of the President, the person having the greatest number of votes of the Electors shall be the Vice-President. But if there should remain two or more who have equal votes, the Senate shall choose from them by ballot, the Vice-President.

4. The Congress may determine the time of choosing the Electors, and the day on which they shall give their votes; which day shall be the same throughout the United States.

5. No person, except a natural-born citizen, or a citizen of the United States at the time of the adoption of this Constitution, shall be eligible to the office of President; neither shall any person be eligible to that office who shall not have attained to the age of thirty-five years, and been fourteen years a resident within the United States.

6. In case of the removal of the President from office, or of his death, resignation, or inability to discharge the powers and duties of the said office, the same shall develop on the Vice-President; and the Congress may by law provide for the case of removal, death, resignation, or inability, both of the President and Vice-President, declaring what officer shall then act as President, and such officer shall act accordingly, until the disability be removed, or a President shall be elected.

8. The President shall, at stated times, receive for his services a compensation, which shall neither be increased nor diminished during the period for which he shall have been elected, and he shall not receive within that period any other emolument from the United States, or any of them.

8. Before he enter on the execution of his office, he shall take the following oath or affirmation :—

" I do solemnly swear (or affirm) that I will faithfully execute the office of President of the United States ; and will, to the best of my ability, preserve, protect, and defend the Constitution of the United States."

SECTION II.

1. The President shall be commander-in-chief of the army and navy of the United States, and of the militia of the several States when called into the actual service of the United States ; he may require the opinion, in writing, of the principal officer in each of the Executive departments, upon any subject relating to the duties of their respective offices, and he shall have power to grant reprieves and pardons for offences against the United States, except in cases of impeachment.

2. He shall have power, by and with the advice and consent of the Senate, to make treaties, provided two thirds of the Senators present concur ; and he shall nominate, 'and by and with the advice and consent of the Senate, shall appoint ambassadors, other public ministers, and consuls, judges of the Supreme Court, and all other officers of the United States whose appointments are not herein otherwise provided for, and which shall be established by law ; but the Congress may by law vest the appointment of such inferior officers as they think proper in the President alone, in the courts of law, or in the heads of departments.

3. The President shall have power to fill up all vacancies that may happen during the recess of the Senate, by granting commissions which shall expire at the end of their next session.

SECTION III.

He shall, from time to time, give to the Congress information of the State of the Union, and recommend to their consideration such measures as he shall judge necessary and expedient : he may, on extraordinary occasions, convene both Houses, or either of them, and in case of disagreement between them with respect to the time of adjournment, he may adjourn them to such time as he shall think proper ; he shall receive ambassadors and other public ministers ; he shall take care that the laws be faithfully executed, and shall commission all the officers of the United States.

SECTION IV.

The President, Vice-President, and all civil officers of the United States, shall be removed from office on impeachment for, and conviction of treason, bribery, or other high crimes and misdemeanors.

ARTICLE III.

SECTION I.

Ths Judicial power of United States shall be vested in one Supreme Court, and in such inferior courts as the Congress may, from time to time, ordain and establish. The judges, both of the supreme and inferior courts, shall hold their offices during good behaviour, and shall, at stated times, receive for their services, a compensation which shall not be diminished during their continuance in office.

SECTION II.

1. The judicial power shall extend to all cases in law and equity arising under this Constitution, the laws of the United States, and treaties made, or which shall be made, under their authority; to all cases affecting ambassadors; other public ministers, and consuls; to all cases of admiralty and maritime jurisdiction; to controversies to which the United States shall be a party; to controversies between two or more States; between a State and citizens of another State; between citizens of different States; between citizens of the same State claiming lands under grants of different States; and between a State, or the citizens thereof and foreign States, citizens, or subjects.

2. In all cases affecting ambassadors, other public ministers, and consuls, and those in which a State shall be a party, the Supreme Court shall have original jurisdiction. In all the other cases before mentioned, the Supreme Court shall have appellate jurisdiction, both as to law and fact, with such exceptions, and under such regulations, as the Congress shall make.

3. The trial of all crimes, except in cases of impeachment, shall be by jury, and such trial shall be held in the State where the said crimes shall have been committed; but when not committed within any State, the trial shall be at such place or places as the Congress may by law have directed.

SECTION III.

1. Treason against the United States shall consist only in levying war against them, or in adhering to their enemies, giving them aid and comfort. No person shall be convicted of treason unless on the testimony of two witnesses to the same overt act, or on confession in open court.

2. The Congress shall have power to declare the punishment of treason; but no attainder of treason shall work corruption of blood or forfeiture, except during the life of the person attainted.

ARTICLE IV.

SECTION I.

Full faith and credit shall be given, in each State, to the public acts, records, and judicial proceedings of every other State. And the Congress may, by general laws, prescribe the manner in which such acts, records, and proceedings shall be proved, and the effect therof.

SECTION II.

1. The citizens of each State shall be entitled to all privileges and immunities of citizens in the several States.

2. A person charged in any state with treason, felony, or other crime, who shall flee from justice and be found in another State, shall, on demand of the Executive authority of the State from which he fled, be delivered up, to be removed to the State having jurisdiction of the crime.

3. No person, held to service or labor in one State under the laws thereof, escaping into another, shall, in consequence of any law or regulation therein, be discharged from such service or labor ; but shall be delivered up on claim of the party to whom such service or labor may be due.

SECTION III.

1. New States may be admitted by the Congress into this Union ; but no new States shall be formed or erected within the jurisdiction of any other State ; nor any State be formed by the junction of two or more States, or parts of States, without the consent of the Legislature of the States concerned, as well as of the Congress.

2. The Congress shall have power to dispose of and make all needful rules and regulations respecting the territory or other property belonging to the United States ; and nothing in this Constitution shall be so construed as to prejudice any claims of the United States, or of any particular State.

SECTION IV.

The United States shall guarantee to every State in this Union a republican form of government, and shall protect each of them against invasion ; and on application of the Legislature, or of the Executive, (when the Legislature cannot be convened,) against domestic violence.

ARTICLE V.

The Congress, whenever two thirds of both Houses shall deem it necessary, shall propose amendments to this Constitution, or, on the application of the legislatures of two thirds of the several States, shall call a convention for proposing amendments ; which, in either case, shall be valid to all intents and purposes, as part of this Constitution, when ratified by the legislatures of three fourths of the several States, or by conventions in three fourths thereof, as the one or the other mode of ratification may be proposed by the Congress : Provided that no amendment which may be made prior to the year one thousand eight hundred and eight, shall in any manner affect the first and fourth clauses in the ninth section of the first article ; and that no State, without its consent, shall be deprived of its equal suffrage in the Senate.

ARTICLE VI.

1. All debts contracted, and engagements entered into before the adoption of this Constitution, shall be as valid against the United States under this constitution as under the Confederation.

2. This Constitution, and the laws of the United States which shall be made in pursuance thereof, and all treaties made, or which shall be made, under the authority of the United States, shall be the supreme law of the land, and the judges in every State shall be bound thereby, anything in the Constitution or laws of any State to the contrary notwithstanding.

3. The Senators and Representatives before mentioned, and the members of the several State Legislatures, and all Executive and Judicial officers, both of the United States and of the several States, shall be bound, by oath or affirmation, to support this Constitution; but no religious test shall ever be required as a qualification to any office or public trust under the United States.

ARTICLE VII.

The ratification of the convention of nine States shall be sufficient for the establishment of this Constitution between the States so ratifying the same.

Done in Convention by the unanimous consent of the States present, the seventeenth day of September, in the year of our Lord one thousand seven hundred and eighty-seven, and of the independence of the United States of America the twelfth. In witness whereof, we have hereunto subscribed our names.

GEORGE WASHINGTON, *President.*
and Deputy from Virginia. (a)

(a) The names of the other deputies follow.

AMENDMENTS.

The following articles in addition to, and amendment of, the Constitution of the United States, having been ratified by the Legislatures of nine States, are equally obligatory with the Constitution itself.

I. Congress shall make no law respecting an establishment of religion, or prohibiting the free exercise thereof, or abridging the freedom of speech or of the press; or the right of the people peaceably to assemble, and to petition the Government for a redress of grievances.

II. A well-regulated militia being necessary to the security of a free State, the right of the people to keep and bear arms shall not be infringed.

III. No soldier shall, in time of peace, be quartered in any house without the consent of the owner; nor in time of war, but in a manner to be prescribed by law

The right of the people to be secure in their persons, houses, papers, and effects, against unreasonable searches and seizures, shall not be violated; and no warrants shall issue, but upon probable cause, supported by oath or affirmation, and particularly describing the place to be searched, and the persons or things to be seized.

V. No person shall be held to answer for a capital or otherwise infamous crime, unless on a presentment or indictment of a grand-jury, except in cases arising in the land or naval forces, or in the militia, when in actual service, in time of war, or public danger; nor shall any person be subject, for the same offence to be twice put in jeopardy of life or limb; nor shall be compelled, in any criminal case, to be witness against himself; nor be deprived of life, liberty, or property, without due process of law; nor shall private property be taken for public use, without just compensation.

VI. In all criminal prosecutions, the accused shall enjoy the right to a speedy and public trial, by an impartial jury, of the State and district wherein the crime shall have been committed; which district shall have been previously ascertained by law; and to be informed of the nature and cause of the accusation; to be confronted with the witnesses against him; to have compulsory process for obtaining witnesses in his favor; and to have the assistance of counsel for his defence.

VII. In suits at common law where the value in controversy shall exceed twenty dollars, the right of trial by jury shall be preserved; and no fact tried by a jury shall be otherwise re-examined in any court of the United States than according to the rules of the common law.

VIII. Excessive bail shall not be required, nor excessive fines be imposed, nor cruel and unusual punishments inflicted.

IX. The enumeration in the Constitution of certain rights shall not be, construed to deny or disparage others retained by the people.

X. The powers not delegated to the United States by the Constitution, nor prohibited by it to the States, are reserved to the States respectively or to the people.

XI. The Judicial power of the United States shall not be construed to extend to any suit in law or equity commenced or prosecuted against one of the United States by citizens of another State, or by citizens or subjects of any foreign State.

XII. § 1. The electors shall meet in their respective States, and vote by ballot for President and Vice-President, one of whom at least, shall not be an inhabitant of the same State with themselves; they shall name in their ballots the person voted for as President, and in distinct ballots the person voted for as Vice-President; and they shall make distinct lists of all persons voted for as President, and of all persons voted for as Vice-President, and of the number of votes for each, which list they shall sign and certify, and transmit sealed to the Government of the United States, directed to the President of the Senate; the President of the Senate shall, in the presence of the Senate and House of Representatives, open all the certificates, and the votes shall then be counted; the person having the greatest number of votes for President shall be the President, if such number be a majority of the whole number of the Electors appointed; and if no person have such majority, then from the persons having the highest numbers not exceeding three on the list of those voted for as President, the House of Representatives shall choose immediately, by ballot, the President. But, in choosing the President, the votes shall be taken by States, the representation from each State having one vote; a quorum for this purpose shall consist of a member or members from two thirds of the States, and a majority of all the States shall be necessary to a choice. And if the House of Representatives shall not choose a President whenever the right of choice shall devolve upon them, before the fourth day of March next following, then the Vice-President shall act as President, as in the case of the death or other constitutional disability of the President. § 2. The person having the greatest number of votes as Vice-President shall be Vice-President, if such number be a majority of the whole number of Electors appointed; and if no person have a majority, then from the two highest numbers on the list the Senate shall choose the Vice-President; a quorum for the purpose shall consist of two thirds of the whole number of Senators, and a majority of the whole number shall be necessary to a choice. § 3. But no person constitutionally ineligible to the office of President shall be eligible to that of Vice-President of the United States.

XIII—1. Neither slavery nor involuntary servitude, except as a punishment for crime, whereof the party shall have been duly convicted, shall exist within the United States, or any place subject to their jurisdiction.

XIV—1. All persons born or naturalized in the United States, and subject to the jurisdiction thereof, are citizens of the United States and of the States wherein they reside. No State shall make or enforce any law which shall abridge the privileges or immunities of citizens of the United States; nor shall any State deprive any person of life, liberty, or property, without due process of law; nor deny to any person within its jurisdiction the equal protection of the laws.

2. Representatives shall be apportioned among the several States according to their respective numbers, counting the whole number of persons in each State, excluding Indians not taxed; but, whenever the right to vote at any election for the choice of electors for President and Vice-President of the United States, Representatives in Congress, the executive and judicial officers of a State, or members of the Legislature thereof, is denied to any of the male inhabitants of such State, being twenty-one years of age and citizens of the United States, or in any way abridged, except for participation in rebellion or other crime, the basis of representation therein shall be reduced in the proportion which the number of such male citizens shall bear to the whole number of male citizens twenty-one years of age in such State.

3. No person shall be a Senator or Representative in Congress, or elector of President and Vice-President, or hold any office, civil or military, under the United States, or under any State, who, having previously taken an oath as a member of Congress, or as an officer of the United States, or as a member of any State legislature, or as an executive or judicial officer of any State, to support the Constitution of the United States, shall have engaged in insurrection or rebellion against the same, or given aid or comfort to the enemies thereof: but Congress may, by a vote of two-thirds of each House, remove such disability.

4. The validity of the public debt of the United States authorized by law, including debts incurred for the payment of pensions and bounties for services in suppressing insurrection or rebellion, shall not be questioned. But neither the United States, nor any State, shall assume or pay any debt or obligation incurred in aid of insurrection or rebellion against the United States, or any claim for the loss or emancipation of any slave; but all such debts, obligations and claims shall be held illegal and void.

5. The Congress shall have power to enforce, by appropriate legislation, the provisions of this article.

XV—1. The right of citizens of the United States to vote shall not be denied or abridged by the United States, or by any State, on account of race, colour, or previous condition of servitude.

2. The Congress shall have power to enforce this article by appropriate legislation.

THE CONSTITUTION OF CANADA.

IMP. ACT 30-31 VICT. c. 3.

An Act for the Union of Canada, Nova Scotia, and New Brunswick, and the Government thereof ; and for purposes connected therewith.

[*29th March*, 1867.]

Whereas the Provinces of Canada, Nova Scotia, and New Brunswick, have expressed their desire to be federally united into one Dominion under the Crown of the United Kingdom of Great Britain and Ireland, with a Constitution similar in principle to that of the United Kingdom :

And whereas such a Union would conduce to the welfare of the Provinces and promote the interests of the British Empire :

And whereas on the establishment of the Union by authority of Parliament it is expedient, not only that the Constitution of the Legislative Authority in the Dominion be provided for, but also that the nature of the Executive Government therein be declared :

And whereas it is expedient that provision be made for the eventual admission into the Union of other parts of British North America :

Be it therefore enacted and declared by the Queen's Most Excellent Majesty, by and with the advice and consent of the Lords Spiritual and Temporal, and Commons, in this present Parliament assembled, and by the authority of the same, as follows : (*a*)

(*a*) The Quebec Resolutions were adopted by the Canadas, New Brunswick, Nova Scotia, Prince Edward Island, and Newfoundland in October, 1864.

Compare the preamble with the following :

The best interests and present and future prosperity of British North America will be promoted by a Federal Union under the Crown of Great Britain, provided such union can be affected on principles just to the several Provinces.

In the Federation of the British North American Provinces, the system of Government best adapted under existing circumstances to protect the diversified interests of the several provinces, and secure

I.—Preliminary.

1. This Act may be cited as " The British North America Act, 1867."

2. The provisions of this Act referring to Her Majesty the Queen extend also to the heirs and successors of Her Majesty, Kings and Queens of the United Kingdom of Great Britain and Ireland.

II.—Union.

3. It shall be lawful for the Queen, by and with the advice of Her Majesty's Most Honourable Privy Council, to declare by proclamation that on and after a day therein appointed, not being more than six months after the passing of this Act, the provinces of Canada, Nova Scotia and New Brunswick shall form and be one Dominion under the name of Canada; and on and after that day those three provinces shall form and be one Dominion under that name accordingly.

4. The subsequent provisions of this Act shall, unless it is otherwise expressed or implied, commence and have effect on and after the Union, that is to say, on and after the Union taking effect in the Queen's proclamation; and in the same provisions, unless it is otherwise expressed or implied, the name Canada shall be taken to mean Canada as constituted under this Act.

5. Canada shall be divided into four provinces, named Ontario, Quebec, Nova Scotia, and New Brunswick.

6. The parts of the province of Canada (as it exists at the passing of this Act) which formerly constituted respectively the provinces of Upper Canada and Lower Canada shall be deemed to be severed, and shall form two separate provinces. The part which formerly constituted the province of Upper Canada shall constitute the province of Ontario; and the part which formerly constituted the province of Lower Canada shall constitute the province of Quebec.

---

efficiency, harmony and permanency in the working of the Union, would be a General Government charged with matters of common interest to the whole country, and Local Governments for each of the Canadas, and for the provinces of Nova Scotia, New Brunswick and Prince Edward Island, charged with the control of local matters in their respective sections,—provision being made for the admission into the Union, on equitable terms, of Newfoundland, the North-West Territory, British Columbia and Vancouver.

In framing a Constitution for the general government, the conference, with a view to the perpetuation of our connection with the Mother Country, and the promotion of the best interests of the people of these provinces, desire to follow the model of the British Constitution, so far as our circumstances will permit.

The sanction of the Imperial and Local Parliaments shall be sought for the Union of the provinces, on the principles adopted by the Conference. (Resolutions 1, 2, 3, and 90.)

7. The provinces of Nova Scotia and New Brunswick shall have tho same limits as at the passing of this Act.

8. In the general census of the population of Canada which is hereby required to be taken in the year one thousand eight hundred and seventy-one, and in every tenth year thereafter, the respective populations of the four provinces shall be distinguished;

III.—EXECUTIVE POWER. (b)

9. The executive government and authority of and over Canada is hereby declared to continue and be vested in the Queen.

10. The provisions of this Act referring to the Governor-General extend and apply to the Governor-General for the time being of Canada, or other the chief executive officer or administrator for the time being carrying on the government of Canada on behalf and in the name of the Queen, by whatever title he is designated.

11. There shall be a council to aid and advise in the government of Canada, to be styled the Queen's Privy Council for Canada; and the persons who are to be members of that council shall be from time to time chosen and summoned by the Governor-General and sworn in as privy councillors, and members thereof may be from time to time removed by the Governor-General.

12. (*See this section, ante, page* 31.)

13. The provisions of this Act referring to the Governor-General in council shall be construed as referring to the Governor-General acting by and with the advice of the Queen's Privy Council for Canada.

14. It shall be lawful for the Queen, if Her Majesty thinks fit, to authorize the Governor-General from time to time to appoint any person or any persons jointly or severally to be his deputy or deputies within any part or parts of Canada, and in that capacity to exercise during the pleasure of the Governor-General such of the powers, authorities, and functions of the Governor-General as the Governor-General deems it necessary or expedient to assign to him or them, subject to any limitations or directions expressed or given by the Queen; but the appointment of such a deputy or deputies shall not affect the exercise by the Governor-General himself of any power, authority or function.

15. The commander-in-chief of the land and naval militia, and of all naval and military forces, of and in Canada, is hereby declared to continue and be vested in the Queen.

(b) The Executive Authority or Government shall be vested in the Sovereign of the United Kingdom of Great Britain and Ireland, and be administered according to the well understood principles of the British Constitution, by the Sovereign personally, or by the Representative of the Sovereign duly authorized. (Resolution 4.)

16. Until the Queen otherwise direct, the seat of government of Canada shall be Ottawa.

IV.—Legislative Power.

17. There shall be one parliament for Canada, consisting of the Queen, an Upper House, styled the Senate, and the House of Commons. (c)

[*Section 18 was repealed by Imperial Act 38 & 39 Vict. c. 38, and the following section substituted therefor.*

18. The privileges, immunities, and powers to be held, enjoyed and exercised by the Senate and by the House of Commons and by the members thereof respectively shall be such as are from time to time defined by Act of the Parliament of Canada, but so that any Act of the Parliament of Canada defining such privileges, immunities and powers shall not confer any privileges, immunities, or powers exceeding those at the passing of such Act held, enjoyed and exercised by the Commons House of Parliament of the United Kingdom of Great Britain and Ireland and by the members thereof.]

19. The Parliament of Canada shall be called together not later than six months after the Union.

20. There shall be a session of the Parliament of Canada once at least in every year, so that twelve months shall not intervene between the last sitting of the Parliament in one session and its first sitting in the next session.

The Senate. (d)

21. The Senate shall, subject to the provisions of this Act, consist of seventy-two members, who shall be styled senators.

22. In relation to the constitution of the senate, Canada shall be deemed to consist of three divisions—

1. Ontario;

2. Quebec;

3. The Maritime Provinces, Nova Scotia and New Brunswick; which three divisions shall (subject to the provisions of this Act) be equally represented in the senate as follows: Ontario by twenty-four senators;

(c) There shall be a general Legislature or Parliament for the federated provinces, composed of a Legislative Council and a House of Commons.

(d) The members of the Legislative Council shall be appointed by the Crown under the Great Seal of the General Government, and shall hold office during life: if any Legislative Councillor shall for two consecutive sessions of Parliament, fail to give his attendance in the said Council, his seat shall thereby become vacant. (Resolutions 7, 11.)

Quebec by twenty-four senators; and the Maritime Provinces by twenty-four senators, twelve thereof representing Nova Scotia, and twelve thereof representing New Brunswick.

In the case of Quebec each of the twenty-four senators representing that province shall be appointed for one of the twenty-four electoral divisions of Lower Canada specified in Schedule A. to chapter one of the Consolidated Statutes of Canada.

23. (*See ante, page* 41).

24. The Governor-General shall from time to time, in the Queen's name, by instrument under the Great Seal of Canada, summon qualified persons to the senate; and, subject to the provisions of this Act, every person so summoned shall become and be a member of the senate and a senator.

25. Such persons shall be first summoned to the senate as the Queen by warrant under Her Majesty's Royal Sign Manual thinks fit to approve, and their names shall be inserted in the Queen's Proclamation of Union.

26. If at any time on the recommendation of the Governor-General the Queen thinks fit to direct that three or six members be added to the senate, the Governor-General may by summons to three or six qualified persons (as the case may be), representing equally the three divisions of Canada, add to the senate accordingly.

27. In case of such addition being at any time made the Governor-General shall not summon any person to the senate, except on a further like direction by the Queen on the like recommendation, until each of the three divisions of Canada is represented by twenty-four senators and no more.

28. The number of senators shall not at any time exceed seventy-eight.

29. A senator shall, subject to the provisions of this Act, hold his place in the senate for life.

30. A senator may by writing under his hand addressed to the Governor-General resign his place in the senate, and thereupon the same shall be vacant.

31. (*See ante, page* 42).

32. When a vacancy happens in the senate by resignation, death, or otherwise, the Governor-General shall by summons to a fit and qualified person fill the vacancy.

33. If any question arises respecting the qualification of a senator or a vacancy in the senate the same shall be heard and determined by the senate.

34. The Governor-General may from time to time, by instrument under the Great Seal of Canada, appoint a senator to be speaker of the senate, and may remove him and appoint another in his stead.

35. Until the parliament of Canada otherwise provides, the presence of at least fifteen senators, including the speaker, shall be necessary to constitute a meeting of the senate for the exercise of its powers.

36. Questions arising in the senate shall be decided by a majority of voices, and the speaker shall in all cases have a vote and when the voices are equal the decision shall be deemed to be in the negative.

The House of Commons.

37. The House of Commons shall, subject to the provisions of this Act, consist of one hundred and eighty-one members, of whom eighty-two shall be elected for Ontario, sixty-five for Quebec, nineteen for Nova Scotia, and fifteen for New Brunswick. (*e*)

38. The Governor-General shall from time to time, in the Queen's name, by instrument under the Great Seal of Canada, summon and call together the House of Commons.

39. A senator shall not be capable of being elected or of sitting or voting as a member of the House of Commons.

40. Until the parliament of Canada otherwise provides, Ontario, Quebec, Nova Scotia and New Brunswick shall, for the purposes of the election of members to serve in the House of Commons, be divided into electoral districts as follows:— (*f*)

41. Until the parliament of Canada otherwise provides, all laws in force in the several provinces at the union relate to the following matters or any of them, namely,—the qualifications and disqualifications of persons to be elected or to sit or vote as members of the House of Assembly or Legislative Assembly in the several provinces, the voters at elections of such members, the oaths to be taken by voters, the returning officers, their powers and duties, the proceedings at elections, the periods during which elections may be continued, the trial of controverted elections, and proceedings incident thereto, the vacating of seats of members, and the execution of new writs in case of seats vacated

---

(*e*) The basis of representation in the House of Commons shall be population, as determined by the official census every ten years; and the number of members at first shall be 194, distributed as follows:

Upper Canada........, ...	82
Lower Canada...............................	64
Nova Scotia................................	19
New Brunswick.............................	15
Newfoundland	8
Prince Edward Island......................	5

(Resolution 17.)

(*f*) As this has been changed it is unnecessary to insert it here.

otherwise than by dissolution—shall respectively apply to elections of members to serve in the House of Commons for the same several provinces.

Provided that, until the parliament of Canada otherwise provides, at any election for a member of the House of Commons for the district of Algoma, in addition to persons qualified by the law of the province of Canada to vote, every male British subject aged twenty-one years and upwards, being a householder, shall have a vote.

42. For the first election of members to serve in the House of Commons the Governor-General shall cause writs to be issued by such persons, in such form, and addressed to such returning officers as he thinks fit.

The person issuing writs under this section shall have the like powers as are possessed at the union by the officers charged with the issuing of writs for the election of members to serve in the respective House of Assembly or Legislative Assembly of the province of Canada, Nova Scotia, or New Brunswick; and the returning officers to whom writs are directed under this section shall have the like powers as are possessed at the union by the officers charged with the returning of writs for the election of members to serve in the same respective House of Assembly or Legislative Assembly.

43. In case a vacancy in the representation in the House of Commons of any electoral district happens before the meeting of the parliament, or after the meeting of the parliament before the provision is made by the parliament in this behalf, the provision of the last foregoing section of this Act shall extend and apply to the issuing and returning of a writ in respect of such vacant district.

44. The House of Commons on its first assembling after a general election shall proceed with all practical speed to elect one of its members to be speaker.

45. In case of a vacancy happening in the office of speaker by death, resignation or otherwise, the House of Commons shall with all practicable speed proceed to elect another of its members to be speaker.

46. The speaker shall preside at all meetings of the House of Commons.

47. Until the parliament of Canada otherwise provides, in case of the absence for any reason of the speaker from the chair of the House of Commons for a period of forty-eight consecutive hours, the House may elect another of its members to act as speaker, and the member so elected shall during the continuance of such absence of the speaker have and execute all the powers, privileges, and duties of speaker.

48. The presence of at least twenty members of the House of Commons shall be necessary to constitute a meeting of the House for the exercise of its powers, and for that purpose the speaker shall be reckoned as a member.

49. Questions arising in the House of Commons shall be decided by a majority of voices other than that of the speaker and when the voices are equal, but not otherwise, the speaker shall have a vote.

50. Every House of Commons shall continue for five years from the day of the return of the writs for choosing the House (subject to be sooner dissolved by the Governor-General), and no longer.

51. On the completion of the census in the year one thousand eight hundred and seventy-one, and of each subsequent decennial census the representation of the four provinces shall be readjusted by such authority, in such manner and from such time as the parliament of Canada from time to time provides subject and according to the following rules :—

(1.) Quebec shall have the fixed number of sixty-five members.

(2.) There shall be assigned to each of the other provinces such a number of members as will bear the same proportion to the number of its population (ascertained at such census) as the number sixty-five bears to the number of the population of Quebec (so ascertained).

(3.) In the computation of the number of members for a province a fractional part not exceeding one half of the whole number requisite for entitling the province to a member shall be disregarded ; but a fractional part exceeding one half of that number shall be equivalent to the whole number.

(4.) On any such readjustment the number of members for a province shall not be reduced unless the proportion which the number of the population of the province bore to the number of the aggregate population of Canada at the then last preceding re-adjustment of the number of members for the province is ascertained at the then last census to be diminished by one twentieth part or upwards.

(5.) Such re-adjustment shall not take effect until the termination of the then existing parliament.

52. The number of members of the House of Commons may be from time to time increased by the Parliament of Canada, provided the proportionate representation of the provinces prescribed by this Act is not thereby disturbed.

Money Votes ; Royal Assent.

53. Bills for appropriating any part of the public revenue, or for imposing any tax or impost, shall originate in the House of Commons.

54. It shall not be lawful for the House of Commons to adopt or pass any vote, resolution, address, or bill for the appropriation of any part of the public revenue, or of any tax or impost, to any purpose that has not been first recommended to that house by message of the Governor-General in the session in which such vote, resolution, address, or bill is proposed.

55. Where a bill passed by the Houses of the Parliament is presented to the Governor-General for the Queen's assent, he shall declare, according to his discretion, but subject to the provisions of this Act and to Her Majesty's instructions, either that he assents thereto in the Queen's name, or that he withholds the Queen's assent, or that he reserves the bill for the signification of the Queen's pleasure.

56. Where the Governor-General assents to a bill in the Queen's name, he shall by the first convenient opportunity send an authentic copy of the Act to one of Her Majesty's principal secretaries of state; and if the Queen in council within two years after the receipt thereof by the secretary of state of the day on which the Act was received by him) being signified by the Governor-General, by speech or message to each of the Houses of the Parliament, or by proclamation, shall annul the Act from and after the day of such signification.

57. A bill reserved for the signification of the Queen's pleasure shall not have any force unless and until within two years from the day on which it was presented to the Governor-General for the Queen's assent, the Governor-General signifies by speech or message to each of the Houses of the Parliament or by proclamation, that it has received the assent of the Queen in council.

An entry of every such speech, message, or proclamation shall be made in the journal of each House, and a duplicate thereof duly attested shall be delivered to the proper officer to be kept among the records of Canada.

V.—Provincial Constitutions. (g)

Executive Power.

58. For each province there shall be an officer, styled the Lieutenant-Governor, appointed by the Governor-General in council by instrument under the Great Seal of Canada.

(g) The Local Government and Legislature of each province shall be constructed in such manner as the existing Legislature of each such province shall provide.

The Local Legislature shall have power to alter or amend their Constitution from time to time.

The power of respiting, reprieving, and pardoning prisoners convicted of crimes, and of commuting and remitting of sentences in whole or in part, which belongs of right to the Crown, shall be administered by the Lieutenant-Governor of each province in council, subject to any instructions he may, from time to time receive from the General Government, and subject to any provisions that may be made in this behalf by the General Parliament. (Resolutions 41, 42 and 44.)

59. A Lieutenant-Governor shall hold office during the pleasure of the Governor-General; but any Lieutenant-Governor appointed after the commencement of the first session of the Parliament of Canada shall not be removable within five years from his appointment, except for cause assigned, which shall be communicated to him in writing within one month after the order for his removal is made, and shall be communicated by message to the Senate and to the House of Commons within one week thereafter if the Parliament is then sitting, and if not then within one week after the commencement of the next session of the Parliament.

60. The salaries of the Lieutenant-Governors shall be fixed and provided by the Parliament of Canada.

61. Every Lieutenant-Governor shall, before assuming the duties of his office, make and subscribe before the Governor-General or some person authorized by him, oaths of allegiance and office similar to those taken by the Governor-General.

62. The provisions of this Act referring to the Lieutenant-Governor extend and apply to the Lieutenant-Governor for the time being of each province or other the chief executive officer or administrator for the time being carrying on the government of the province, by whatever title he is designated.

63. The executive council of Ontario and of Quebec shall be composed of such persons as the Lieutenant-Governor from time to time thinks fit, and in the first instance of the following officers, namely:—the attorney-general, the secretary and registrar of the province, the commissioner of crown lands, and the commissioner of agriculture and public works, within Quebec, the speaker of the legislative council and the solicitor-general.

64. The Constitution of the executive authority in each of the Provinces of Nova Scotia and New Brunswick shall, subject to the provisions of this Act, continue as it exists at the Union until altered under the authority of this Act.

65. (*See ante, page* 140).

66. The provisions of this Act referring to the Lieutenant-Governor in Council shall be construed as referring to the Lieutenant-Governor of the Province acting by and with the advice of the Executive Council thereof.

67. The Governor-General in Council may from time to time appoint an administrator to execute the office and functions of Lieutenant-Governor during his absence, illness, or other inability.

68. Unless and until the Executive Government of any Province otherwise directs with respect to that Province, the seats of Government of the Provinces shall be as follows, namely,—of Ontario, the City of Toronto; of Quebec, the City of Quebec; of Nova Scotia, the City of Halifax; and of New Brunswick, the City of Fredericton.

Legislative Powers. (h)

1.—ONTARIO.

69. There shall be a legislature for Ontario consisting of the Lieutenant-Governor and of one House, styled the Legislative Assembly of Ontario.

70. The Legislative Assembly of Ontario shall be composed of eighty-two members, to be elected to represent the eighty-two electoral districts set forth in the first schedule to the Act.

2—QUEBEC.

71. There shall be a Legislature for Quebec consisting of the Lieutenant-Governor and of two Houses, styled the Legislative Council of Quebec and the Legislative Assembly of Quebec.

72. The Legislative Council of Quebec shall be composed of twenty-four members, to be appointed by the Lieutenant-Governor in the Queen's name, by instrument under the Great Seal of Quebec, one being appointed to represent each of the twenty-four electoral divisions of Lower Canada, in this Act referred to, and each holding office for the term of his life, unless the Legislature of Quebec otherwise provides under the provisions of this Act.

73. The qualifications of the Legislative Councillors of Quebec shall be the same as those of the Senators for Quebec.

74. The place of a Legislative Councillor of Quebec shall become vacant in the cases *mutatis mutandis*, in which the place of Senator becomes vacant.

75. When a vacancy happens in the Legislative Council of Quebec, by resignation, death, or otherwise, the Lieutenant-Governor, in the Queen's name by instrument under the Great Seal of Quebec, shall appoint a fit and qualified person to fill the vacancy.

76. If any question arises respecting the qualification of a Legislative Councillor of Quebec, or a vacancy in the Legislative Council of Quebec, the same shall be heard and determined by the Legislative Council.

77. The Lieutenant-Governor may from time to time, by instrument under the Great Seal of Quebec, appoint a member of the Legislative Council of Quebec to be Speaker thereof, and may remove him and appoint another in his stead.

(h) The resolutions are silent as to the matters from secs. 69 to 90 both inclusive and 131 to 144 also.

78. Until the Legislature of Quebec otherwise provides, the presence of at least ten members of the Legislative Council, including the Speaker, shall be necessary to constitute a meeting for the exercise of its powers.

79. Questions arising in the Legislative Council of Quebec shall be decided by a majority of voices, and the Speaker shall in all cases have a vote, and when the voices are equal the decisions shall be deemed to be in the negative.

80. The Legislative Assembly of Quebec shall be composed of sixty-five members, to be elected to represent the sixty five electoral divisions or districts of Lower Canada in this Act referred to, subject to alteration thereof by the Legislature of Quebec : Provided that it shall not be lawful to present to the Lieutenant-Governor of Quebec for assent any bill for altering the limits of any of the electoral divisions or districts mentioned in the second schedule to this Act, unless the second and third readings of such bill have been passed in the Legislative Assembly with the concurrence of the majority of the members representing all those electoral divisions or districts, and the assent shall not be given to such bill unless an address has been presented by the Legislative Assembly to the Lieutenant-Governor stating that it has been so passed. (*g*)

3.—ONTARIO AND QUEBEC.

81. The Legislatures of Ontario and Quebec respectively shall be called together not later than six months after the Union.

82. The Lieutenant-Governor of Ontario and of Quebec shall from time to time, in the Queen's name, by instrument of the Great Seal of the Province, summon and call together the Legislative Assembly of the Province.

83. Until the Legislature of Ontario or of Quebec otherwise provides, a person accepting or holding in Ontario or Quebec any office, commission, or employment, permanent or temporary, at the nomination of the Lieutenant-Governor, to which an annual salary, or any fee, allowance, emolument, or profit of any kind or amount whatever, from the Province is attached, shall not be eligible as a member of the Legislative Assembly of the respective Province, nor shall he sit or vote as such ; but nothing in this section shall make eligible any person being a member of the Executive Council of the respective Province, or holding any of the following offices, that is to say, the offices of Attorney General, Secretary and Registrar of the Province, Treasurer of the Province, Commissioner of Crown Lands, and Commissioner of Agriculture and Public Works, and in Quebec, Solicitor-General, or shall disqualify him to sit or vote in the House for which he is elected, provided he is elected while holding such office.

84. Until the Legislatures of Ontario and Quebec respectively otherwise provide, all laws which at the Union are in force in those Provinces respectively, relate to the following matters, or any of them, namely, – the qualification and disqualifications of persons to be elected or to sit or vote as members of the Assembly of Canada, the qualifications or disqualifications of voters, the oaths to be taken by voters, the returning officers, their powers and duties, the proceedings at elections, the period during which such elections may be continued, and the trial of controverted elections and the proceedings incident thereto, the vacating of the seats of members and the issuing and execution new writs in case of seats vacated otherwise than by dissolution shall respectively apply to elections of members to serve in the respective Legislative Assemblies of Ontario and Quebec.

Provided that until the Legislature of Ontario otherwise provides, at any election for a member of the Legislative Assembly of Ontario for the District of Algoma, in addition to persons qualified by the law of the Province of Canada to vote, every male British subject, aged twenty-one years or upwards, being a householder, shall have a vote.

85. Every Legislative Assembly of Ontario and every Legislative Assembly of Quebec shall continue for four years from the day of the return of the writs for choosing the same (subject nevertheless to either the Legislative Assembly of Ontario or the Legislative Assembly of Quebec being sooner dissolved by the Lieutenant-Governor of the Province), and no longer.

86. There shall be a Session of the Legislature of Ontario and of that of Quebec once at least in every year, so that twelve months shall not intervene between the last sitting of the Legislature in each Province in one session and its first sitting in the next Session.

87. The following provision of this Act respecting the House of Commons of Canada shall extend and apply to the Legislative Assemblies of Ontario and Quebec, that is to say,--the provisions relating to the election of a Speaker originally and on vacancies, the duties of the Speaker, the absence of the Speaker, the quorum, the mode of voting, as if those provisions were here re-enacted and made applicable in terms to each such Legislative Assembly.

4.—NOVA SCOTIA AND NEW BRUNSWICK.

88. The constitution of the Legislature of each of the Provinces of Nova Scotia and New Brunswick shall, subject to the provisions of this Act, continue as it exists at the Union until altered under the authority of this Act; and the House of Assembly of New Brunswick existing at the passing of this Act shall, unless sooner dissolved, continue for the period for which it was elected.

5.—ONTARIO, QUEBEC, AND NOVA SCOTIA.

89. Each of the Lieutenant-Governors of Ontario, Quebec and Nova Scotia shall cause writs to be issued for the first election of members of the Legislative Assembly thereof in such form and by such person as he thinks fit, and at such time and address to such Returning Officer as the Governor-General directs, and so that the first election of member of Assembly for any Electoral District or any sub-division thereof shall be held at the same time and at the same places as the election for a member to serve in the House of Commons of Canada for that electoral district.

O'S. G. C. 22

6.—THE FOUR PROVINCES.

90. The following provisions of this Act respecting the Parliament of Canada, namely,—the provisions relating to appropriation and tax bills, the recommendation of money votes, the assent to bills, the disallowance of Acts, and the signification of pleasure on bills reserved,— shall extend and apply to the legislatures of the several provinces as if those provisions were re-enacted and made applicable in terms to the respective provinces and the legislatures thereof, with the substitution of the Lieutenant-Governors of the Province, for the Governor-General, of the Governor-General for the Queen and for a Secretary of State, of one year for two years, and of the Province for Canada.

91. See page 99 for this and the next section. (*i*)

(*i*) 29th Resolution is as follows :

The General Parliament shall have power to make laws for the peace, welfare and good government of the federated provinces (saving the Sovereignty of England) and especially laws respecting the following subjects : [Then follows a list not differing materially from the classes in sec. 91; the last one being as follows:] And generally respecting all matters of a general character, not specially and exclusively reserved for the Local Government and Legislatures.

The 43rd resolution is as follows :

The Local Legislatures shall have power to make laws respecting the following subjects :

1. Direct taxation, and in New Brunswick the imposition of duties on the export of timber, logs, masts, spars, deals and sawn lumber ; and in Nova Scotia, of coals and other minerals.

2. Borrowing money on the credit of the province.

3. The establishment and tenure of local offices, and the appointment and payment of local officers.

4. Agriculture.

5. Immigration.

6. Education ; saving the rights and privileges which the Protestant or Catholic minority in both Canadas may possess as to their denominational schools, at the time when the union goes into operation

7. The sale and management of both public lands, excepting lands belonging to the general government.

8. Sea coast and inland fisheries.

9. The establishment, maintenance and management of penitentiaries and public and reformatory prisons.

10. The establishment, maintenance and management of hospitals, asylums, charities, and eleemosynary institutions.

11. Municipal institutions.

12. Shop, saloon, tavern, auctioneer and other licenses.

13. Local works.

14. The incorporation of private or local companies, except such as relate to matters assigned to the general parliament

Education. (j)

93. In and for each province the legislature may exclusively make laws in relation to education, subject and according to the following provisions : —

    (1.) Nothing in any such law shall prejudicially affect any right or privilege with respect to denominational schools which any class of persons have by-law in the Province at the Union : —

    (2.) All powers, privileges, and duties at the Union by law conferred and imposed in Upper Canada on the separate schools and school trustees of the Queen's Roman Catholic subjects shall be and the same are hereby extended to the dissential schools of the Queen's Protestant and Roman Catholic subjects in Quebec.

    (3). Where in any Province a system of separate or dissentient schools exists by law at the Union or is thereafter established by the Legislature of the Province, an appeal shall lie to the Governor-General in Council from any Act or decision of any provincial authority affecting any right or privilege of the Protestant or Roman Catholic minority of the Queen's subjects in relation to education.

    (4). In case any such provincial law as from time to time seems to the Governor-General in Council requisite for the due execution of the provisions of this section is not made, or in case any decision of the Governor-General in Council on any appeal under this sectio.1 is not duly executed by the proper Provincial authority in that behalf, then and in every such case, and as far only as the circumstances of each case require, the Parliament of Canada may make remedial laws for the due execution for the provisions of this section and of any decisions of the Governor-General in Council under this section.

Uniformity of Laws in Ontario, Nova Scotia and New Brunswick.

94. Notwithstanding anything in this Act, the Parliament of Canada may make provision for the uniformity of all or any of the laws relative to property and civil rights in Ontario, Nova Scotia and New Brunswick, and of the procedure of all or any of the Courts in those three

---

15. Property and civil rights, excepting those portions thereof assigned to the general parliament.

16. Inflicting punishment by fine, penalties, imprisonment or otherwise. for the breach of laws passed in relation with any subject within their jurisdiction.

17. The administration of justice, including the constitution maintenance and organization of the courts both of civil and criminal jurisdiction, and including also the procedure in civil matters.

18. And generally all matters of a private or local nature not assigned to the general parliament.

(j) See the preceeding note.

provinces ; and from and after the passing of any Act in that behalf the power of the Parliament of Canada to make law in relation to any matter comprised in any such Act shall, notwithstanding anything in this Act, be unrestricted ; but any Act of the Parliament of Canada making provision for such uniformity shall not have effect in any province unless and until it is adopted and enacted as law by the Legislature thereof.

Agriculture and Immigration.

95. In each Province the Legislature may make laws in relation to agriculture in the Province, and to immigration into the Province ; and it is hereby declared that the Parliament of Canada may from time to time make laws in relation to Agriculture in all or any of the Provinces, and to immigration into all or any of the Provinces ; and any law of the Legislature of a Province relative to agriculture or to immigration shall have effect in and for the Province as long and as far only as it is not repugnant to any Act of the Parliament of Canada.

VII.—JUDICATURE.

96. The Governor-General shall appoint the judges of the Superior, District and County Courts in each Province, except those of the Courts of Probate in Nova Scotia and New Brunswick.

97. Until the laws relative to property and civil rights in Ontario, Nova Scotia, and New Brunswick, and the procedure of the courts in those Provinces, are made uniform, the judges of the courts of those Provinces appointed by the Governor-General shall be selected from the respective bars of those Provinces.

98. The Judges of the Courts of Quebec shall be selected from the Bar of that Province.

99. The Judges of the Superior Courts shall hold office during good behaviour, but shall be removable by the Governor-General on address of the Senate and House of Commons.

100. The salaries, allowances and pensions of the Judges of the Superior, District and County Courts (except the Courts of Probate in Nova Scotia and New Brunswick,) and of the Admiralty Courts in cases where the Judges thereof are for the time being paid by salary, shall be fixed and provided by the Parliament of Canada.

101. See page 181, *ante.* *Supreme Court*

VIII.—REVENUES ; DEBTS ; ASSETS ; TAXATION.

102. All duties and revenues over which the respective Legislatures of Canada, Nova Scotia and New Brunswick before and at the Union had and have power of appropriation, except such portions thereof as are by this Act reserved to the respective legislatures of the province, or are raised by them in accordance with the special powers conferred on them by this Act, shall form one consolidated revenue fund, to be appropriated for the public service of Canada in the manner and subject to the charges in this Act provided.

103. The consolidated revenue fund of Canada shall be permanently charged with the costs, charges, and expenses incident to the collection, management, and receipt thereof, and the same shall form the first charge thereon, subject to be reviewed and audited in such manner as shall be ordered by the Governor-General in Council until the Parliament otherwise provides.

104. The annual interest of the public debt of the several Provinces of Canada, Nova Scotia, and New Brunswick at the Union, shall form the second charge on the consolidated revenue fund of Canada.

105. Unless altered by the Parliament of Canada, the salary of the Governor-General shall be ten thousand pounds sterling money of the United Kingdom of Great Britain and Ireland, payable out of the consolidated Revenue Fund of Canada, and the same shall form the third charge thereon.

106. Subject to the several payments by this Act charged on the consolidated revenue fund of Canada, the same shall be appropriated by the Parliament of Canada for the public service.

107. All stocks, cash, banker's balances, and securities for money belonging to each Province at the time of the Union, except as in this Act mentioned, shall be the property of Canada, and shall be taken in reduction of the amount of the respective debts of the Provinces at the Union.

108. The public works and property of each province enumerated in the third schedule to this Act, shall be the property of Canada. (k)

109. All lands, mines, minerals, and royalties belonging to the several Provinces of Canada, Nova Scotia and New Brunswick at the Union, and all sums then due or payable for such lands, mines, minerals, or royalties, shall belong to the several Provinces of Ontario, Quebec, Nova Scotia, and New Brunswick in which the same are situate or arise, subject to any trusts existing in respect thereof, and to any interest other than that of the province in the same.

110. All assets connected with such portion of the public debt of each Province as are assumed by that Province shall belong to that Province.

111. Canada shall be liable for the debts and liabilities of each Province existing at the Union.

112. Ontario and Quebec conjointly shall be liable to Canada for the amount (if any) by which the debt of the Province of Canada exceeds at the Union sixty-two million five hundred thousand dollars, and shall be charged with interest at the rate of five per centum per annum thereon.

(k) See *ante*, page 115 for this schedule.

113. The assets enumerated in the fourth schedule to the Act belonging at the Union to the Province of Canada shall be the property of Ontario and Quebec conjointly. (*l*)

114. Nova Scotia shall be liable to Canada for the amount (if any) by which its public debt exceeds at the Union eight million dollars, and shall be charged with interest at the rate of five per centum per annum thereon.

115. New Brunswick shall be liable to Canada for the amount (if any) by which its public debts exceeds at the Union seven million dollars, and shall be charged with interest at the rate of five per centum per annum.

116. In case the public debt of Nova Scotia and New Brunswick do not at the Union amount to eight million and seven million dollars respectively, they shall respectively receive by half-yearly payments in advance from the Government of Canada interest at five per centum per annum on the difference between the actual amounts of their respective debts and such stipulated amounts.

117. The several provinces shall retain their respective public property not otherwise disposed of in this Act, subject to the right of Canada to assume any lands or public property required for fortifications or for the defence of the country.

118. The following sums shall be paid yearly by Canada to the several provinces for the support of their governments and legislatures :

		Dollars.
Ontario	- - - - - - -	Eighty thousand.
Quebec	- - - - - - -	Seventy thousand.
Nova Scotia	- - - - - - -	Sixty thousand.
New Brunswick	- - - - - - -	Fifty thousand.

Two hundred and sixty thousand ; and an annual grant in aid of each province shall be made, equal to eighty cents per head of the population as ascertained by the census of one thousand eight hundred and sixty-one, and in the case of Nova Scotia and New Brunswick, by each subsequent decennial census until the population of each of those two provinces amounts to four hundred thousand souls, at which rate such grant shall thereafter remain. Such grants shall be in full settlement of all future demands on Canada, and shall be paid half-yearly in advance to each province ; but the Government of Canada shall deduct from such grants, as against any province, all sums chargeable as interest on the public debt of that province in excess of the several amounts stipulated in this Act.

119. New Brunswick shall receive by half-yearly payments in advance from Canada for the period of ten years from the Union an additional allowance of sixty-three thousand dollars per annum ; but as long as the public debt of that province remains under seven million dollars, a

---

(*i*) See *ante*, page 118 for this schedule.

deduction equal to the interest at five per centum per annum on such deficiency shall be made from the allowance of sixty-three thousand dollars.

120. All payments to be made under this Act, or in discharge of liabilities created under any Act of the province of Canada, Nova Scotia, and New Brunswick respectively, and assumed by Canada, shall, until the Parliament of Canada otherwise directs, be made in such form and manner as may from time to time be ordered by the Governor-General in council.

121. All articles of the growth, produce, or manufacture of any one of the provinces shall from and after the Union, be admitted free into each of the other provinces.

122. The customs and excise laws of each province shall, subject to the provisions of this Act, continue in force until altered by the Parliament of Canada.

123. Where customs duties are, at the Union, leviable on any goods, or merchandises in any two provinces, those goods, wares, or merchandises may, from and after the Union, be imported from one of those provinces into the other of them on proof of payment of the customs duty leviable thereon in the province of exportation, and on payment of such further amount (if any) of customs duty as is leviable thereon in the province of importation.

124. Nothing in this Act shall affect the right of New Brunswick to levy the lumber dues provided in chapter fifteen of title three of the Revised Statutes of New Brunswick, or in any Act amending that Act before or after the Union, and not increasing the amount of such dues; but the lumber of any of the provinces other than New Brunswick shall not be subjected to such dues.

125. No lands or property belonging to Canada or any province shall be liable to taxation.

126. Such portions of the duties and revenues over which the respective legislatures of Canada, Nova Scotia, and New Brunswick had before the Union power of appropriation as are by the Act reserved to the respective governments or legislatures of the provinces, and all duties and revenues raised by them in accordance with the special powers conferred upon them by this Act, shall in each province form one consolidated revenue fund to be appropriated for the public service of the province.

IX.—MISCELLANEOUS PROVISIONS.

General.

127. If any person being at the passing of this Act a member of the legislative council of Canada, Nova Scotia, or New Brunswick, to whom a place in the senate is offered, does not within thirty days thereafter, by writing under his hand addressed to the Governor-General of the province of Canada or to the Lieutenant-Governor of Nova Scotia or New Brunswick (as the case may be), accept the same, he shall be deemed to have declined the same; and any person who, being at the passing of this Act a member of the legislative council of Nova Scotia or New Brunswick, accepts a place in the senate shall thereby vacate his seat in such legislative council.

128. Every member of the senate or house of commons of Canada shall before taking his seat therein take and subscribe before the Governor-General or some person authorized by him, and every member of a Legislative Council or a Legislative Assembly of any province shall before taking his seat therein take and subscribe before the Lieutenant-Governor of the province or some person authorized by him, the oath of allegiance contained in the fifth Schedule to this Act; and every member of the senate of Canada and every member of the Legislative Council of Quebec shall also, before taking his seat therein, take and subscribe before the Governor-General, or some person authorized by him, the declaration of qualification contained in the same schedule. (*m*)

129. Except as otherwise provided by this Act, all laws in force in Canada, Nova Scotia, or New Brunswick at the Union and all courts of civil and criminal jurisdiction, and all legal commissions, powers and authorities, and all officers, judicial, administrative and ministerial, existing therein at the Union, shall continue in Ontario, Quebec, Nova Scotia, and New Brunswick respectively, as if the Union had not been made ; subject nevertheless (except with respect to such as are enacted by or exist under Acts of parliament of Great Britain or of the parliament of the United Kingdom of Great Britain and Ireland,) to be repealed, abolished, or altered by the parliament of Canada, or by the Legislature of the respective province, according to the authority of the parliament or of that Legislature under this Act.

130. Until the parliament of Canada otherwise provides, all officers of the several provinces having duties to discharge in relation to matters other than those coming within the classes of subjects by this Act assigned exclusively to the Legislatures of the provinces shall be officers of Canada, and shall continue to discharge the duties of their respective offices under the same liabilities, responsibilities and penalties as if the Union had not been made.

131. Until the parliament of Canada otherwise provides, the Governor-General in council may from time to time appoint such officers as the Governor-General in council deems necessary or proper for the effectual execution of the Act.

132. The parliament and government of Canada shall have all powers necessary or proper for performing the obligations of Canada or of any province thereof, as part of the British Empire, towards foreign countries, arising under treaties between the Empire and such foreign countries.

(*m*) See *ante*, page 43.

133. Either the English or the French language may be used by any person in the debates of the houses of the parliament of Canada and of the houses of the legislature of Quebec; and both those languages shall be used in the respective records and journals of those houses ; and either of those languages may be used by any person or in any pleading or process in or issuing from any court in Canada established under this Act, and in or from all or any of the courts of Quebec.

The Acts of the parliament of Canada and of the legislature of Quebec shall be printed and published in both those languages.

Ontario and Quebec.

134. Until the legislature of Ontario or of Quebec otherwise provides the Lieutenant-Governors of Ontario and Quebec may each appoint under the great seal of the province the following officers, to hold office during pleasure, that is to say—the Attorney-General the Secretary, and Registrar of the Province, the Treasurer of the Province, the Commissioner of the Crown Lands, and the Commissioner of Agriculture and Public Works, and in the case of Quebec the Solicitor-General ; and may, by order of the Lieutenant-Governor in council, from time to time prescribe the duties of those officers and of the several departments over which they shall preside or to which they shall belong, and of the officers and clerks thereof ; and may also appoint other and additional officers to hold office during pleasure, and may from time to time prescribe the duties of those officers, and of the several departments over which they shall preside, or to which they shall belong, and of the officers and clerks thereof.

135. Until the legislature of Ontario or Quebec otherwise provides, all rights, powers, duties, functions, responsibilities, or authorities at the passing of this Act vested in or imposed on the Attorney-General, Solicitor-General, Secretary and Registrar of the Province of Canada, Minister of Finance, Commissioner of Crown Lands, Commissioner of Public Works, and Minister of Agriculture and Receiver-General, by any law, statute or ordinance of Upper Canada, Lower Canada, or Canada, and not repugnant to this Act, shall be vested in or imposed on any officer to be appointed by the Lieutenant-Governor for the discharge of the same or any of them ; and the Commissioner of Agriculture and Public Works shall perform the duties and functions of the office of Minister of Agriculture at the passing of this Act imposed by the law of the province of Canada, as well as those of the Commissioner of Public Works.

136. Until altered by the Lieutenant-Governor in council, the great seals of Ontario and Quebec respectively shall be the same or of the same design as those used in the provinces of Upper Canada and Lower Canada respectively before their Union as the province of Canada.

137. The words " and from thence to the end of the then next ensuing session of the legislature," or words to the same effect, used in any temporary Act of the Province of Canada not expired before the union, shall be construed to extend and apply to the next session of the Parliament of Canada, if the subject matter of the Act is within the powers of the same, as defined by this Act, or to the next sessions of the legislatures of Ontario and Quebec respectively, if the subject matter of the Act is within the powers of the same as defined by this Act.

138. From and after the Union, the use of the words " Upper Canada " instead of " Ontario," or " Lower Canada " instead of " Quebec," in any deed, writ, process, pleading, document, matter, or thing, shall not invalidate the same.

139. Any proclamation under the Great Seal of the Province of Canada issued before the Union to take effect at a time which is subsequent to the Union, whether relating to that Province, or to Upper Canada, or to Lower Canada, and the several matters and things therein proclaimed shall be and continue of like force and effect as if the Union had not been made.

140. Any proclamation which is authorized by any Act of the legislature of the Province cf Canada to be issued under the Great Seal of the Province of Cana.la, whether relating to that Province, or to Upper Canada, or to Lower Canada, and which is now issued before the Union, may be issued by the Lieutenant-Governor of Ontario or of Quebec, as its subject matter requires, under the Great Seal thereof ; and from and after the issue of such proclamation the same and the several matters and things therein proclaimed shall be and continue of the like force and effect in Ontario or Quebec as if the Union had not been made.

141. The penitentiary of the Province of Canada shall, until the Parliament of Canada otherwise provides, be and continue the penitentiary of Ontario and of Quebec.

142. The division and adjustment of the debts, credits, liabilities, properties and assets of Upper Canada and Lower Canada shall be referred to the arbitrament of three arbitrators, one chosen by the Government of Ontario, one by the Government of Quebec, and one by the Government of Canada ; and the selection of the arbitrators shall not be made until the Parliament of Canada and the Legislatures of Ontario and Quebec have met; and the arbitrator chosen by the Government of Canada shall not be a resident in Ontario or in Quebec.

143. The Governor-General in council may from time to time order that such and so many of the records, books, and documents of the Province of Canada as he thinks fit shall be appropriated and delivered either to Ontario or to Quebec, and the same shall thenceforth be the property of that Province; and any copy thereof or extract therefrom, duly certified by the officer having charge of the original thereof shall be admitted as evidence.

144. The Lieutenant-Governor of Quebec may from time to time by proclamation under the Great Seal of the Province, to take effect from a day to be appointed therein, constitute townships in those parts of the Province of Quebec in which townships are not then already constituted, and fix the metes and bounds thereof.

X.—INTERCOLONIAL RAILWAY.

145. Inasmuch as the Provinces of Canada, Nova Scotia and New Brunswick have joined in a declaration that the construction of the Intercolonial Railway is essential to the consolidation of the Union of British North America, and to the assent thereto of Nova Scotia and New Brunswick, and have consequently agreed that provision should be made for its immediate construction by the Government of Canada: Therefore, in order to give effect to that agreement, it shall be the duty of the Government and Parliament of Canada to provide for the commencement within six months after the Union, of a railway connecting the River St. Lawrence with city of Halifax in Nova Scotia, and for the construction thereof without intermission, and the completion thereof with all practicable speed.

XI.—ADMISSION OF OTHER COLONIES.

146. It shall be lawful for the Queen, by and with the advice of Her Majesty's Most Honourable Privy Council, on addresses from the Houses of Parliament of Canada, and from the Houses of the respective legislatures of the Colonies or Provinces of Newfoundland, Prince Edward Island, and British Columbia, to admit those colonies or provinces, or any of them, into the Union, and on address from the Houses of the Parliament in Canada to admit Rupert's Land and the North-Western Territory, or either of them, into the Union, on such terms and conditions in each case as are in the addresses expressed and as the Queen thinks fit to approve, subject to the provisions of this Act; and the provisions of any order in council in that behalf shall have effect as if they had been enacted by the Parliament of the United Kingdom of Great Britain and Ireland.

147. In case of the admission of Newfoundland and Prince Edward Island, or either of them, each shall be entitled to a representation in the Senate of Canada of four members, and (notwithstanding anything in this Act) in case of the admission of Newfoundland the normal number of Senators shall be seventy-six and their maximum number shall be eighty-two; but Prince Edward Island when admitted shall be deemed to be comprised in the third of the three divisions into which Canada is, in relation to the constitution of the Senate, divided by this Act, and accordingly, after the admission of Prince Edward Island, whether Newfoundland is admitted or not, the representation of each of those Provinces shall not be increased at any time beyond ten, except under the provisions of this Act for the appointment of three or six additional Senators under the direction of the Queen.

THE B. N. A. ACT, 34-35 VICT. c. 28.

An Act respecting the establishment of Provinces in the Dominion of Canada.

[29th June, 1871.]

Whereas doubts have been entertained respecting the powers of the Parliament of Canada to establish provinces in Territories admitted, or which may hereafter be admitted into the Dominion of Canada, and to provide for the representation of such provinces in the said parliament, and it is expedient to remove such doubts, and to vest such powers in the said parliament :

Be it enacted by the Queen's most excellent Majesty, by and with the advice and consent of the Lords Spiritual and Temporal, and Commons, in this present parliament assembled, and by the authority of the same, as follows :

1. This Act may be cited for all purposes as the " British North America Act, 1871."

2. The parliament of Canada may from time to time establish new provinces in any territories forming for the time being part of the Dominion of Canada, but not included in any province thereof, and may, at the time of such establishment, make provision for the constitution and administration of any such province, and for the passing of laws for the peace, order, and good government of such province, and for its representation in the said parliament.

3. The parliament of Canada may from time to time, with the consent of the Legislature of any province of the said Dominion, increase, diminish, or otherwise alter the limits of such province, upon such terms and conditions as may be agreed to by the said Legislature, and may, with the like consent, make provision respecting the effect and operation of any such increase or diminution or alteration of territory in relation to any province affected thereby.

4. The parliament of Canada may from time to time make provision for the administration, peace, order and good government of any territory not for the time being included in any province.

5. The following Acts passed by the said parliament of Canada, and intituled respectfully : " An Act for the temporary government of Rupert's Land and the North-Western Territory when united with Canada," and " An Act to amend and continue the Act thirty-two and thirty-three Victoria, chapter three, and to establish and provide for the government of the province of Manitoba," shall be and be deemed to have been valid and effectual for all purposes whatsoever from the date at which they respectively received the assent, in the Queen's name, of the Governor-General of the said Dominion of Canada.

6. Except as provided by the third section of this Act, it shall not be competent for the parliament of Canada to alter the provisions of the last mentioned Act of the said parliament, in so far as it relates to the province of Manitoba, or of any other Act hereafter establishing new provinces in the said Dominion, subject always to the right of the Legislature of the province of Manitoba to alter from time to time the provisions of any law respecting the qualification of electors and members of the Legislative Assembly, and to make laws respecting elections in the said province.

THE PARLIAMENT OF CANADA ACT, 1875.

This Act was passed to amend section 18 of the B. N. A. Act of 1867 already referred to in that Act, section 2 is as follows :

The Act of the parliament of Canada passed in the thirty-first year of the reign of Her present Majesty, chapter twenty-four, intituled "An Act to provide for oaths to witnesses being administered in certain cases for the purposes of either House of Parliament " shall be deemed to be valid, and to have been valid as from the date at which the Royal Assent was given thereto by the Governor-General of the Dominion of Canada.

INDEX.

D

Q

R

S

KEHOE'S CHOSES IN ACTION. An exposition of the Law relating to the assignment and Transfer of Securities, with the practice thereunder. By J. J. Kehoe. Cloth, $2 ; 1881, Half-calf, $2.50.

LEGGO'S FORMS AND PRECEDENTS of Pleadings in the Court of Chancery. Second edition. By W. Leggo, 1876. Half-calf, $5.

LEWIS' (E. N.) INDEX TO ONTARIO STATUTES. An Alphabetical Index to Ontario Statutes, down to and including the year 1884, including the Revised Statutes of Ontario down to and including 1884, including the Revised Statutes of Ontario. 1884. Cloth, $2.50 ; Half calf or sheep, $3.

LEWIS' JUSTICES MANUAL. Containing a short Summary of the usual practice and manner of procedure in ordinary cases, coming under the observation of Justices of the Peace, Coroners, Constables, Landlords, Bailiffs, etc. By E. N. Lewis. Cloth, $1.50 ; Half-calf, $2.

LEWIS (E. N.) ON SHIPPING. A Treatise on the Law of Shipping respecting Inland and Sea coast Shipping of Canada and the United States. 1885. Half-calf or Sheep, $5.

LOWER CANADA JURIST. A collection of Decisions, 1857-1875. 20 vols. Half-calf, $100. N.B.—This Series is continued to date.

LOWER CANADA LAW JOURNAL and Magazine of Jurisprudence, containing cases not elsewhere reported. 1866-8, 4 vols. Half-calf, $10.

MACLENNAN'S (JAS., Q.C.) JUDICATURE ACT 1881, and subsequent Rules of the Supreme Court of Judicature and the High Court of Justice, with the orders of the Court of Appeal. Second edition. By Thos. Langton, M.A., LL.B. Half-calf, $5.

MANITOBA REPORTS. (Temp. Wood). A collection of Decisions in the court of Q.B. of Manitoba, in the time of Chief Justice Wood. Half-calf, $10.

MARITIME COURT RULES. The General Rules of the Maritime Court of Ontario to date with Forms, Tariff of Costs and Fees. 1878. $1.

CARSWELL & CO., LAW PUBLISHERS, Etc.,

26 & 28 Adelaide Street East, Toronto.

NEW BRUNSWICK REPORTS. Reports of Cases determined by the Supreme Court of N. B. Subscription in advance $6. Half-calf $7 per vol. as follows :—

    N. B. R. vol. 2 (Berton.)
    " " " " 10 & 11 (Allen vols. 5 & 6.)
    " " " " 12 & 13 (Hannay 2 vols.)
    " " " " 14, 15 & 16 (Pugsley 3 vols.)
    " " " " 17 to 20 (Pugsley and Burbidge 4 vols.)
    " " " " 21-24.

NOVA SCOTIA REPORTS. Subscription $5 per vol.

    N. S. R. vol. 2 (James.)
    N. S. R. " 19, 20 (Russell and Geldert 7, 8.)

O'SULLIVAN'S CONVEYANCER. A Manual of Practical Conveyancing, with Forms, Precedents and References. By D. A. O'Sullivan, LL.B. 1882. Half-calf, $4.

O'SULLIVAN'S (D. A., LL.B.) HOW TO DRAW A SIMPLE WILL 1883. Paper, $1.

O'SULLIVAN'S (D. A., M.A., D.C.L.) MANUAL OF GOVERNMENT. A Manual of Government in Canada; or the principles and institutions of our Federal Constitutions. 2nd edition, 1887. Cloth, $3.25; Half-calf, $4.

ROGERS' (R. VASHON, Jr.) LAW AND MEDICAL MEN. A Treatise on the law relating to Physicians, Dentists and Druggists. 1881. Cloth, $1.50; Half-calf, $2.

ROGERS' (R. VASHON, Jr.) LAW OF THE ROAD; or the Wrongs and Rights of a Traveller. 1881. Cloth, $1 50; Half-calf, $2.

SPLINTERS. A collection of humorous anecdotes from various sources. Cloth, $1.50.

STEPHENS' (C. H.) JOINT STOCK COMPANIES. A practical exposition of the law of Joint Stock Associations, including the Canada Clauses Act, 1877, and the Acts of Ontario and Quebec. 1881. Half-calf, $7.

STEVENS (J. G., Judge), on Indictable Offences and Summary Convictions. 1880. Cloth, $1.50. Half-calf, $2.00.

STEVEN'S (J. G., Judge) DIGEST of the reported and unreported cases of the Supreme Court of New Brunswick from 1825-1879. Second Edition. Half-calf, $13.00.

STEVEN'S, DITTO, from 1880—1887. 1888. Half-calf, $5.00.

TACHE'S (Louis II.) LEGAL HAND BOOK AND LAW LIST for the Dominion of Canada and a Book of Parliamentary and General Information. 1888. Cloth, $3.00.

CARSWELL & CO., LAW PUBLISHERS, Etc.,

26 & 28 Adelaide Street East, Toronto.

TASCHEREAU'S (Hon Mr. Justice) CRIMINAL LAW. Consolidation and Amendment Acts in force on 1st day of March, 1887. 2nd Edition. 1888. Half-calf or circuit, $10.00.

TAYLOR'S EQUITY JURISPRUDENCE. A Commentary on Equity Jurisprudence, founded on Story. By T. W. (now Chief Justice) Taylor, M.A., Q.C. 1875. Half-calf, $5.00.

TAYLOR'S PRESBYTERIAN STATUTES. A collection of the Public Statutes relating to the Presbyterian Church in Canada, with Acts and Resolutions of the General Assembly and By-laws for the government of the Colleges and schemes of the Church. By T. W. (now Chief Justice) Taylor, M.A., Q.C. Cloth, 75c.

TIFFANY'S (E. H.) REGISTRATION OF TITLES. Registry Offices—Registrars —Books of Office—Instruments to be Registered—Proof of Registration—Manner of Registering—Effects of Registering or omitting to Register—Fees—Forms, etc. 1881. Half-calf, $5.00.

TODD'S BRITISH COLONIES. Parliamentary Government in British Colonies. By Alpheus Todd. 1880. Cloth, $5.00 Half-calf, $6.00.

TRAVIS' (J.) CONSTITUTIONAL LAW. A Treatise on the Constitutional Powers of Parliament and of the Local Legislature under the British North America Act. 1884. Paper, $1.00 ; Cloth, $1.25.

WATSON'S POWERS OF CANADIAN PARLIAMENTS. By S. J. Watson, late Librarian of the Parliament of Ontario. 1880. Cloth, $1.00.

UPPER CANADA REPORTS, 1823 to 1867, 70 vols., as follows :
Taylor's K. B., 1 vol ; Draper's K. B., 1 vol.; Q. B. O. S., 6 vols.; Q. B., 25 vols.; C. P., 16 vols.; Chy., 12 vols. ; Chy. Cha., 1 vol.; Prac., 3 vols. ; Error and Appeal, 3 vols. C. L. Cha., 2 vols.

WALKEM ON WILLS (R. T., Q.C.). A Treatise on the law relating to the Execution and Revocation of Wills and to testamentary capacity. 1873. Half-calf, $5.00.

YOUNG'S VICE-ADMIRALTY DECISIONS. The decisions of Sir Wm. Young, Kt., LL.B., Judge of the Court of Vice-Admiralty for the Province of Nova Scotia. 1865-1880. Edited by J. M. Oxley. Half-calf, $6.00.

The above named books are published and owned by us, and will be sent to any address carriage prepaid, on receipt of the price.

CARSWELL & CO., LAW PUBLISHERS, Etc.,

26 & 28 Adelaide Street East, Toronto.